CHOCOLATE ALCHEMY

A Bean to Bar Primer

Creating Your Own Truffles, Candies,
Cakes, Fudge and Sipping Chocolates

KRISTEN HARD

RIZZOLI
NEW YORK

New York Paris London Milan

I would like to dedicate this book to my daughter, Delphine, and my best friend Caline, the two ladies in my life who inspire me to keep going and to stay true to my vision.

First published in the United States of America in 2018
by Rizzoli International Publications, Inc.
300 Park Avenue South
New York, NY 10010
www.rizzoliusa.com

© 2018 Kristen Hard
Text © 2018 Bill Addison

Designer: Jennifer S. Muller

Rizzoli Editor: Martynka Wawrzyniak
Additional writing and recipe editor: Janice Shay / Pinafore Press
Photography: Chia Chong
Additional photography, pages 16, 17, 19, 20: Audra Melton
Food and prop stylist: Libbie Summers

2018 2019 2020 2021 / 10 9 8 7 6 5 4 3 2 1

Distributed in the U.S. trade by Random House, New York

Printed in China

Trade ISBN: 978-0-8478-5841-5
Deluxe ISBN: 978-0-8478-6197-2

Library of Congress Control Number: 2017955898

CHOCOLATE ALCHEMY

FOREWORD

It was on an early spring day in 2009 when I first walked into Cacao Atlanta Chocolate Company, then located in Atlanta's historic Inman Park neighborhood. The temperature inside the shop (which doubled as a factory) felt pleasantly cool, and to say that chocolate perfumed the building undersells the effect. Its very essence ionized the air. Simply breathing in was a pleasure. A quiet but radiant five-foot-four woman greeted me from behind the shop's counter. She wore a white lab coat whose panels were smeared with chocolate in ways that struck me as almost artistic, like cocoa-colored Rothkos. This was my introduction to Kristen Hard.

As a food writer who'd made desserts in restaurants in a previous life, I knew about the nascent movement of bean to bar makers across the country–the obsessives who tracked down cacao from tropical farms around the globe, and who roasted, ground, melted, and formed chocolate into bars far more nuanced than anything previously available. Cacao Atlanta Chocolate Company offered the expected bars, but the counter also displayed meticulous rows of velvety-looking truffles. I picked one out called the Italian Cowboy, flavored with bourbon and espresso, and lobbed a casual inquiry to Kristen about where she sourced her cacao beans.

A light suddenly flickered on behind her eyes. She'd been asked the magic question. Before the truffle had entirely melted on my tongue, Kristen had not only detailed her thoughts on beans from the Dominican Republic versus Venezuela, but she had also zigzagged through treatises on cacao-farming techniques, how farmers might achieve more consistent results with fermentation, and why too much chocolate gets roasted at too high a temperature. She finished with a rapid-fire rundown of chocolate's little-known health benefits.

Meanwhile, the exquisite flavors of the truffle performed somersaults over my taste buds. I nodded, fascinated, through most of our conversation. Then I asked for a bar studded with dried cherries and picked out a few more truffles–one spiked with seductive Aztec spices, another scented with rosemary and cardamom, a last one with the intriguing duo of Earl Grey tea and Aperol. I left the store dizzy on a chocolate high, asking myself, *whom exactly did I just meet?*

That question answered itself a year later when, reporting on a feature for *Atlanta* magazine, I joined Kristen on a trip to Trinidad and Tobago, where she was visiting farms and meeting with scientists in the cacao research unit at the University of the West Indies. One afternoon we trekked into Tobago's northern mountains. Kristen navigated a Jeep over dirt roads two inches from the edge of a cliff, and then she took up a machete in a cacao grove like Katniss Everdeen in a jungle *Hunger Games* challenge. Another day she scoured charts on genetic strands of cacao hybrids, all the while discussing crop yields and (her favorite subject) degrees of seed fermentation. It was nearly impossible to keep up with her that week. As a journalist, it was also a once-in-a-lifetime education in the complex fundamentals of this everyday indulgence.

Kristen Hard is the renaissance woman of the chocolate industry, and this book is your invitation into her world. As a businessperson, she understands that bewitchingly delicious chocolate is her bottom line, but her curiosity and rigorous standards make the subject of *Theobroma cacao* ("food of the gods") so much bigger than a delicate truffle or decadent slice of cake. As an author, she takes the same approach: Precise and conversational recipes for treat after treat fill these pages. But in discussing her background and philosophies and definitions, she also puts the universe of chocolate under a microscope and guides you through what you're seeing and touching and tasting.

None of it ever gets too lofty. This is a practical course in understanding chocolate on every level. There's a step in the master technique for making bean to bar chocolate that involves a hair dryer. That's so Kristen. She can be romantic about dreamy flavor combinations, and theoretical about the future of cacao farming, but she's also deeply pragmatic. Her readers will understand the mechanics behind the magic.

Chocolate Alchemy covers the breadth of Kristen's inspired creations, the delights that have defined her career. I see the beckoning shelves and counters of Cacao Atlanta Chocolate Company when I read the secrets for making truffles, macarons, silky sipping chocolate with passion fruit marshmallows, chocolate-dipped oatmeal cream pies, and bark with cocoa nibs and almonds. Notice the subtle Southern allusions that thread through the book: jellies and pâte de fruit made with mayhaw (a fruit of the Georgia summer), bourbon cake, hickory-smoked caramels, pecan pie truffles. Chocolate may grow in the tropics, but Kristen infuses her life's work with her own singular sense of place.

With this book, you'll find your place in the chocolate universe, too.

–**Bill Addison**, restaurant editor and national food critic, *Eater*

AN EPIPHANY AMONG THE TREES

When I was in my 20s, I worked as a chef on a yacht sailing the world's oceans, seas' and waterways. At each port, I was constantly on the hunt for food to stock the boat's small larder. My favorite ports of call were on the islands of the Caribbean. There, the simplest ingredients, such as tomatoes and lettuce, are difficult to find; but the things that grow in abundance can be wondrous–foods I'd never seen on a grocery store shelf or at farmers' markets back in the States. Everywhere I went in these lush green islands, I marveled at beautiful trees that lined the village streets–trees that were heavy with big, brightly colored fruit–cacao pods, I was told, which are the source of chocolate.

With this discovery, it was as if the stars suddenly aligned. My scientific-leaning brain and my lifelong passion for sweets sparked an obsession with making fine chocolate. I wanted to know everything about these amazing seedpods, but soon learned how little written knowledge was available on how to make chocolate using these source seeds, or beans. How could this be? I had eaten chocolate all my life. These seeds were the source of a food familiar and beloved to almost everyone around the world. Why wasn't more known about cacao beans? It became the puzzle that fueled my research and would map my future as a chocolatier who would one day lease farmland to grow my own beans, and take an active part in trying to change the chocolate and cacao industry.

When I first became interested in the creation of chocolate, I read everything I could find about its history: how its popularity spread, who the industry players were around the world (there are a lot of different perspectives on these subjects). At roughly the same time I was investigating chocolate makers and industry standards and practices, the general buying public was becoming aware of the many different types and tastes of chocolate, its health benefits, and how it is produced from the cacao bean. The more I worked with the raw chocolate I acquired in the beginning of my foray into chocolate making, the more respect I had for the mysterious seeds that held so many overlooked and underestimated health benefits.

Today, I am a chef and a chocolatier and a chocolate maker. There are differences. A chef makes food inspired by ingredients and recipes to create particular flavors. A chocolatier takes that love affair with flavor and incorporates it into chocolate. A chocolate maker is one who uses the raw ingredient, the seeds, to create chocolate bars. Wearing all three of these hats, I combine the science of creating chocolate with the art of flavor sensation, playing up the delicate nature and variety of the beans.

Why is my chocolate story part of this cookbook? Only recently, thanks to the bean to bar movement, has machinery become available to make chocolate in the home. Any home cook has the capability of learning how to make chocolate from scratch. I know because I learned the hard way: I taught myself.

The chocolate used for cooking has traditionally been available primarily through mass-produced bars. For many home cooks, it's a bit of a maze to navigate the many types of artisanal chocolate offered on the market today, and almost impossible to calculate how to substitute one chocolate for another when cooking from recipes. With this book, I want to share my knowledge, clarify the terminology, explain the origins of beans and present-day farming practices, simplify how to read labels, and address how to taste and buy chocolate. Plus—and this is an exciting plus—this book will show home cooks how to make their own healthy, delicious chocolate. In this way I hope to share my passion for chocolate making with you.

THE DISCOVERY OF CHOCOLATE'S HEALTH BENEFITS

The history of chocolate dates back to pre-Columbian Mexico, to about 2,800 years ago when the Mayans (and later the Aztecs) enjoyed a drink made from the beans of the cocoa tree. Via the conquistadors, the Spanish brought the beans to Europe in 1528, along with the recipe for drinking chocolate. The first recorded shipment of cacao beans arrived in Seville in 1585.

In 1828 and 1838, respectively, Casparus van Houten and his son, Coenraad, developed methods that greatly enhanced chocolate as an ingredient in cooking. Casparus developed a way to create a cocoa powder, which allowed chocolate to be used in cooking, and Coenraad found a technique to alkalize cacao in order to lessen the bitterness and enhance the flavor. By the Industrial Age of the early 1800s, new machinery enabled the processing of chocolate for mass production. What had originally been enjoyed mainly as a drink consumed by the upper classes became affordable to a broad spectrum of society, and in a wide variety of forms. It became an instant sensation.

The first bars of solid chocolate were produced in 1847 by the English firm J. S. Fry & Sons. Because of its coarse, gritty texture, these first solid forms of chocolate didn't gain much popularity until 1876, when a clever Swiss chocolatier, searching for flavor solutions to sweeten the bitter cacao taste, found the perfect additive: milk. By the 1930s, milk chocolate was the most popular consumer choice of chocolate. Unfortunately, the buying public was unaware that methods used in the production of mass market chocolates over the preceding 150 years greatly reduced the health benefits of cacao.

It wasn't until the latter half of the 20th century that the cocoa bean was discovered to be an antioxidant whose healthy properties are lost during processing. Cacao powder is made by cold pressing unroasted cacao beans, which retain the living enzymes, but removes the fat. Although it looks similar, cocoa powder—used by most large-scale chocolate manufacturers to make their chocolate—is a product of cacao beans that are roasted at high temperatures, thereby reducing the live enzymes and lowering the nutritional value.

In the last decade, single-origin and bean to bar chocolates have gained popularity, and changed the buying habits of many people. Consumers have begun to demand chocolate with less sugar—a darker chocolate, with greater health benefits. This is where my story picks up again. My initial studies of cacao intersected with the first glimmerings of public awareness about the chocolate industry.

I began experimenting with cacao in its raw form in 1999. Having bought seasonal produce wherever we docked when I worked on a yacht, and having lived in Italy—the home of the Slow Food Movement—I always prefer to cook using fresh, local foods. With this in mind, I guessed there should be no reason to feel guilty for eating chocolate if it was made with cacao. How could eating something made from the seeds of this beautiful fruit be bad for you? And, if it wasn't bad for you, how was it good?

At that time, there was only a small national conversation on the subject of cacao. The organic consumer was the only group that understood cocoa nibs were nutritious. The health focus was mainly on the seeds—where and how they were grown and harvested, and the percentage of cacao in bars—not on how the processing of cacao affected its nutritional value. It wasn't until the year 2000, when I was working with a good source of chocolate (I hadn't yet

worked with the seeds, but was direct sourcing single origin chocolate), that I became aware of the wealth of antioxidants found in dark chocolate made from cacao. Here are a few benefits of modest consumption of dark chocolate that are recognized by the FDA:

- Cacao is rich in minerals: magnesium, iron, potassium, calcium, zinc, copper, and manganese.

- It contains antioxidants called "flavonoids" (compounds found primarily in plants), that can help protect your skin.

- Cacao improves blood flow, through blood-thinning properties similar to those contained in aspirin.

- Cacao is high in resveratrol, a potent antioxidant also found in red wine that helps protect your nervous system and shields nerve cells from damage.

- The flavonoids in dark chocolate have inflammation-fighting properties, and can help reduce the risk of heart disease.

- The flavonoids in cacao can significantly lower systolic blood pressure and diastolic blood pressure by improving blood flow, with beneficial effects on blood pressure and decreased risks of heart attack.

- The antioxidants in cacao guard against toxins and can repair the damage caused by free radicals.

- Chocolate boosts your general mood and helps fight stress. Eating a modest amount of chocolate can increase levels of certain neurotransmitters that promote a sense of well-being. Phenylethylamine, a chemical released when we experience deep feelings of love, is also found in chocolate.

There are many good reasons to eat dark chocolate, and it's high time for chocolate to shed the stigma of being merely a guilty pleasure! To that end, some researchers claim the feelings of guilt we have while eating chocolate release an enzyme in the mouth that destroys the flavors of real, unprocessed chocolate. I remember worrying I had to fix this perception, because if the flavor is destroyed, then the delicacy of my chocolate creations would be lost!

Most chocolate made and sold in America contains 90 percent sugar with additives such as soy lecithin, a soybean-based product used to emulsify cocoa butter in chocolate. It also minimizes bloom and adds a smoother texture. (I don't use lecithin in chocolate because it is extracted using harsh chemicals, and is usually derived from genetically modified plants.) The USDA requires that a minimum of 10 percent real chocolate, or cacao, must be present in a bar for it to be labeled "chocolate." Cacao, you must understand, is expensive, so many of the big chocolate companies meet only the minimum requirement in their products. If consumers only buy this kind of processed chocolate, they've never experienced the health benefits of real chocolate.

In addition, most dark chocolate bars on the market are loaded with vanilla and made with a mixed quality of cacao beans. (Traditionally, farmers grow trees of differing quality beans, and mix them together to sell at market.) These factors dilute the quality of the dark chocolate, so the consumer actually only gets about 50 percent chocolate in a bar. To experience the health benefits, it's best to buy a 70 percent chocolate. It's frustrating to have to pay more to buy the higher-quality chocolate on the market these days, but it's useful to understand that a $2 bar has 10 percent dark chocolate, and a $6 bar has 70 percent or 75 percent. I know it's a generalization, but if you pay more, it's likely you'll get more health benefits from the chocolate. So, the obvious question becomes: Why do we buy a diluted chocolate? We wouldn't dilute a good wine.

In the last couple of years, it has been recognized that Dutching, or the Dutch process of making cocoa, is not particularly healthy. This is cocoa made with alkali as an additive, which darkens the color and reduces the bitterness, so people feel it is a richer chocolate. Alkali has been proven to be an unhealthy addition to chocolate, because it reduces the level of beneficial flavonoid (the powerful antioxidants in chocolate). The U.S. labeling regulations presently require alkalized cocoa powder be declared as such. There are different regulations in other countries, so the consumer can't be certain if their imported chocolate has been through the Dutching process.

In many ways, the practices implemented by the mass market chocolate industry have been no different than those followed by other companies who have used chemicals in the preparation of processed food over the last century. Thankfully, popular opinion is now leaning toward buying chocolate that contains a healthy percentage of cacao, and the public palate is moving away from milk chocolate. Food can do two things for us: it can wake up the cells in the body, or it can put them to sleep. Good chocolate is not only nutritious, but it's a mood enhancer, it's low glycemic, and it's a food we all love. What other food on earth is so healthy and seductive?

The bottom line is this: chocolate that's minimally processed and devoid of chemical additives is nutritious and beneficial to our well-being. It can improve brain, heart, and digestive function as well as skin quality. And there's more good news for the home cook: you never have to worry about the nutritional aspect and the cost effectiveness of the chocolate you make at home.

THE BEAN FIELDS: SOURCING & GROWING CACAO

Armed with the knowledge that quality cacao is an important part of making good, healthy chocolate, I set out to find the best chocolate mass to buy. I wasn't yet sourcing the beans, but I wanted to know which beans were being used to make the raw chocolate I was buying. What I discovered about the commodification and future of cacao beans was life-changing.

It's well known that cacao beans grown in a particular habitat, or country, will produce distinctive taste characteristics, like a good wine, according to the chemistry of the soil and the climate and conditions of growing. These characteristics are said to have "terroir." For example, cacao from Madagascar often tastes fruity, whereas cacao from Venezuela has a nuttier profile.

Most large chocolate manufacturers use a single-source mash-up of beans, which can differ vastly in quality. Poor-quality beans can render a flat taste, requiring an experienced chocolatier to enhance the flavor. The cocoa industry is a $5.1 billion market. West Africa alone grows more than half of the 3 million tons of beans sold annually, according to the World Cocoa Foundation. Soil, climate, and market prices make Africa a longtime favorite region for growing cacao.

The problem with much of our chocolate coming from one region is that the majority of the beans will tend to have a one-note taste, and rely on sugar and additives to enhance flavors. But there is an even greater problem that can be traced to industry practices. In 2000, I began to make chocolate using a good source of couverture acquired from a vendor in New York who bought Ecuadorian seeds and transformed them into couverture for the market. The result was 75 percent chocolate, which wasn't popular in the United States at that time because it wasn't sweet enough. I began to add infusions and extractions of herbs, such as rhodiola and ginkgo biloba, to stimulate the brain. Occasionally, I would add a fresh herb, such as lavender, rosemary, or chamomile. Eventually, I knew I was ready and eager to make my own bar chocolate from cacao beans.

I knew from traveling in the Caribbean that the trees I saw there had pods and seeds vastly dissimilar in shape, size, and even color; so I guessed that different beans would produce different tastes. In trying to discover why the industry was using basically one type of bean, I unearthed papers that dealt with the development and genetics of chocolate. This research showed me that the individual flavor of beans was always lost in overprocessing. Why use different types of beans if you planned to add back the flavor that was lost in overprocessing? It became clear to me that the health benefits and therefore the flavor profiles of cocoa beans had been intentionally discarded. It was a simple matter of money: quantity over quality.

When I started my business, Cacao Atlanta Chocolate Company, in 2008, small quantities of beans were not readily available in the United States, so I called a broker and asked if I could buy 100 pounds of cacao beans. He just laughed at the small quantity I required and said, "We could sweep some off the floor for you if you want." Typically a large chocolate-maker buys beans by the ton–not the pound–to transform into chocolate bars for the marketplace. The only way for me to get a small amount of beans would be to purchase them directly from a small farmer.

I traveled to the Dominican Republic where I knew a lot of cacao was being farmed. These small farmers didn't take phone orders and they didn't have access to the internet. Visiting a farm in person was the only way to find out more about the beans I would be buying, and where and how they were grown. This was buying local at the most basic level!

For the first year, I traveled back and forth to the Dominican Republic, bringing burlap sacks of beans back to the United States in a suitcase. Although it was legal to do so, I always felt like I was smuggling. I'm sure the guy at the Department of Agriculture office at the Atlanta airport didn't know what to think of me. He saw me so often he came to know me by name.

Eventually I found small farms that would ship beans to me. It was then that I began to notice the beans I received were not all the same quality. There were big differences in size and color within each shipment, all jumbled together in the bags.

I learned most farmers had no quality controls in place for what they grew and sold, and there was no comprehension of the diversity of their product. This wasn't entirely the growers' fault–big companies didn't want to buy the highest quality beans because they needed to keep their price points stable for the end product. Plus, low-quality cacao trees typically produce bigger pods with more and bigger seeds, bringing in more money for the farmer. High-quality cacao trees are smaller and produce fewer beans, so they just weren't worth the farmers' efforts.

Shipments from farms always consist of a combination of beans of differing qualities ranging from poor to good. To achieve consistency, we inaugurated a system of hand sorting the beans according to quality when shipments arrived. We also analyzed the level of fermentation, the possibility of disease, and the presence of bugs. It was easy to spot the genetic differences among seeds by their shape, size, color, and the taste of the pulp. Smaller beans are typically from the highest-quality cacao trees. The larger beans are from the lower-tier quality of cacao.

One of our first big shipments of beans ($40,000 worth) looked bad. Most of them were old, overfermented and moldy. I found someone in New Jersey to test the beans to see if I could recoup some of my investment by proving I had been sent bad beans. His analysis results were an eye opener. He reported that, within the range of our samples, all were deemed acceptable by U.S. standards!

This led me to begin studying the genetics of cacao, and why farmers are not motivated to grow, sell, and ship better-quality beans. In 2012, I began testing the pulp and sugar content of the pulp, analyzing pods directly on the farms, before the beans are shipped.

There are three basic genetic types of cacao trees that subspecies are based upon. The Criollo tree originated centuries ago in Mexico and Central America. It has a reddish or white bean with complex flavors of nuts, caramel, vanilla, and tobacco, and a sweet taste requiring less sugar when produced as chocolate. The rare Criollo tree is a small, fragile tree that needs to be sheltered from wind by other taller trees, and yields smaller pods with fewer beans. The Criollo bean

represents the highest-quality cacao. Venezuela grows various varietals based on this bean.

The second genetic type of cacao is Forastero. Originally from the Amazon, many types of this tree are now grown all over the world, especially in Brazil and West Africa. The Forastero bean and its subspecies account for 80 percent of the world's cacao bean supply.

Trinitario, the third genetic type, is a hybrid of Criollo and Forastero trees. Originally from Trinidad, it is now grown–along with its varietals–in Venezuela, Mexico, the Caribbean, Ecuador, Colombia, Cameroon, Samoa, Sri Lanka, Java, and Papua New Guinea, as well as other Asian countries. It is a middle-quality bean, and most farms grow a mix of the Trinitario trees, as well as the Forastero.

Different genetic varieties of cacao are identified by the flavor of the pulp. Some are sour, some sweet, but all have fruit flavors affecting the bean and the end flavor of the chocolate. All beans are affected by the soil they are grown in and other regional factors. I began making chocolate from beans featuring the flavor profiles of the cacao grown on farms in Venezuela. One varietal, grown in Patanemo, expresses the natural flavors of bread pudding, cinnamon, caramel, and dried cherries. The first time I roasted, shelled, and husked the beans, transformed them into chocolate, and dipped my spoon in to taste it, I burst into tears. I had never tasted anything that good before and I knew my efforts had been worthwhile.

Each of the beans present a distinctive taste that is also affected by the terroir, or region where it is grown. There is a great deal of genetic and flavor diversity in cacao beans. I quickly learned most farmers didn't know the differences in what they were growing and selling–to them it was just one raw material. The farmers knew that diversity in their seeds affected the taste, but they had been told by the large chocolate companies (who have set the commodity prices for cacao for generations) to grow larger pods with more seeds, so their trees could produce more seeds per square foot. This earned the farmers more money, but also allowed the big companies to set the growing standards.

Additionally, industry scientists were breeding the trees to produce large pods while ignoring the flavor factor in deference to the production of more beans and resistance to disease. Farmers were caught in a box: they needed to make enough money to feed their family; larger cacao pods meant a sure income; and the big companies were telling them to grow the lesser-quality cacao trees. There was just no incentive to grow the top-quality Criollo tree.

Historically, many cacao farms were owned by the large chocolate companies to the tune of hundreds of thousands of acres. Companies offered only basic quality control of the crops, mainly consisting of information on pruning. As a result, farmers depended on the chocolate makers to tell them what to plant if they were to sell their crops. Interestingly, I learned that the great majority of famers I met had never eaten chocolate beyond tasting the ground beans in a drink. The flavor and taste of their product was not even on their radar.

Armed with this information, and wanting to find quality beans to make my chocolate, I set out to work directly with the farmers, and expanded my search for quality beans to other countries. I looked for farmers who cared about the quality of the soil as well as the trees, so that I could control the quality of the raw material of chocolate, as well as grow the genetic varieties I needed. About one in 15 farmers in Venezuela cared about the artistry of growing quality cacao, and I focused on those growers.

Currently, a majority of the world's cacao is grown on small family farms. There are around 6 million farmers who grow and sell cacao beans, and that number is rising along with the popular demand for chocolate. To be productive and economically viable, cacao crops must be constantly protected from the elements, as well as from pests and disease. Most farmers can't afford to replant. One hectare of cocoa trees costs at least $1,000, and that amount doesn't include fertilizer and other tools needed to care for the saplings. And worse news: genetics are tricky when it comes to the reproduction of new trees. Quality seeds from one tree won't necessarily produce quality beans in a new tree. Plus, trees don't yield marketable pods until their fifth year.

I often visit 15 farms in a week, so I have a checklist of things to assess. Does the farmer care about his trees? Is he honest? How does he feel about the industry he's supplying? How deep is his knowledge of what he grows? How long does he wait to remove the beans from the pods after the harvest? Is the fermentation done at the farm, or are the beans taken to a centralized facility? The answers to these questions tell me a lot about his product, and whether he is astute about post-harvest practices such as fermentation and drying, which are critical to the quality of the bean.

I have found that many farmers had almost no knowledge of such simple contemporary practices such as pruning and fertilizing their trees, calculating soil information to aid in growth, or polycropping to feed the soil. Post-harvesting practices matter greatly, too. The grower may have quality trees, but if the seeds are moldy when they make it to market, they will be useless. I identified 14 points of possible failure of quality before the cacao even leaves the farm, all practices farmers could easily be taught to correct. Perhaps, most troubling to me was, for the most part, growers do not understand the importance of genetic diversity to the contemporary chocolate maker.

The recent popularity of bean to bar chocolate has fueled a rebirth in the cacao industry, with a handful of small chocolate businesses like my own, who purchase their beans direct from farmers. I believe that through efforts like mine, farmers can become more knowledgeable about the quality of their crops, and their respective countries will–and have begun to support farmers' efforts to expand their business through fair trade practices. Growing my own cacao was a major step toward establishing the pillars of my company, which are sustainability, transparency in business practices, and quality of product.

Now that I knew the problems the farmers had growing quality beans for the market, I thought perhaps I could create a market environment wherein I could invest in the farmer, and have more say over the quality of cacao trees he grew. As I mentioned, most small farmers grow a genetic mix of trees but get only one price for their beans, so they simply throw the good in with the lesser-quality beans. I thought, how great would it be for consumers and farmers if more of the quality beans could be grown, and priced at market according to their actual quality? Could I actually affect cacao prices with this idea?

THE FUTURE OF CHOCOLATE

To have an impact on the industry, I had to find a new way to align consumer needs and the manner in which cacao was grown. It didn't make sense for me to ask a customer to pay high prices for a bar of chocolate just because it was part of a "small batch" production from a single source. I believed the genetics of the bean plus good post-harvest practices should define the quality rating of the chocolate and dictate price point for the consumer. This was a new concept for the industry, but one I strongly believed would benefit both the farmer and the consumer.

In 2011, I was invited to be a judge at the International Cocoa Awards, a global competition hosted by Cocoa of Excellence, an international nonprofit organization that promotes the genetic diversity and quality of cacao on farms. My vocabulary of cacao expanded as I tested the quality of beans from hundreds of farms, and gained a heightened ability to detect flaws in chocolate on a minute scale.

At first I wanted to own my own farm, but quickly realized that alone wouldn't have enough impact to change the industry. One farm growing different genetic beans and pricing them accordingly wouldn't make a significant difference. While pondering the problem, in 2015, I decided to try to close the loop on the chocolate industry's source strategy by providing farmers with a better outlet to sell what were they producing. The stability of the price point for cacao has traditionally been all on the side of the chocolate companies at the cost of the farmer. Prices fluctuate based on the market, and farmers are told what to grow by the industry, and sometimes the government, based on market prices.

The problem with creating quality trees is that trees aren't propagated from saved seeds. They have to be alive. Most farmers cut down type one trees to grow type three, because it produces more crop. The quality pods and beans are smaller in general, more delicate, harder to grow, and require more attention. Farmers have to have an incentive to grow them, because the big companies don't differentiate between beans, so the lesser-quality trees produce more and are more attractive for farmers.

I wanted to change that dynamic; and in doing so, I hoped to change the industry as a whole.

At our factory in Atlanta, we now produce bars for each quality type; all the bars are the same size but all are priced based on quality. We pay the farmer according to the tier of bean, not one price for all their beans. Plus, we offer the farmer trees to grow the top-quality trees so they can make more money for those beans, and we guarantee the purchase of those cacao beans.

In 2016 we launched a new industry concept to help farmers grow more quality trees on their land. This sustainability effort, named twigg & co., works on various levels for both the farmer and the consumer. The idea is this: Farmers can apply for quality trees, telling us how many trees they will grow on their land, and we put them on a waiting list. For every bar of twigg & co. chocolate sold, we buy a cacao tree for a farmer, so when we sell 1,000 bars, the first farmer on the waiting list gets 1,000 trees. We choose and identify the tiers of quality trees and set cacao prices for them. This permits farmers to grow more quality cacao and make significantly more money doing so.

We plan to hold a competition among farmers to see who can produce the best quality cacao bean based on a stringent set of criteria. Those who are producing such qaality are awarded a significant amount of money to provide a simple and true incentive–a better quality of life. Additionally, we hope to help famers with related issues such as water shortages.

twigg & co. also plans to launch a holistic brand, utilizing natural ingredients. Recently, we have begun creating chocolates made with natural healing elements, such as ginko biloba and gotu kola. We have forged partnerships with doctors that prescribe our chocolate for some female ailments, and have created custom blends for cancer patients.

This is a unique chocolate concept wherein we can support those who cope with medical challenges, as well as those who seek natural and holistic remedies as an alternative to traditional medicine.

Right now, it's a relatively small movement that I hope will grow along with the cacao trees. By its nature, chocolate is a luxury. I would love for the highest-quality cacao to be the standard, and still be affordable for everyone.

THE LANGUAGE *of* CHOCOLATE

These definitions will help you understand more about chocolate as you learn about its properties, processes, and health benefits.

Bean to bar

If a label says the chocolate is "bean to bar," it means the maker has taken whole cacao beans and roasted, ground, and tempered them into chocolate from scratch.

Bittersweet chocolate

Not to be confused with unsweetened or semisweet chocolate, this slightly sweetened dark chocolate is used primarily for baking. The U.S. Food and Drug Administration (FDA) requires that bittersweet chocolate must contain at least 35 percent chocolate liquor.

Bloom

If the cocoa butter separates (breaks) from the cocoa solids, the surface of the chocolate will begin to turn white; this is called "bloom." Usually bloom is caused by an extreme or sudden change in temperature, but it may also occur over time. When chocolate is not tempered properly, cocoa butter separates from the chocolate and rises to the surface when the chocolate is cooled, which can cause bloom. The chocolate may be remelted and retempered to return it to its bloom-free state.

Cocoa or cacao tree

A small tropical evergreen tree (*Theobroma cacao*) that grows in regions within 20 degrees north or south of the equator. The beans in the pod it produces are the source of chocolate, cocoa powder, and cocoa butter. Cacao trees need five years to bear their first fruit, and will produce quality beans for another 10 years. They grow well only as understory and thus require "mother trees" (usually banana or palm trees) to shade them. Most cacao plantations grow a genetic mix of varietals, and are typically small farms due to the intense amount of skilled hand labor required for the trees' maintenance and harvest.

Cacao

A term used for the purest raw product of the cacao tree, made by cold pressing the unroasted cacao beans. This keeps the enzymes in the cocoa alive and removes the fat (cocoa butter). "Cocoa" and "cacao" are often used interchangeably.

Cacao beans, *also called* cacao seeds

These are the source of all chocolate. Cacao beans are found in the pods of the cacao tree.

Cacao nibs

The kernels of cacao seeds are called "nibs," and are the basic ingredient from which chocolate is made. The nibs contain a live enzyme that makes them nutrient dense, full of antioxidants, minerals, and vitamins.

Cocoa pods

The fruit of the cacao tree are fleshy football-shaped pods, between 6 and 12 inches in length, and ranging in color from green to bright reddish-orange or purple. When ripe, they are harvested with machetes and split open. The pod contains a pulp embedded with 20 to 60 seeds.

Chocolate liquor, *also called* cacao liquor or cacao paste

(Not to be confused with a liquor—cacao liquor doesn't contain any alcohol.) The basis of all chocolate, this is 100 percent chocolate, made from the finely ground nibs of the cacao bean. Nibs are ground to a thick paste, which becomes liquid when heated. It is sometimes commercially referred to as "cacao mass."

Cocoa butter

A cacao bean is approximately 50 percent cocoa butter. This fatty substance is obtained from chocolate liquor during processing. Under high pressure, the cocoa butter separates (breaks) from the cacao liquor, and the remaining material is pulverized to make cocoa powder. The two are combined again with sugar and other ingredients to make chocolate. Cocoa butter is not a dairy product, and it is also used in cosmetics and moisturizers. Cocoa butter melts at body temperature, which is why chocolate will "melt in your mouth."

Cocoa powder

When raw cacao is roasted and processed at high temperatures—resulting in the loss of the live enzymes—it forms a powder, which is referred to as "cocoa powder." Cocoa powder doesn't provide the many health benefits that are present in cacao. It is used often for drinking chocolate and in cooking.

Couverture

A high-quality coating chocolate that contains between 32 to 39 percent cocoa butter. The cocoa butter helps form a thinner coating shell than non-couverture chocolate.

Dark chocolate

Chocolate that contains more than 50 percent cacao content. Besides chocolate liquor, it often contains added cocoa butter, sugar, vanilla, and may also contain soy lecithin, which helps keep the cacao solids and cocoa butter from separating.

Ganache

A rich, silky mixture made by combining chopped milk, dark, or white chocolate with boiling cream, which is stirred until the mixture has a smooth, glossy sheen. (Sometimes cocoa butter is also added.) If cooled slightly, ganache will remain liquid and can be used to top cakes and other desserts. When it is chilled, ganache is used to make truffles.

Milk chocolate

Chocolate liquor to which milk, sugar, vanilla, and, often, lecithin have been added. Quality milk chocolate should contain a minimum of 30 percent chocolate liquor.

Single-origin chocolate

A chocolate that is made using cacao beans from one particular place or "origin." The bean to bar movement has made single-origin chocolate popular. Single-origin chocolates focus on the specific terroir (or region) and the types of beans grown, which produce varied indigenous flavors.

Tempering

The process of bringing chocolate to a temperature high enough that the cocoa butter achieves a stable crystal form. Proper tempering to the right heat, followed by proper cooling, produces a glossy shine, good "mouthfeel," and distinctive snap. [per p38]

Unsweetened chocolate

This is chocolate in its simplest form; it is made from cacao solids and cocoa butter. Unsweetened chocolate is not good for eating because it is so bitter, but it can be used for baking and cooking. Not to be confused with bittersweet or dark chocolates, which have some sugar added.

White chocolate

This is not considered real chocolate, although it contains cocoa butter, because it does not contain chocolate liquor. White chocolate is made from cocoa butter, milk, sugar, and vanilla.

HOW TO TASTE CHOCOLATE

You don't need to be a professional chocolatier to learn to taste, and truly savor chocolate. You just need to know a few things, and then practice–always the fun part! For me, the upside of cooking with good chocolate is apparent in these recipes, such as the Chocolate Pots de Crème (page 115), in which the delicate flavors of the chocolate and other ingredients are easily accessible to the palate.

As you prepare and taste some of the recipes in this book, you'll realize chocolate is not a one-dimensional flavor. The relationship between the chocolate and the other ingredients creates a dynamic layering of new tastes. For instance, if you pair a chocolate that has a flavor note of raisins in a recipe using rum as an ingredient, you'll create a great new rum-raisin taste.

Here's a primer on how to taste chocolate:

• Some say the best time to taste is in the morning before you've eaten anything that day. If you don't want to eat chocolate in the morning, just be sure to have a clean palate. Don't wait until after a meal or a cocktail to taste test your chocolate.

• Choose a plain chocolate bar that doesn't have any nuts, salt, or inclusions of flavor. Allow it to come to room temperature; never taste it cold. In fact, it's best to store chocolate in a cool cabinet rather than a refrigerator. Chocolate is porous and absorbs the scents of its neighbors in a regrigerator.

• Look at the chocolate to make sure there are no white patches that signify bloom, which can alter the taste. Then check the color: milk chocolate will be lighter than dark or semisweet chocolate, and the color will vary according to the country of origin of the bean. Milk chocolate usually also contains more sugar.

• Good chocolate should not feel brittle when you break it, but you don't want it to be too soft, either. Put the chocolate on a napkin so you don't add the smell of your hands to this experience, and smell the broken chocolate to see if you can determine any special aromas. Does it smell sweet like vanilla? Or does it have another aroma?

• Put the chocolate in your mouth, but don't eat it right away. If you must, chew a couple of times, then let it melt a little on your tongue. Note: The melting point of chocolate is our standard body temperature, so it's true that chocolate "melts in your mouth." Close your eyes. What do you taste? You might detect a note of berries or almonds. A good chocolate will suggest different tastes at the beginning, middle, and finish as you slowly eat it.

• Try this taste-testing ritual with a variety of chocolate bars and see if you can detect the flavor differences.

CHOCOLATE LABELS: THE DEVIL IS IN THE DETAILS

When you find a chocolate that fits your sensibilities, check the label to learn a little more about what you're eating. Is it single origin? Fair trade? Bean to bar? Here's a guide to the tiny details.

Information on the label of a chocolate bar helps you know exactly what you're buying. Sometimes what you'll notice are things to avoid, such as industrial overprocessing, fake flavoring, Dutching and the addition of alkali, or soy lecithin. These things can destroy the health benefits or the delicate flavor of chocolate– or both.

• Check the percentage of cacao that's in the bar. If a bar is labeled 70 percent chocolate, it means it is 70 percent cacao mass (or ground cocoa seeds), which is a mixture of cacao solids and cocoa butter. The other 30 percent is usually a mixture of sugar and vanilla, as well as any added flavors, such as nuts, berries, herbs, etc. Dark chocolate has a higher percentage of cacao than milk chocolate. A good chocolate maker will sometimes list only two ingredients, cacao beans and sugar. Many use added cocoa butter and vanilla for texture and taste. If the label lists artificial sweeteners, milk substitutes, non-cocoa butter fats, such as vegetable oil, then the bar isn't real chocolate and will likely be labeled as "made with chocolate." In the United States, a chocolate maker must put only a minimum of 10 percent cacao in a chocolate to call it chocolate, whereas in Europe the minimum standard is 22 percent.

• If the label says "bean to bar," then the chocolate is made from cacao beans. If it isn't bean to bar chocolate, then the bar has likely been prepared from premade chocolate and, in most cases, this premade chocolate is mass produced.

• If the bar is marked "single origin," the label will list the name of the country where the cacao was grown, such as Ecuador or Venezuela. Generally, single origin chocolate is carefully crafted to express the flavors of the varietals from that area.

• The use of the term "fair trade" on the label will tell you the beans were more than likely grown ethically and more sustainably. Fair trade certification ensures farmers are paid a fraction more than what the commodity market offers.

• Don't forget to check if there's an expiration date–chocolate can indeed expire, but some labels don't denote a date. This is rarely a problem, but it's good to check for a date anyway, to make sure you're not buying a bar that has bloom.By the way, no need to put your chocolate in the refrigerator. It may take on the flavors of whatever food is in there as chocolate is like a sponge.

• Labels also will list flavoring inclusions, and these are not to be confused with chemical additives. These days, bars can include everything from sea salt and toffee to pretzels and peppermint.

THE CHOCOLATIER'S PANTRY

Spirits
Allspice liqueur
Aperol
Beer (ideally, something local from a smaller brewery)
Bourbon
Ginger beer
Rum
Scotch whisky
Tequila

Fruits and Preserves
Apples
Bananas
Blueberries
Cherries
Lemon
Lime
Mayhaws
Passion fruit (fresh) or ready-made puree
Peppers (assorted, including Habanero)
Strawberries
Blueberry jam
Fig jam
Orange marmalade
Raspberry jam
Candied ginger
Candied oranges
Dried apricots
Dried cherries
Raisins

Nuts
Almonds (raw)
Cashews
Shredded coconut
Hazelnuts
Peanuts
Peanut butter
Pecans
Pumpkin seeds

Herbs, Spices and Essential Oils
Allspice
Cardamom
Cayenne pepper
Chamomile flowers
Chili powder
Cinnamon
Cloves
Earl Grey tea (loose leaf)
Fennel seeds
Fleur de sel
Ginseng powder
Lavender flowers
Nutmeg
Paprika
Pink peppercorn
Red pepper
Rosemary (fresh)
Thyme (fresh)
Almond extract
Cinnamon oil
Lemon balm extract
Orange blossom oil
Peppermint essential oil
Vanilla extract
Vanilla bean

Baking Necessities
70% percent dark chocolate (if making it from scratch, cacao beans or nibs, sugar)
Cocoa nibs
Cocoa powder (natural, non-alkalized)
All-purpose flour
Almond flour
Baking powder
Baking soda
Rolled oats
Brown rice syrup
Confectioners' sugar
Glucose
Honey (preferably local)
Invert sugar
Maple syrup
Molasses
Organic raw cane sugar
Coconut oil
Vegetable oil
Vegetable shortening

Dairy
Butter
Buttermilk
Mascarpone
Sweetened condensed milk
Heavy whipping cream
Whole milk
Eggs

Miscellaneous
Amaretti biscuits
Bacon
Apple cider vinegar
Balsamic vinegar (aged)
Coffee (ground)
Apple pectin
Gelatin
Marshmallows
Malt powder
Matcha green tea powder
Sprinkles

1.

BEAN TO BAR CHOCOLATE

BAR TALK

Through this book, I want to demystify bean to bar production completely, so home cooks understand what defines each bar of chocolate, what properties to look for in their own homemade chocolate, and the importance of using quality chocolate in these recipes. I'm not writing to convince my readers to buy my Cacao Atlanta chocolate, although I certainly don't mind if they do. I simply want to show how using healthy, homemade chocolate in these recipes can result in fabulous desserts.

Please note: It isn't necessary for you to make your own chocolate from scratch–although I do urge you to give it a try. If you choose, you can substitute store-bought chocolate bars in all of the recipes in this book. Just be sure to choose high-quality chocolate to get the luscious results you desire. From tempering chocolate to making truffles to dipping a wide variety of chocolates and desserts in a chocolate coating, we've created recipes a home cook can produce using little more than basic utensils and their new-found knowledge of chocolate.

If, however, you're interested in making chocolate from scratch in your kitchen, this book will simplify the process, and create a comfort level that will add a myriad of chocolate confections to your skill set. Given that making chocolate has, for the most part, eluded home cooks, I've written this book in such a way that you can simply and inexpensively produce your own bar chocolate.

You might ask, *How do I know where and what kind of cacao seeds to buy?* I have recommended a couple of different varieties of cacao that can be sourced easily on the internet (see page 196).

If I choose to make chocolate from the bean, what basic equipment will I need and where can I get it? Foremost, you'll need a mélangeur (a tabletop electric grinder, available for about the price of a good stand mixer); a hair dryer; a cracker to break the cacao beans into pieces and then separate (or winnow) the husk from the nib, or a rolling pin if you prefer to do this by hand. (See page 44.)

I've refined the ganache recipes so they don't require molds, but I've included sources for molds if you wish to create your own chocolate confections (see Source Guide, page 196). Personally, I love to hand-dip

chocolates. It requires a patience I've had to learn, but there is a real beauty in the process. Patience is indeed a fundamental asset to making all chocolates. I don't mean to imply chocolate-making is time-consuming. Instead, I mean it simply requires that a cook take the time to learn slowly, to know the "feel" of working with chocolate. You'll be building a relationship with chocolate.

To truly understand chocolate requires a blended knowledge of the scientific basis as it relates to the physical aspects of chocolate-making. For example, the tempering process allows you to understand the science of the heating, cooling, and movement of chocolate, as you will simultaneously see the physical changes as they correspond to this process.

A good reason–if you still need one by this time–to make your own chocolate from scratch is that homemade chocolate gives you greater control over what you and your family eat. As you now know, the health benefits of eating chocolate made from cacao is far greater than popular opinion concedes. There is no reason anymore for guilt!

How do I know what percentage of cacao to use for these recipes? First you ask yourself "how sweet do I like my chocolate." The lower the percentage of cacao, the sweeter the chocolate. With a higher percentage, the chocolate is darker and less sweet.

The cacao content for bean to bar chocolate in this book will fall between 60 and 70 percent for the final homemade version. If you prefer not to make your chocolate bars at home, you will still enjoy making the recipes in this cookbook. When I indicate dark chocolate as a recipe ingredient, I recommend you choose a chocolate with between 60 and 70 percent cacao. For me, this percentage balances the intensity of the cacao with sweetness nicely. The higher percentage of cacao may also offer the following health benefits:

• Potentially lowers blood pressure
• Decreases LDL ("bad") cholesterol levels
• Lowers risk of blood clots
• Increases blood flow throughout the body, including in the arteries and the heart
• Boosts mood, thanks to increased serotonin and endorphin levels
• Supplies certain minerals such as magnesium and potassium

The higher the percentage of cacao, the richer and more intense the taste of chocolate will be. (See the chart on how to achieve different cacao percentages, page 51.)

If you choose to make your own chocolate from the bean, check out "Flavor Profiles of Cacao Beans," indicating source countries of origin and what flavors the beans present, so that you can choose a taste you prefer. The Source Guide on page 196, will lead you to information on how to order from the different distributors.

I hope a more complete awareness of what you buy as packaged bars will inform your cooking as well as your buying practices, and lead to more transparency in an industry that has always seemed mysterious and unknowable. I believe information arms us, and the more we know about what we eat–and where and how it's grown, harvested, processed, and marketed– the more we are able to take control of our own and our family's health.

Home cooks who make their own bars will have the knowledge and pride that their chocolate treats are truly "from scratch." Knowing how to handle chocolate in its primary form is a wonderful education and introduction to understanding its amazing properties–as well as offering an incredible sense of accomplishment.

I wrote this book to dispel any fear you may have of making and cooking with chocolate, and to offer new and layered recipes for desserts based on chocolate as an ingredient. I hope you will have as much fun with these recipes as I do!

FLAVOR PROFILES OF CACAO BEANS

Cacao is a bean that lends the unique taste and bitterness to chocolate. Cacao is grown in most countries within 20 degrees north and south of the equator. The terroir of different countries of origin—and even the soil of different farms within the same country—will affect the unique flavor profile of that crop. In general, here are the flavors associated with the genetic profiles of the beans.

Criollo
Grown mostly in Central America, Criollo trees produce thin-shelled pods that contain large round white or light purple beans. Considered the highest quality cacao bean, these beans have low astringency with complex mild, nutty, sweet flavor notes.

Forastero
About 80 percent of the world's cacao beans come from these highly productive trees. Grown largely in South America and West Africa, the thick-shelled yellow pods contain flat purple beans. Forastero beans produce a strong chocolate taste with a slightly bitter flavor.

Nacional varietal, grown in Ecuador and Peru, is believed to be a rare rediscovered member of the Forastero family, thought to be extinct. The Nacional bean presents a full cacao flavor with floral and spicy notes.

Trinitario
Grown in all cacao regions of the world, Trinitario originated in Trinidad as a hybrid of the Criollo and Forastero varieties, then spread to Cameroon, Samoa, Sri Lanka, Java, and Papua New Guinea. Trinitario combines the higher-quality aromatic flavor of Criollo with the hardiness and productivity of Forastero. It presents spicy, earthy, and fruity flavor notes.

HOW TO MAKE HOMEMADE CHOCOLATE FROM CACAO BEANS

As described in detail above, chocolate is a solid mixture composed of ground cacao beans, cocoa butter, and some type of sweetener, such as sugar in its most basic form. There are several steps to get from cacao bean to bar chocolate, or couverture. And, of course, prior to the purchase of the beans, there are many steps that are very important to flavor development, including the harvest, when the cacao fruit is cracked open, and the fermentation, which lets the microorganisms heat and kill the seed and develops the chocolate flavor. Once fermented, the beans are sun dried and cleaned.

At this point, the beans are ready for the chocolate-making process. You start by **roasting** the beans to bring out the flavor; next you use a rolling pin to **crack** them into pieces, breaking the shell or husk. Cracking allows you to separate the nib from the husk; then the nibs (which are broken beans) are dehulled, or **winnowed**, to remove the husk, which is then discarded; then the nibs are **ground** with the addition of cane sugar, and the resulting couverture is poured into an airtight container and stored at room temperature for one to two weeks to further develop the flavor of the chocolate. When you have a fine chocolate, the flavor seems to unify over time as it sits. I have not quite come up with a scientific explanation for why this happens, but I have tried and tested different methods and, from what I have observed, the flavor develops over the first six months and I like the results.

For this cookbook, I refer to the couverture in the ingredients list for recipes as the "chocolate base." If you prefer to make any of these recipes using store-bought chocolate, choose a bar with the percentage of cacao you need. I do not recommend using the bar chocolate that is found in the baking section of a grocery store, because it may be a lesser-quality chocolate. Traditionally, I have found that when people view chocolate as an ingredient for baking, the expectation of a lower prices exists–an expectation that inhibits the chocolate maker from producing a higher-quality bar.

The next step in creating your own homemade chocolate is **tempering**, a heating and cooling of the chocolate that crystallizes the cocoa butter within the chocolate to form a solid that is easy to snap. (For instructions, see page 52.)

To begin your own personal chocolate-making journey, you will need a few things. On the next page I've listed items that relate not only to bean to bar making, but also tempering, and other chocolate recipes included in the book so you will have them on hand when you're ready to make your chocolate. Get excited, you are about to take a very fun step!

CHOCOLATE–MAKING EQUIPMENT

See Source Guide, page 196, for suggestions on
how and where to purchase these items.

Tabletop electric grinder/mélangeur with cover

Heat gun

Hair dryer

High–heat rubber spatula

Flat plastic container with a lid, large enough to hold 5 pounds of chocolate

Candy thermometer, ideally a laser thermometer

Double boiler (2– to 8–quart size) or a metal mixing bowl that fits
snuggly into a saucepan to create your own double boiler

Large metal spoon

Parchment paper

Several cookie sheets

Master Technique:
Roasting Your Own Cacao Beans

Roasting the cacao bean is critical for the flavor development of your chocolate. Every person who roasts cacao beans has different flavor prefereces, so as you become more familiar with the process, you'll want to time- and taste-test to find the optimal flavor for you. In this recipe, I suggest a temperature that in my experience works well for chocolate; however, once you perfect this process, I urge you to develop your chocolate's own flavor profile through roasting.

5 pounds whole unroasted cacao beans
(see Source Guide, page 196)

1. Preheat the oven to 250°F.

2. Place the cacao beans on a large baking sheet and sort them, removing and discarding any beans that are shriveled, broken, or have holes.

3. Spread the unroasted beans out on the baking sheet in a single layer.

4. Bake on the center rack of the preheated oven for 45 minutes total. After 20 minutes, stir the beans around on the baking sheet to ensure that they bake evenly, then continue to roast them. While they are roasting, notice the smell they emit. It should turn from a slight vinegary smell to a chocolate brownie aroma. You may also hear the beans begin to snap or crack. This is the shells cracking due to the change in their moisture content. This sound means they are close to being done.

5. After 45 minutes, take the baking sheet out of the oven and pour them into a metal bowl to cool for several hours. You will need to repeat this process if your beans don't all fit in one layer on the baking sheet.

Master Technique:
Cracking the Roasted Cacao Beans

Once the beans are cool, the task of cracking or breaking begins. This step is probably one of the most critical. I think of the shell as a tannin. The only difference between this tannin and the compounds in wine is the tannin in wine is on some level good and desired by the winemaker, while it is never good for the flavor of chocolate.

1. You may have three or four full pans of roasted beans to crack, so you might choose to crack two pans' worth at a time, then repeat the process. Line two large sheet pans with large kitchen towels (linen or cotton rather than terrycloth), then spread a single layer of roasted cacao beans on the towels, leaving 2 inches around the edges of the each towel.

2. Place additional towels on top of the beans, and use a rolling pin to tap or roll over the beans to crack them. As the beans break, the hull will separate from the bean. You want to break all the beans. Check under the towel often, and continue until all the beans are separated from their husks.

3. Repeat this process until you've cracked all the beans. It usually takes about 30 minutes to crack 5 pounds of roasted beans.

Master Technique: Winnowing or Dehulling the Roasted Cacao Beans

The goal of this step is to get every single piece of shell out of the beans. Remember the tannins and how stray pieces of shell can throw off the flavor of the end product. It may sound like a frustrating task, but I assure you the result will be well worth the effort. In the early days of our business we dehulled by hand and found it to be a good time for meditation—or at least a quiet time to think about your plans for the week.

1. Once you've cracked all the beans, remove the towels that cover them and pour your sheet pans of beans into a large metal wide-mouth bowl. Ideally, you will take the bowl outdoors and set up a hairdryer on an extension cord–winnowing is a dirty job. If you can't get outside, you can do this indoors, but be prepared to make a *big* mess. However, it is nothing a good vacuum can't clean up.

2. Aiming the dryer away from the beans, turn the hair dryer on low speed, then slowly bring it around and across the beans, without pointing it directly at them. The husk is lighter than the nibs and so it will blow off in the gentle breeze from the dryer. Just be careful not to blow your nibs right out of the bowl. (This is a learned technique, so expect to lose some nibs the first time you do this.) You can shake the bowl just a bit in-between blasts so that the light husks rise to the surface. Scoop these husks out of the bowl and discard them.

3. Once you've removed the majority of the husks, you can then dump the nibs and leftover husks out of the bowl and onto a baking sheet. You'll have better visibility to differentiate between the husks and the nibs. They are similar in size, but the husks are paper thin and the nibs are heavier. Weight is the main way to differentiate between the two.

4. Remove the remaining husks by hand. This usually takes me about 1 hour per large baking sheet of beans (about 5 pounds of beans).

Tip: Don't throw the husks away. They're full of nutrients and great for replenishing your soil, so add it to compost, or mix it into potting soil.

Master Recipe:
70% Cacao Base Chocolate

Makes 5 pounds couverture (70% cacao base chocolate)

An electric grinder/mélangeur is the key piece of equipment you need to make quality chocolate at home (see Source Guide, page 196). It needs to be powerful enough to grind the beans into very small particles. The best grinders have a granite base and granite wheels inside that rotate against each other. If this is your first time running your grinder, be aware that the stones are going to generate a certain amount of granite dust as they grind. This can greatly affect the flavor of the chocolate. It's best to run a much smaller batch of inferior nibs, or melted cocoa butter, through the machine before making the chocolate you plan to consume. This will allow the stones to not only get rid of their powdery coating but also to begin absorbing the fat from the nibs or cocoa butter. This fat will make the stones turn a much darker shade of gray. After doing a few initial runs to prime the stones and get rid of their dust, you're ready to make some tasty chocolate.

Note: Be aware the initial process of loading the beans into the grinder can take up to 2 hours, so be prepared to stay with it throughout the entire time period.

3½ pounds cacao nibs, cleaned and winnowed (see Tip page 44) (or 3½ pounds store-bought cacao liquor or cacao paste, chopped into small pieces)

1½ pounds sugar

1. Before you begin, make sure your grinder and its stones are clean and dry. You do not want moisture in your chocolate, as it will cause the chocolate to seize up. Turn on the grinder and use a scoop or measuring cup to begin loading your nibs into the grinder immediately, starting with just ½ cup. Initially it will sound like loose stones being thrown around a metal drum, but as the nibs get broken down to smaller pieces, the extraction of the cocoa butter begins.

2. Add a little heat to the wheels of the grinder using a heat gun or hair dryer. Hold the gun 2 inches from the wheel and heat it in 10-second intervals. Be careful not to add too much heat, because you could scorch your nibs. After about 10 minutes, you'll see the nibs start to break down. You'll notice the nibs aren't as noisy as they were at first. At this point, they're beginning to break down, and you should stop adding heat.

3. Once the nibs are broken down enough that they no longer sound like stones bouncing around, you can begin adding your next few scoops of nibs, gradually adding 1 cup at a time and applying heat in the same manner between each addition. You should spend 10 to 15 seconds adding heat between each scoop. This will ensure that the cocoa butter begins to extract and melt before you add more nibs. Watch for the beans to break down before you add another scoop.

4. When you have added about one third of the total nibs, pay particular attention to the nibs inside the grinder. This first stage requires the most delicate touch, because the nibs have not yet reached a fluid state. If you add more nibs too quickly at this stage, you may notice a "donut" forming around the center of the grinder. This donut forms when nibs are added before the previous scoops have broken down. If the "donut" is allowed to grow too large, it will break under its own weight and potentially block your stones, and you risk your machine seizing up.

In fact, the cacao has essentially merged to form one large nib, which has wedged itself under the stones. Avoid the "donut" at all costs! If you notice it starting to build up, just add a little more heat before your next scoop, and everything should keep operating smoothly. (If a donut does cause your machine to seize up, you must remove the donut, break it up, and start the process again while the grinder is running. But you don't want to stop the machine for long, because you need to maintain the heat to break down the nibs. It's not necessary to clean the grinder. Just start the grinder again and repeat the process.)

Some grinders have a lid with an opening to put the nibs through, but if you have a solid lidded grinder, just remove the lid when you're adding the nibs. As you're adding more scoops of nibs, you may notice some small pieces flying out of the grinder. This is normal, but take precautions. You may want to put on protective glasses or goggles, and use the lid that came with the grinder to cover it until everything calms down a bit. If you don't, there will be a large mess to clean up, and you'll also lose product! Then continue adding your nibs.

5. After about 45 minutes to 1 hour, when the first third of the nibs have been added to the grinder, your chocolate should have the consistency of oatmeal. That's because the cocoa butter is finally beginning to melt.

You can begin to add more scoops at a time now, but still apply extra heat every 3 or 4 scoops. Continue to avoid the donut, and try to keep as much of the chocolate from flying out as possible. Finish adding your remaining nibs in this fashion.

6. Once all the nibs are in, the mixture will begin to decrease in volume. At this point, watch for unground nibs that get left behind on the walls of the grinder. Use a hard rubber spatula to scrape down this residue, but don't use too much pressure as you don't want to scratch the grinder.

As you continue grinding, the mixture should start to resemble buttercream in consistency. Now you are ready to begin adding the sugar, 1 cup at a time. Continue running the grinder for a few seconds after each addition to let those crystals break down before adding more sugar.

7. When you've finished adding all the sugar, use a rubber spatula to thoroughly scrape down the surfaces inside the grinder. You want to make sure you get all the nibs and sugar crystals that were left behind and incorporate them into your chocolate.

8. Let the grinder run for 1 hour more, then check again that the sides are still clean and scraped. Replace the lid, and let the grinder continue to run undisturbed for at least 24 hours, to finish the process. The liquid couverture is finished when it looks smooth and glossy and is still pourable. Taste it to make sure it isn't gritty. If it is, continue to grind the couverture for another 2 to 4 hours, then taste it again. Don't worry if it takes longer to achieve perfection. Just repeat the process until the couverture is smooth. It won't hurt to grind for another 24 hours if you need or want to do so. Each type of bean requires different grinding times in order to remove the grittiness from the chocolate. Conversely, if you like a rough texture to the chocolate, then you can decide to stop at an earlier point.

9. When the couverture is ready, stop the grinder. Immediately pour it into lidded plastic containers and let it set for 1 to 2 weeks before you use it in a recipe. Once the chocolate sets, it will lose the smooth, glossy texture and may have white spots, or bloom. Do not worry, this is because the chocolate has not yet been tempered. This base chocolate can be coarsely chopped, and either melted or tempered for use in the recipes in the cookbook; follow the directions within the ingredients list of each recipe with care.

Tip: In making bean to bar chocolate, my preference is not to add extra cocoa butter. Natural cocoa butter already exists in the beans that will be maintained in the grinding process. This natural cocoa butter defines the texture of your chocolate. Adding more cocoa butter–which is adding more fat–changes the melting point of the finished chocolate, so it will melt faster in your mouth. I prefer to use only the butter that is present within the cacao bean. You also must be vigilant if you buy extra cocoa butter to use, as it may not be fresh, or it can have a different aroma from the butter in your bean. Both things will affect the taste of your chocolate.

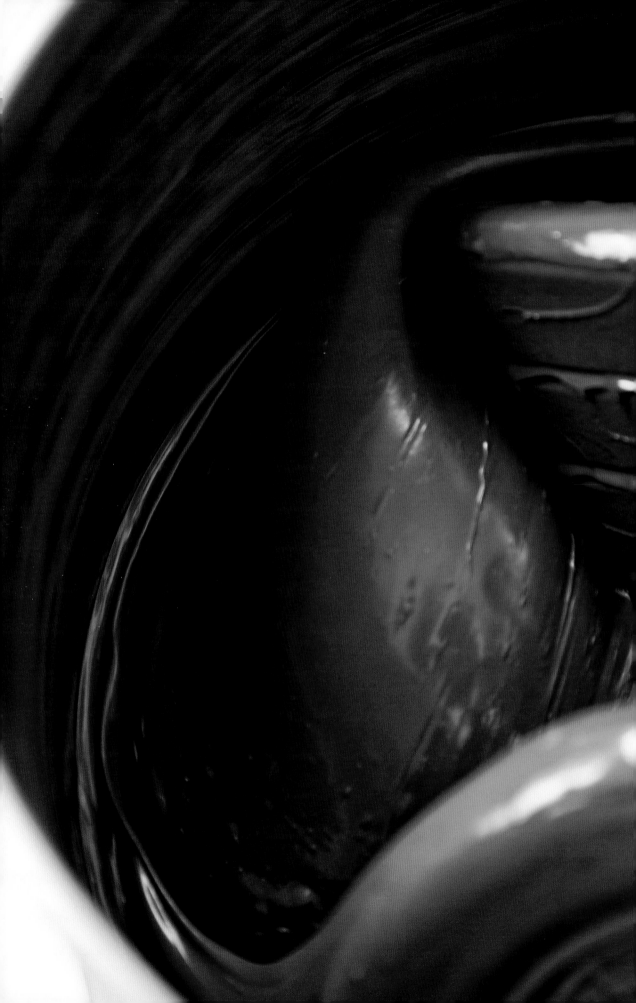

HOW DARK DO YOU LIKE YOUR CHOCOLATE : A GUIDE FOR HOW TO ACHIEVE DIFFERENT CACAO PERCENTAGES

The recipes in this book all call for 70% cacao, but if you prefer a darker chocolate with more cacao, use this chart to figure out your amounts of nibs and sugar to use.

$3\frac{1}{2}$ pounds nibs plus $1\frac{1}{2}$ pounds sugar = 70% cacao

4 pounds nibs plus 1 pound sugar = 80% cacao

$4\frac{1}{2}$ pounds nibs plus $\frac{1}{2}$ pound sugar = 90% cacao

5 pounds nibs = 100% cacao

Master Technique: Tempering the Chocolate

Tempering is an essential step in bringing out the best attributes (the smooth mouthfeel and stability) of chocolate. When chocolate is melted at a temperature high enough to break down the fatty acid crystals of cocoa butter, tempering aligns the crystals in a more stable form.

Tempered chocolate presents a smooth glossy surface for dipping (or enrobing), and prevents the dull, gray color and waxy texture that results when cocoa fat separates out. Tempered chocolate has a crisp snap when you bite into it.

Tempered chocolate can be kept and re-used when you are ready to cook with it. Nothing will be wasted! You may start with less chocolate if you wish, but you will use this tempered chocolate in most of the recipes in this cookbook. Nothing will be wasted!

The Tabling Method

For the recipes in this book, we use the tabling method of tempering. This method will give you a better understanding of the complexity and texture of chocolate, and will familiarize you with the handling of it.

There is a freedom and creativity in cooking with chocolate. To begin, you must allow yourself the freedom to make a mess and make mistakes as you learn the methods. Making chocolate from scratch should be fun! These first steps will help you build a relationship with the chocolate and help you overcome any fear you may have of working with it.

You may start with less chocolate if you wish, but you will use this tempered chocolate in most of the recipes in this cookbook. Nothing will be wasted!

When making chocolate, I work in a room that is around 68°F. It's very difficult to distinguish the exact effect the room temperature and humidity have while working with chocolate. What I can tell you is that the data I have collected over the years leads me to believe extreme highs and lows in room temperature and humidity (like when it is raining outside) make a big difference in your success rate. So, for best results, especially depending on the time of year and conditions of where you live, you may need to adjust the temperature in the room.

1. Melt 2 to 5 pounds 70 percent cacao chocolate in a double boiler over medium heat, just until melted. Use a laser candy thermometer in the pot of chocolate and keep the temperature between 104°F and 113°F.

2. Remove the double boiler from the heat. Allowing yourself at least 3 feet of workspace on a clean marble, stone, or granite surface, pour half the liquid chocolate onto the countertop. Do not use wood or grouted tile. If you don't have a stone countertop, see the Source Guide, page 196, for alternative work surfaces.

3. Using a high-heat rubber offset spatula, simply move the chocolate around: scrape it, mound it, see how it flows from the spatula, let it drip, spread it out, gather it together, and repeat. Don't worry about making a mess when you table the chocolate–just move it around. These motions lower the temperature of the chocolate and allow you time to learn the feel of it. Crystallization begins to take place when the chocolate has cooled 4 or 5 degrees.

4. After several minutes, you'll feel the chocolate begin to thicken, which means it has begun to set up. Before it solidifies completely, use the spatula to transfer it back to the double boiler. With the heat on low, stir to reincorporate with any chocolate left in the pan, then test the chocolate.

Use a butter knife (rather than your spatula as the rubber holds heat and the metal does not) to stir the chocolate mixture until it liquefies again. Lift the knife out of the pot, scrape the chocolate from the back of the knife on the side of the pan, and leave the rest of the chocolate on the face of the knife. Place the knife on the countertop face up and let it sit for a couple of minutes at room temperature. If the chocolate has tempered, it will have a nice sheen when it sets up. This should take only a few minutes.

If the chocolate you have worked doesn't set up quickly, or if it develops a white powder coating (a fat bloom, or sugar bloom), don't worry. The chocolate can be tempered again. If the chocolate is streaky in color, it may have been melted over too high a temperature for too long, or it took too long to cool. Again, don't worry. You can temper it again to correct this.

Keep your tempered chocolate in an airtight container, and store it in a dry, well-ventilated space. The ideal temperature for storing chocolate is 68 F. Tempered chocolate can keep for up to 6 months.

2.

TRUFFLES, GANACHE SQUARES & LAYERED GANACHE CHOCOLATES

Master Technique: Making Ganache

A ganache is simply a combination of chocolate and cream (and any flavorings) that are brought together at optimal temperatures to create a smooth and well-blended mixture called an emulsion. Ganache is used in glazes, icing, sauces, pastries, and truffles. When freshly made, ganache is warm and liquid. In order for it to be used for cut ganache, it needs to cool and set, a process often referred to as allowing it to "harden" (but don't take that term literally, as it actually means something closer to stiffen).

To begin, we will show you how to create ganache chocolates, either cut into squares, rolled into round balls, or layered with pâte de fruit, a fruit gel confection (see page 181). (The term "truffle" refers to any of these chocolate shapes, with possible additions such as cocoa powder, chopped nuts, coconut, etc.) I also use ganache in cake and cookie recipes in this cookbook, and you will find recipes for cream-based ganache chocolates and even vegan ganache.

1. There are two important tips to keep in mind as you are making ganache. First, the size of the bowl you use matters. If you are making a ganache you plan to cut, use a wider bowl; if you are using the ganache in a mold, you want it to remain liquid longer, so use a smaller bowl. A smaller, deeper bowl will hold residual heat longer, extending the amount of time it takes for the ganache to cool and set. A wider bowl, with more surface area exposed to air, will allow the ganache to cool and set faster.

2. Second, ambient temperature matters. Chocolate in general cools, sets, or hardens faster and more easily in cooler, drier atmospheres than in hot and humid ones. If you are making ganache on a summer day, in a kitchen that is not air-conditioned, you may need to pop your ganache in the refrigerator for a little bit to help it cool.

3. If you have followed all the instructions and your ganache is still not smooth, but has a streaky or grainy look, this means the ganache has not emulsified properly and has "broken." Slowly whisk in a small amount of cold heavy cream until you achieve the proper consistency, then continue as directed in the recipe.

4. Be aware that the finished ganache needs to cool to room temperature in order to set. This cooling process can take up to 4 hours depending on the ambient air temperature.

5. Once your ganache has cooled to the consistency of peanut butter, it's ready to be transformed into finished chocolates. You may shape it into truffles, ganache squares, or layered ganaches–just choose from among the master ganache recipes.

Tip: Most of the ganache recipes in this book can be converted to vegan or sugar free by swapping in coconut oil for the dairy, or eliminating the sugar. Note that eliminating sugar in the recipe will not yield an entirely sugar-free chocolate unless the couverture (chocolate coating) is made using 100 percent cacao; see "How to Achieve Different Cacao Percentages," page 51.

Master Technique:
How to Dip Truffles and Other Ingredients in Chocolate

Dipping chocolates with a fork can be tricky as this is one of the steps that you will notice will need work to fine tune. As a chocolatier, one of the ways we perfect our craft is to balance the outer shell with the ganache inside. If the shell is too thick, it overpowers the chocolate piece and if it is too thin, you miss the texture that makes it what it is. You will find that as you work the chocolate will change temperature and thus the shell will change thickness. My suggestion is to work on this step over and over till you get the hang of it. Don't beat yourself up, as even the pieces that are not perfect will still taste great.

1. The ganache chocolates will be delicious lightly dusted with cocoa powder; however, if you like, the shaped chocolates may be dipped, or enrobed, in tempered chocolate to create a smooth, glossy finish and an extra layer of chocolaty goodness.

2. To dip one batch of truffles made following any one of the master ganache recipes, you'll need to temper 1 pound of 70 percent chocolate. (For tempering instructions, see page 52).

Set your baking sheet of truffles, ganache squares, or layered ganaches on your work surface, where you can reach them. (The chocolates may be easily lifted from the parchment using a spatula, or your hand.) Line a second sheet pan with parchment paper and set it aside. Temper your chocolate according to the directions and place the bowl of tempered chocolate in your workspace.

3. Working one at a time and using a chocolate dipping fork (or a regular dinner fork with long tines), gently place one truffle on the end of the fork tines (don't skewer it) and dunk the truffle into the tempered chocolate, keeping the truffle balanced on the end of the fork as you submerge it until it is completely covered in the melted chocolate. Gently bounce the fork a few times so that the ganache is well coated in the tempered chocolate. Slowly remove the fork and truffle from the chocolate, and gently tap the fork against the side of the bowl to allow any excess chocolate to drip off the truffle and back into the bowl.

Too much extra chocolate on the truffle will form a puddle around the truffle as the chocolate sets, and you want to avoid that. Carefully release the piece of chocolate-enrobed ganache from the dipping fork onto the parchment paper–lined pan to set. (You may tap the fork on the side of the bowl to help gently release the truffle from the fork tines.)

4. If your tempered chocolate starts to harden, return it to the double boiler and stir for a few seconds over medium heat to remelt the chocolate. However, if your chocolate has hardened completely, you will need to temper it again.

This process of enrobing truffles in chocolate takes between 10 and 20 seconds per truffle. Practice makes perfect, so don't worry if you don't achieve perfection on your first batch. The truffles will still taste great!

Tip: If you want to add another layer of flavor or texture to your truffles, you can roll them in a variety of toppings (such as cocoa powder, coconut flakes, or ground nuts) immediately after removing them from the tempered chocolate, before the chocolate hardens.

Allow 1 to 1½ hours for the finished truffles to set. They will keep, refrigerated, in an airtight container, with wax paper or parchment paper separating the layers, for 2 weeks.

Master Recipe:
Cream-Based Dark Chocolate Ganache Truffles

Makes about 2 dozen round or square truffles

These classic truffles are made from chocolate ganache, butter, and sugar, shaped into balls or squares, and coated with cocoa. To make 2 dozen sugar-free truffles, omit both the cane and invert sugar and double the quantities of the cream and use 100% base chocolate.

$3^{1}/_{4}$ cups cane sugar

$^{3}/_{4}$ cup invert sugar (see Source Guide, page 196)

$^{3}/_{4}$ cup heavy cream

12 ounces 70% Cacao Base Chocolate (page 47) or highest-quality store-bought chocolate, coarsely chopped ($1^{1}/_{4}$ cups), melted and kept lukewarm

2 cups natural (non-alkalized) cocoa powder, for coating

Step 1. In a medium saucepan over medium-low heat, combine half of the heavy cream, the cane sugar, and invert sugar, stirring constantly until both sugars dissolve. Remove the pan from the heat and pour into a medium-sized glass or stainless steel mixing bowl.

Step 2. Add the remaining heavy cream to the bowl and slowly whisk in the melted chocolate until the mixture is emulsified.

Step 3. Set the bowl aside to cool for at least 1 hour, until the ganache sets and is firm to the touch but not solid.

Note: if you are making square ganache chocolates instead of round truffles, at this stage you should pour the ganache into a 9 x 12-inch baking sheet or frame (see Source Guide, page 196). Let it set at room temperature for 4 to 6 hours, then slice into 1- to $1^{1}/_{2}$-inch squares using a long, slender, sharp chef's knife.

Step 4. To make round truffles, use a small ($^{1}/_{3}$-ounce) ice cream scoop with a squeeze handle or a melon baller to scoop the cooled ganache into twenty-four 1 to $1^{1}/_{2}$-inch balls, placing them on a parchment paper-lined baking sheet or pan. You also can also use a teaspoon to scoop the ganache and shape it into balls by hand. It's okay if they're not perfectly round.

Step 5. Put the cocoa powder in a medium bowl. Working one at a time, use your hands to roll the balls in the cocoa until well coated, returning them to the baking sheet until all the balls are coated. Transfer the truffles to the refrigerator for at least 2 hours or until chilled before serving.

The finished truffles will keep, refrigerated, in an airtight container between layers of wax or parchment paper, for up to 1 month.

Master Recipe:
Vegan Dark Chocolate Ganache Truffles

Makes about 2 dozen round or square truffles

You can make equally delicious vegan ganache truffles by swapping coconut oil for heavy cream in the recipes. Glucose is a sugar syrup made mainly from the starch of corn, potatoes, or wheat. Glucose is used as a substitute for sugar and it can be purchased online (see Source Guide, page 196) and in some grocery stores. Brown rice syrup, a natural sweetener with a butterscotch-like flavor, can be substituted in place of the glucose, if you prefer. It is available at health food stores or grocery store chains specializing in natural foods. I don't recommend substituting corn syrup because high-fructose corn syrup can spike sugar levels.

Make sure that all of the ingredients are lukewarm, between 90 and 105°F before you combine them. Any ingredient that is too hot will cause the ganache to separate or break. If the ganache separates, stop mixing and put it into the freezer. Every 5 to 8 minutes, take it out of the freezer and mix it again until it comes back together. If the ganache becomes too hard, pop it in the microwave on high for 5-second intervals until a creamy consistency is achieved.

$3/4$ cup coconut oil, melted and cooled to lukewarm

Scant 3 tablespoons glucose or brown rice syrup (see above), at room temperature

1 pound 15 ounces 70% Cacao Base Chocolate (page 47) or highest-quality store-bought chocolate bars, coarsely chopped ($3^1/4$ cups), melted and kept lukewarm

$3/4$ cup room temperature water

2 cups natural (non-alkalized) cocoa powder

Step 1. Combine the coconut oil and glucose in a wide glass or metal mixing bowl and whisk to combine.

Step 2. Add the melted chocolate and stir with a silicone spatula until smooth and emulsified.

Step 3. Stir in the water, being careful not to overmix as this may cause the ganache to separate (see Tip). Stop stirring as soon as the ganache begins to slowly come together and thicken.

Note: If you're making square ganache chocolates instead of round truffles, at this stage you should pour the ganache into a 9 x 12-inch baking sheet or frame (see Source Guide, page 196)). Let it set at room temperature for 4 to 6 hours, then slice into 1- to 1½-inch squares with a long, slender, sharp chef's knife.

Step 4. To make round truffles, set the bowl of ganache aside to cool at room temperature until the chocolate has set to the consistency of pudding.

Step 5. Use a small (⅓-ounce) ice cream scoop with a squeeze handle or a melon baller to scoop the cooled ganache into twenty-four 1 to 1½-inch balls, placing them on a parchment paper–lined baking sheet or pan. You can also use a teaspoon and scoop the ganache and shape it into balls by hand. It's okay if they're not perfectly round.

Step 6. Put the cocoa powder in a medium bowl. Working one at a time, roll the balls in the cocoa powder until well coated, returning them to the baking sheet until all the balls are coated. Transfer the truffles to the refrigerator for at least 2 hours or until chilled before serving. The finished truffles will keep in an airtight container in the refrigerator for up to 1 month.

One-Step Ganache Variations

Either of the master recipes for Cream-Based Dark Chocolate Ganach or Vegan Dark Chocolate Ganache (pages 60-62) can be flavored according to the variations below. Simply mix in the additional ingredients called for in your variation of choice, as specified. Cool the ganache as described in Step 4 of all of the master recipes, then dip in tempered chocolate to finish to create a smooth, glossy finish (see "Master Technique: How to Dip Truffles and Other Ingredients in Chocolate," page 58).

Aztec Ganache Chocolates

These chocolates have a tempered spice that builds very nicely on your palate as you consume them. You can adjust the cayenne, chile powder, or red pepper quantities depending on how spicy you want your ganache to be.

Add 1 to 2 teaspoons Aztec Powder (page 177) to the warm cream or coconut oil in Step 2 of the master recipe, and stir to combine before adding the melted chocolate.

Fig and Balsamic Ganache Chocolates

Be sure to choose an aged balsamic when preparing this variation. The older the balsamic vinegar, the more sweetness it adds to the ganache.

In Step 3 of the master recipe, add $1/4$ cup fig jam, 1 tablespoon aged balsamic vinegar, and 2 teaspoons vanilla extract to the emulsified ganache. Mix thoroughly to combine and set aside to cool.

Coconut-Caramel Ganache Chocolates

This recipe calls for sweetened shredded coconut from a package. If you want to substitute fresh grated coconut, add sugar by the teaspoonful, tasting as you go, to balance the sweetness of the recipe. Also, be careful not to let the caramel sauce get too hot in Step 3, or it will become too firm when it cools. If your caramel is rock hard, then you've let it overheat.

In Step 3 of the master recipe, add $1/4$ cup thick, homemade Whisky Caramel Sauce (page 195) or your favorite brand of store-bought caramel sauce, and $1/3$ cup toasted, shredded sweetened coconut to the emulsified ganache. Mix thoroughly to combine and set aside to cool.

Note: This recipe cannot be made using the vegan master dark chocolate ganache recipes.

Orange Ganache Chocolates

This recipe is light on the orange flavor, but if you love the orange-chocolate combination, don't hesitate to use more candied orange or orange marmalade. In Step 3 of the master recipe, add $1^{1}/2$ tablespoons chopped candied orange and $1/4$ cup orange marmalade to the emulsified ganache. Mix thoroughly to combine and set aside to cool.

Lemon Ganache Chocolates

Dark chocolate paired with lemon tastes really delectable. Use a Meyer lemon when making the candied lemon peel, because it has a thicker peel and will contribute more lemon flavor overall than a regular lemon.

In Step 3 of the master recipe, add $1^{1}/2$ tablespoons chopped candied lemon peel (see page 190) and $1/4$ cup lemon curd (page 187) to the emulsified chocolate, mix thoroughly to combine, and set aside to cool.

Pink Peppercorn–Ginger Ganache Chocolates

If you think this sounds like a spicy recipe, then eat a pink peppercorn and you'll understand that it has a floral, rather than a spicy, taste. You can purchase the candied ginger at most grocery stores.

In Step 3 of the master recipe, add 1 tablespoon crushed pink peppercorns and $1/4$ cup chopped candied ginger to the emulsified ganache. Mix thoroughly to combine and set aside to cool.

Mint Ganache Chocolates

Use a peppermint essential oil for the flavoring, but be aware that there is no standardized strength among the different peppermint oil brands. Taste test the oil before you use, and remember it's always easier to use less than a recipe calls for at first, then add more if needed.

In Step 3, add up to $1/8$ teaspoon peppermint essential oil to the emulsified ganache. (I suggest adding less at first, then taste for strength before adding the rest.) Mix thoroughly to combine and set aside to cool.

Pecan Pie Ganache Chocolates

If you don't have access to a food processor to chop the pecans, chop them finely and evenly with a sharp chef's knife.

In Step 3, add $1/4$ cup finely chopped pecans and 1 tablespoon molasses to the emulsified ganache. Mix thoroughly to combine and set aside to cool.

Hazelnut Ganache Chocolates

Different varieties of hazelnut express different flavors. Just buy a good-quality shelled hazelnut from your grocer to start.

In Step 3, add $1/4$ cup finely chopped hazelnuts and 1 tablespoon molasses to the emulsified ganache. Mix thoroughly to combine and set aside to cool.

Two-Step Ganache Variations

These two-step variations are only slightly more complicated than the one-step variations above. Either of the master recipes for ganache chocolates or truffles (pages 60-62) can be flavored according to the variations below. Simply mix in the additional ingredients called for in your variation of choice, taking care to add them in the specified steps. Cool the ganache as described in Step 4 of all of the master recipes, then dip in tempered chocolate to finish to create a smooth, glossy finish (see "Master Technique: How to Dip Truffles and Other Ingredients in Chocolate," page 58).

Laphroaig & Ginger Ganache Chocolates

Laphroaig single-malt Scotch whisky, aged 10 years, has a deep peaty taste (think smoky), Scotch drinkers love, particularly the men. This ganache chocolate is a great gift for Father's Day, or for the Scotch drinker in your life on any occasion. Candied ginger is available at any well-stocked grocery store.

In Step 1 of the master recipe, whisk ½ tablespoon Laphroaig Scotch whisky into the ingredients in the saucepan. In Step 3, add ¼ cup candied ginger and 1 teaspoon ground ginger to the emulsified ganache. Mix thoroughly to combine and set aside to cool.

Bourbon–Espresso Ganache Chocolates

Lots of different smaller batch coffees are available on the market today. I recommend using a coffee with a nutty flavor rather than a fruity one. Check the tasting notes on packages to help make your choice. A fruity coffee will clash with the bourbon, and the finished chocolate will have a sour taste.

In Step 1 of the master recipe, whisk 1 tablespoon bourbon into the ingredients in the saucepan. In Step 3, mix ½ teaspoon finely ground espresso beans into the emulsified ganache. Mix thoroughly to combine and set aside to cool.

Rum–Raisin Ganache Chocolates

I have read that rum raisins are good for combatting the symptoms of arthritis, so I like to give these chocolates to my loved elders. If you use a mix of both dark and light raisins, your ganache will have a tasty layering of flavors.

Soak ¼ cup raisins overnight in enough dark rum to cover. The next day, strain and discard the rum, setting the soaked raisins aside.

Prepare the master recipe through Step 2. In Step 3, add up to ⅛ teaspoon cinnamon essential oil and all of the raisins to the emulsified ganache. Mix thoroughly to combine and set aside to cool.

Raspberry–Thyme Ganache Chocolates

In a raspberry thyme preserve, the thyme flavor disappears over time (pardon the pun!). If you want to add fresh thyme to enhance that flavor, first clean it under hot water, and chop it very finely. Add a teaspoon of the chopped fresh thyme to the cream as it comes to a boil. Once the cream comes to a boil, strain it, discarding the thyme.

In Step 1 of the master recipe, add 1½ tablespoons finely chopped thyme leaves to the saucepan. In Step 2, pour the hot cream mixture through a fine-mesh sieve and into a heatproof bowl, discarding the thyme, then stir in the remaining cream. In Step 3, add ¼ cup raspberry jam to the emulsified ganache, mix thoroughly to combine, and set aside to cool.

Note: This variation can't successfully be made using the vegan master ganache recipes because its flavor relies heavily on fresh cream.

Blueberry–Lavender Ganache Chocolates

The strength of the lavender flavor is critical to the success of these chocolates. If the lavender taste is not strong enough for your liking, substitute fresh lavender flowers. Clean the flowers well in hot water and add them to the cream as it comes to a boil. Once the cream comes to a boil, strain it, discarding the lavender flowers.

In Step 1 of the master recipe, add 2 tablespoons freshly chopped, culinary-grade lavender to the saucepan. In Step 2, pour the hot cream mixture through a fine-mesh sieve and into a heatproof bowl, discarding the lavender; stir in the remaining cream. In Step 3, add 1/4 cup Blueberry-Lavender Confiture (page 184) or blueberry jam of your choice to the emulsified ganache, mix thoroughly to combine, and set aside to cool.

Master Recipe:
Cream–Based Ganache Truffles

Makes about 24 (1-inch) chocolates

Cream-based truffles are very familiar to people—they've been included in boxed chocolates for decades. Originally ganache was invented because someone spilled hot cream into chocolate—and it was an instant flavor and texture success. If you prefer to make these chocolates as squares, refer to page 69 for the directions.

2 cups heavy cream

1 pound 12$\frac{1}{2}$ ounces 70% Cacao Base Chocolate
(page 47) or highest-quality store-bought chocolate
bars, coarsely chopped (3 cups), at room temperature

Step 1. Place a medium, heavy-bottomed saucepan on the stovetop and add 1 cup of the heavy cream. Cook over medium-low heat until the cream is just about to come to a boil, then remove the pan from the stovetop.

Step 2. Pour the hot cream into a heatproof bowl. Stir in the remaining 1 cup cream.

Step 3. Mix the chocolate into the warm cream mixture, whisking slowly and continuously until the ganache is smooth and emulsified.

Step 4. Set the bowl aside for 20 to 30 minutes to cool to room temperature and set. When it thickens to the consistency of peanut butter, it's ready.

Step 5: Use a small ($\frac{1}{3}$-ounce) ice cream scoop with a squeeze handle or a melon baller to scoop the cooled ganache into twenty-four 1 to 1 $\frac{1}{2}$-inch) balls, placing them on a parchment paper–lined baking sheet or pan. You can also use a teaspoon to scoop and shape the ganache into balls by hand. It's okay if they aren't perfectly round.

Step 6: Working one at a time, roll each ball in your choice of spices until well coated, returning them to the baking sheet until all the balls are coated. Transfer the truffles to the refrigerator for at least 2 hours or until chilled before serving. The finished chocolates will keep in an airtight container in the refrigerator for up to 1 month.

Master Recipe:
Vegan Dark Chocolate Ganache Squares

Makes about 24 (1-inch) chocolates

While we enjoy historic methods for making ganache, these days there is a popular desire, and sometimes need, to move away from dairy. In these recipes, we substitute coconut oil for the heavy cream—trading a fat for a fat; glucose or brown rice syrup are sweeteners with a clean taste. There are other flavors on the market, but be aware that they all have different flavors and will affect the taste of your ganache.

$^3/_4$ cup coconut oil, melted and kept warm

Scant 3 tablespoons glucose or brown rice syrup (see Source Guide, page 196), at room temperature

1 pound 15 ounces 70% Cacao Base Chocolate (page 47) or highest-quality store-bought chocolate bars, coarsely chopped ($3^1/_4$ cups), melted and kept lukewarm

$^3/_4$ cup room temperature water

2 cups natural (non-alkalized) cocoa powder

19 ounces 70% Cacao Base Chocolate (page 47) or chocolate bars, coarsely chopped (2 cups), melted, and tempered (see page 52), for dipping

Step 1. Combine the coconut oil and glucose in a medium-sized mixing bowl and whisk to combine.

Step 2. Add the melted chocolate and stir until smooth and emulsified.

Step 3. Stir in the water, being careful not to overmix as this may cause the ganache to separate (break). Stop stirring as soon as the ganache slowly begins to come together and thicken.

Step 4. Set the ganache bowl aside at room temperature to cool until the chocolate has set to the consistency of pudding.

Step 5. Finish by spreading the ganache about $^1/_4$ inch thick onto a parchment paper–lined baking sheet to cool, then cut into 1-inch squares using a sharp, well-oiled knife.

Step 6. Make sure the bowl of warm tempered chocolate is at least 1 inch deep. Working one at a time and using a chocolate dipping fork (or a regular dinner fork with long tines), gently place one ganache square on the end of the fork tines (don't skewer it) and dunk the square into the tempered chocolate, keeping it balanced on the end of the fork as you submerge it, until it is completely covered in the melted chocolate.

Gently bounce the fork a few times so that the ganache square is well coated in the tempered chocolate. Slowly remove the fork and square from the chocolate, and gently tap the fork against the side of the bowl to allow any excess chocolate to drip off the ganache square and back into the bowl. Too much extra chocolate on the square will form a puddle around the square as the chocolate sets, and you want to avoid that. Carefully release the piece of chocolate-enrobed ganache from the dipping fork onto the parchment paper–lined pan to set. (You may use the side of the bowl to lift the truffle just a bit off the fork so that it slides off easily onto the parchment paper.)

This process of enrobing ganache squares in chocolate takes between 10 and 20 seconds per square. Practice makes perfect, so don't worry if you don't achieve perfection on your first batch. The ganache squares will still taste great!

The finished ganache squares will keep in an airtight container in the refrigerator for up to 1 month.

Bourbon–Espresso Vegan Ganache Chocolates

Mix ⅓ cup bourbon, ½ cup brewed room temperature espresso, and 1 tablespoon finely ground espresso beans in a small bowl until combined. Omit the water in Step 3 of the master recipe and instead stir the bourbon–espresso mixture into the emulsified coconut oil and chocolate mixture, being careful to not overmix, as this may cause the ganache to separate (break). Finish by spreading the ganache onto a prepared baking sheet to cool and set, cut into 1-inch squares using a sharp, well-oiled knife, and dip in the tempered chocolate as described.

Orange Blossom Vegan Ganache Chocolates

Orange blossoms lend a very floral taste to these chocolates. I use Neroli oil, an essential oil produced from the blossoms of the bitter orange tree, which has a balanced orange blossom flavor and scent. Use just 3 drops to start, then taste to see if you want to add more.

In Step 3, combine 3 teaspoons orange blossom oil with the water, and add this to the emulsified coconut oil and chocolate mixture, being careful not to overmix, as this may cause the ganache to separate (break). Finish by spreading the ganache onto a prepared baking sheet to cool and set, cut into 1-inch squares using a sharp, well-oiled knife, and dip in the tempered chocolate as described.

Peppermint Vegan Ganache Chocolates

This is a great chocolate for holiday gift-giving, or to keep on hand for a refreshing after dinner sweet. If you are gifting them, these don't need to be individually wrapped. I like to decorate them with a fresh mint leaf pressed into the top of each square after you dip them in the tempered chocolate.

Combine ⅔ teaspoon peppermint extract with the water in Step 3, and add this to the emulsified coconut oil and chocolate mixture, being careful to not overmix, as this may cause the ganache to separate (break). Finish by spreading the ganache onto a prepared baking sheet to cool and set, cut into 1-inch squares using a sharp, well-oiled knife, and dip in the tempered chocolate as described.

Sea Salt–Tequila Vegan Ganache Chocolates

I like to use pink Himalayan sea salt or fleur de sel in my chocolates. Just check the size of the grain, and use less if it's a larger grain. To make a high-end version of this recipe, substitute an aged dark tequila.

Stir ⅓ cup tequila, ⅓ cup water, and 2 teaspoons sea salt (see above) in a small bowl until combined. Omit the water in Step 3 of the master recipe, and instead stir the tequila mixture into the emulsified coconut oil and chocolate mixture, being careful to not overmix, as this may cause the ganache to separate (break). Finish by spreading the ganache onto a prepared baking sheet to cool and set, cut into 1-inch squares using a sharp oiled knife, and dip in the tempered chocolate as described.

Ginger Ganache Vegan Chocolates

This variation contains a trio of gingery ingredients for an extra-spicy ginger taste experience. Both candied ginger and ginger beer are available at most well-stocked grocery stores.

Mix together $3/4$ cup ginger beer, $3/4$ cup chopped candied ginger, and 1 tablespoon powdered ginger in a small bowl until combined. Omit the water in Step 3 of the master recipe, and instead stir the ginger beer mixture into the emulsified coconut oil and chocolate mixture, being careful to not overmix, as this may cause the ganache to separate (break). Finish by spreading the ganache onto a prepared baking sheet to cool and set, then cut into 1-inch squares using a sharp, well-oiled knife, and dip in the tempered chocolate as described.

Honey-Ginseng Vegan Ganache Chocolates

A natural preservative, honey extends the shelf life of these chocolates. In fact, feel free to use a little bit of honey in any of these vegan chocolate variations: it will sweeten them further without changing the viscosity. Use local honey for its healing property. If you prefer, you may substitute light agave syrup for the honey.

Mix $1/3$ cup water, $1/8$ teaspoon organic lemon balm extract, $1/8$ teaspoon ginseng powder, and $1/2$ cup finely chopped Candied Lemon Peel (recipe, page 190, or order online) in a small bowl until well combined. Omit the water in Step 3 of the master recipe, and instead add this lemony mixture to the emulsified coconut oil and dark chocolate mixture, being careful to not overmix, as this may cause the ganache to separate (break). Finish by spreading the ganache onto a prepared baking sheet to cool and set, then cut into 1-inch squares using a sharp, well-oiled knife, and dip in tempered chocolate (see page 58).

Rosemary-Cardamom Vegan Ganache Chocolates

I call this "The Protect" because it produces a subtle feeling of balance that gets you through tough days. The rosemary is a natural analgesic, or painkiller, that pairs with the cardamom to give you a healthy, radiant energy. I clip rosemary out of my yard, but you can also use powdered rosemary for a similar effect.

Rosemary-Cardamom-Infused Coconut Oil

1 cup coconut oil

3 teaspoons freshly chopped rosemary

1 teaspoon ground cardamom

Rosemary-Cardamom Ganache

$^1/_3$ cup Rosemary-Cardamom-Infused Coconut Oil (recipe above), melted and cooled to lukewarm

$^1/_2$ cup coconut oil, melted and cooled to lukewarm

Scant 3 tablespoons glucose (see Source Guide, page 196), at room temperature

$^3/_4$ cup lukewarm water

1 pound 15 ounces 70% Cacao Base Chocolate (page 47) or highest-quality store-bought chocolate bars, coarsely chopped ($3^1/_4$ cups), melted and kept lukewarm

Make the infused oil: In a small, heavy-bottomed saucepan over medium heat, melt the coconut oil. Add the rosemary and cardamom, stirring well to combine, and cook for 5 minutes.

Pour the coconut oil mixture into a heatproof bowl and set aside to cool. When it has reached room temperature, cover and steep overnight in the refrigerator.

The next day, strain the mixture through a fine-mesh sieve and store the infused oil in an airtight container for up to 1 month.

Make the ganache: Line a 9 x 12-inch baking sheet or frame (see Source Guide, page 196) with parchment paper and set aside.

In a small bowl, whisk the infused coconut oil, melted coconut oil, and glucose. Add the melted chocolate and stir until smooth and emulsified.

Incorporate the lukewarm water, stirring continuously but being careful to not overmix, as this may cause the ganache to separate (break). Stop stirring as soon as the ganache begins to come together and thicken. Using an offset spatula, spread the ganache onto the prepared baking sheet, making an even layer about

$^1/_4$ inch thick. Set aside to cool and set until the ganache is firm to the touch, about 20 to 30 minutes.

When the ganache is set, flip the pan upside down to unmold the ganache onto a clean sheet of parchment paper. Peel the parchment paper from the top of the ganache and discard.

Using a paring knife or a pizza cutter, cut the ganache into squares, rectangles, or triangles. Save the scraps and form them into balls, if you like.

The ganache is ready to eat at this point; however, if you like, you may dip the pieces in tempered chocolate (see the master dipping technique, page 58) or dust with cocoa powder (see page 58). The infused chocolates will keep for up to 1 month in an airtight container in the refrigerator.

Smoked Habanero Vegan Ganache Chocolates

To add extra smokiness to the chile pepper's taste, I use tongs to hold the habanero over a burner or grill, scorching it until it's almost black. Just take care that you're scorching only the skin and not the interior of the pepper.

Infused Smoked Habanero Coconut Oil

1 cup coconut oil

1 cup smoked habanero pepper (see above), seeded and chopped

Smoked Habanero Ganache

$1/3$ cup Infused Smoked Habanero Coconut Oil (recipe above), melted and cooled to lukewarm

$1/2$ cup coconut oil, melted and cooled to lukewarm

Scant 3 tablespoons glucose (see page 196), at room temperature

$3/4$ cup lukewarm water

1 pound 15 ounces 70% Cacao Base Chocolate (page 47) or highest-quality chocolate bars, coarsely chopped ($3^1/4$ cups), melted and kept lukewarm

Make the infused oil: In a small, heavy-bottomed saucepan over medium heat, melt the coconut oil. Add the chopped pepper, stirring well to combine, and cook for 5 minutes.

Pour the coconut oil mixture into a heatproof bowl and set aside to cool. When it has reached room temperature, cover and steep overnight in the refrigerator.

The next day, strain the mixture through a fine-mesh sieve and store the infused oil in an airtight container for up to 1 month.

Make the ganache: Line a 9 x 12-inch baking sheet or frame (see Source Guide, page 196) with parchment paper and set aside.

In a small bowl, whisk the infused coconut oil, the melted coconut oil, and the glucose. Add the melted chocolate and stir until smooth and emulsified.

Incorporate the lukewarm water, stirring continuously but being careful to not overmix, as this may cause the ganache to separate (break). Stop stirring as soon as the ganache begins to come together and thicken.

Using an offset spatula, spread the ganache onto the prepared baking sheet, making an even layer $1/4$ inch thick. Set aside to cool and set until the ganache is firm to the touch, about 20 to 30 minutes.

When the ganache is set, flip the pan upside down to release the ganache onto a clean sheet of parchment paper. Peel the parchment paper from the top of the ganache and discard.

Use a paring knife or a pizza cutter, cut the ganache into your desired shapes and sizes. Save the scraps and form them into balls, if you like.

The ganache is ready to eat at this point; however, if you like, you may dip the pieces in tempered chocolate (see the master dipping technique, page 58) or dust with a powder (see page 58). The infused chocolates will keep for up to 1 month in an airtight container in the refrigerator.

Fennel-Lime Vegan Ganache Chocolates

My little girl, Delphine, fell in love with fennel as a baby—I don't particularly like the licorice flavor, but many people love it. The addition of the lime brightens the licorice flavor of the fennel. If you want more lime taste, don't add juice, stir the zest of 1 lime into the ganache when you add the candied lime pieces. If you don't want to make your own candied lime citrus peel (page 190), you can purchase it online, but I recommend that you try my recipe—it's easier than you might think.

Fennel-Infused Lime Coconut Oil

1 cup coconut oil

$1^1/_2$ tablespoons ground fennel seeds

Fennel Lime Ganache

$^1/_3$ cup diced Candied Lime Zest (recipe, page 190)

Zest of 1 lime, optional

$^3/_4$ cup Fennel-Infused Lime Coconut Oil (recipe above), melted and cooled to lukewarm

$^1/_2$ cup coconut oil, melted and cooled to lukewarm

Scant 3 tablespoons glucose (see Source Guide, page 196), at room temperature

1 pound 15 ounces 70% Cacao Base Chocolate (page 47) or highest-quality store-bought chocolate bars, coarsely chopped ($3^1/_4$ cups), melted and kept lukewarm

Make the infused oil: In a small, heavy-bottomed saucepan over medium heat, melt the coconut oil, then stir in the fennel seeds and cook for 5 minutes.

Pour the coconut oil mixture into a heatproof bowl and set aside to cool. When it has reached room temperature, cover and steep overnight in the refrigerator.

The next day, strain the mixture through a fine-mesh sieve and store the infused oil in an airtight container for up to 1 month.

Make the ganache: Line a 9 x 12-inch baking sheet or frame (see page xx) with parchment paper and set aside.

Mix $^3/_4$ cup water, the diced candied lime, and the optional lime zest for deeper lime flavor, if desired, in a small bowl and set aside.

Whisk the infused oil, coconut oil, and glucose in a separate small bowl.

Add the melted chocolate and stir until smooth and emulsified.

Carefully stir in the diced candied lime mixture, being careful to not overmix as this may cause the ganache to separate (break). Stop stirring as soon as the ganache begins to slowly come together and thicken. Using an offset spatula, spread the ganache onto the prepared baking sheet, making an even $^1/_4$-inch-thick layer. Set aside to cool and set until the ganache is firm to the touch, about 20 to 30 minutes.

When the ganache is set, flip the pan upside down to unmold the ganache onto a clean sheet of parchment paper. Peel the parchment paper from the top of the ganache and discard.

Using a paring knife or a pizza cutter, cut the ganache into your desired shapes and sizes. Save the scraps and form them into balls, if you like.

The ganache is ready to eat at this point; however, if you like, you may dip the pieces in tempered chocolate (see the master dipping technique, page 58) or dust with a powder (see page 58). The infused chocolates will keep for up to 1 month in an airtight container in the refrigerator.

Earl Grey–Aperol Vegan Ganache Chocolates

Use any brand of loose leaf Earl Grey tea leaves. Keep in mind that the fresher the tea leaves, the better the end result will taste. Aperol is an Italian aperitif liqueur that is made from bitter oranges and different herbs and spices and can be purchased at most liquor stores. If you prefer not to add alcohol, you may substitute the zest of 1 orange for the Aperol. You can substitute store-bought candied orange, available online, if you prefer.

Earl Grey–Infused Aperol

$^3/_4$ cup Aperol

3 tablespoons loose-leaf Earl Grey tea

Earl Grey–Aperol Ganache

$^3/_4$ cup lukewarm Earl Grey–Infused Aperol (recipe above)

$^3/_4$ cup finely chopped Candied Orange Peel (recipe, page 190)

$^3/_4$ cup coconut oil, melted and cooled to lukewarm

Scant 3 tablespoons glucose (see Source Guide, page 196), at room temperature

1 pound 15 ounces 70% Cacao Base Chocolate (page 47) or highest-quality store-bought chocolate bars, coarsely chopped (3$^1/_4$ cups), melted and kept lukewarm

Make the infused Aperol: Heat the Aperol in a small, heavy-bottomed saucepan over medium heat until just warm. Add the tea leaves, stir well to combine, and cook for 5 minutes.

Pour the Aperol mixture into a heatproof bowl and set aside to cool. When it reaches room temperature, cover and steep overnight in the refrigerator.

The next day, strain the mixture through a fine-mesh sieve and store the Aperol infusion in an airtight container for up to 1 month.

Make the ganache: Line a 9 x 12-inch baking sheet or frame (see Source Guide, page 196) with parchment paper and set aside.
Stir together the infused Aperol and candied orange in a small bowl and set aside.

Whisk together the coconut oil and glucose in another small bowl. Add the melted chocolate and stir until smooth and emulsified.

Carefully stir in the Aperol-orange mixture, being careful to not overmix, as this may cause the ganache to separate (break). Stop stirring as soon as the ganache begins to come together and thicken.

Using an offset spatula, spread the ganache onto the prepared baking sheet, even layer $^1/_4$ inch thick. Set aside to cool and set until it is firm to the touch.

When the ganache is set, flip the pan upside down and unmold the rectangle of ganache onto a clean sheet of parchment paper. Peel the parchment paper from the top of the ganache and discard.

Using a paring knife or a pizza cutter, cut the ganache into your desired shapes and sizes. Save the scraps and form them into balls, if you like.

The ganache is ready to eat at this point; however, if you like, you may dip the pieces in tempered chocolate (see the master dipping technique, page 58) or dust with a powder (see page 58). The infused chocolates will keep for up to 1 month in an airtight container in the refrigerator.

Master Recipe:
Layered Ganache and Pâte de Fruit Squares

Layered ganache and pâte de fruit squares provide a taste experience of two textures and flavors made by layering a fruit paste over a base layer of chocolate. I've provided a variety of different pâte de fruit recipes to choose from, including mayhaw, strawberry, blueberry, and passion fruit. Although this is a slightly advanced technique, the elegant chocolates are well worth the effort.

Step 1: Make the pâte de fruit recipe of your choice (pages 182–183).

Step 2: Line a 9 x 12-inch baking sheet or frame with parchment paper (see Source Guide, page 196). Prepare the ganache according to the Master Recipe: Cream-Based Dark Chocolate Ganache Truffles (recipe, page 60).

Step 3: Pour the ganache onto the prepared baking sheet and let it set at room temperature for 4 to 6 hours.

Step 4. Carefully use your hands to transfer the pâte de fruit with the parchment atop the hardened ganache, turning it over so that the parchment paper can be removed. You can immediately cut the chocolates into 1 to 1½-inch squares using a long, slender, sharp, well-oiled knife.

Strawberry Pâte de Fruit Layered with Dark Chocolate Ganache

Makes 32 (1-inch square) layered chocolates

We do these when strawberries are in season. The pure, sweet taste makes the chocolates so special! But the season is short, and not everyone has easy access to a wild strawberry patch or pick-your-own farm. If you don't have the luxury of picking your own strawberries, buy them at the farmers' market, or use organic strawberries from the grocery store. While you make the recipe, it's always fun to dip a few to enjoy as you go. Bonus: These layered pâte de fruit chocolates, as well as the two pâte de fruit chocolates below, are vegan.

1 recipe Strawberry Pâte de Fruit (page 183)

1 recipe Vegan Dark Chocolate Ganache (page 62)

1 pound 70% Cacao Base Chocolate (page 47) or chocolate bars, coarsely chopped (1½ cups plus 2 tablespoons), melted and tempered (see page 52), for dipping

Make the Strawberry Pâte de Fruit: While it cools on the parchment-lined baking sheet, prepare the chocolate ganache through Step 3.

Using an offset spatula, spread the lukewarm ganache in an even layer on top of the cooled pâte de fruit. Set aside to cool for at least 30 minutes at room temperature.

Use a sharp, well-oiled knife to cut the cooled layered ganache into 1-inch squares.

To prepare to dip the chocolates, line a baking sheet with parchment paper.

Working one at a time and using a chocolate dipping fork (or a regular dinner fork with long tines), gently place one piece of layered ganache on the end of the fork tines (don't skewer it) and dunk it into the tempered chocolate, keeping the piece balanced on the end of the fork as you submerge it until it is completely covered in the melted chocolate. Gently bounce the fork a few times so that the piece of layered ganache is well coated in the tempered chocolate. Slowly remove the fork and coated ganache from the chocolate, and gently tap the fork against the side of the bowl to allow any excess chocolate to drip off the layered ganache and back into the bowl. Too much extra chocolate on the layered ganache will form a puddle around the piece as the chocolate sets, and you want to avoid that. Carefully release the piece of chocolate-enrobed ganache from the dipping fork on the parchment paper–lined pan to set. (You may use the side of the bowl to lift the coated ganache just a bit off the fork so that is slides off easily onto the parchment paper.)

The chocolates will keep in an airtight container at room temperature for up to 2 weeks.

Blueberry Pâte de Fruit Layered with Balsamic–Dark Chocolate Ganache

Makes 32 (1-inch) layered chocolates

Use locally grown blueberries in season when possible, and organic blueberries when seasonal berries aren't available. Use a vintage, aged balsamic for the best results. Partner this chocolate with a mild cheese for a great dessert.

1 recipe Blueberry Pâte de Fruit (page 183)

Balsamic Ganache

$30^{1}/_{2}$ ounces 70% Cacao Base Chocolate (page 47) or highest-quality chocolate bars, coarsely chopped ($3^{1}/_{4}$ cups), melted and kept lukewarm

$^{3}/_{4}$ cup coconut oil, melted and kept warm

$^{1}/_{4}$ cup invert sugar (see Source Guide, page 196)

2 tablespoons glucose (see Source Guide, page 196)

$^{2}/_{3}$ cup room temperature water

$^{1}/_{3}$ cup balsamic vinegar

1 pound 70% Cacao Base Chocolate (page 47) or highest-quality store-bought chocolate bars, coarsely chopped ($1^{1}/_{2}$ cups plus 2 tablespoons), melted and tempered (see page 52), for dipping

Make the Blueberry Pâte de Fruit: While it cools on the parchment-lined baking sheet, prepare the ganache.

Make the ganache: Melt the dark chocolate in the top of a double boiler over medium heat, then remove from the heat. Whisk the coconut oil, invert sugar, and glucose in a small bowl until well combined. Pour the coconut oil mixture into the melted chocolate. Add the balsamic vinegar. Whisk slowly and continuously until the ganache is smooth and emulsified. Set aside to cool at room temperature.

Using an offset spatula, evenly spread the lukewarm ganache on top of the cooled pâte de fruit. Set aside to cool for at least 30 minutes at room temperature.

Using a sharp, well-oiled knife, cut the cooled layered ganache into 1-inch squares.

When you're ready to dip the chocolates, line a baking sheet with parchment paper. Working one at a time and using a chocolate dipping fork (or a regular dinner fork with long tines), gently place one piece of layered ganache on the end of the fork tines (don't skewer it) and dunk it into the tempered chocolate, keeping the piece balanced on the end of the fork as you submerge it until it is completely covered in the melted chocolate. Gently bounce the fork a few times so that the piece of layered ganache is well coated in the tempered chocolate. Slowly remove the fork and coated ganache from the chocolate, and gently tap the fork against the side of the bowl to allow any excess chocolate to drip off the layered ganache and back into the bowl. Too much extra chocolate on the layered ganache will form a puddle around the piece as the chocolate sets, and you want to avoid that. Carefully release the piece of chocolate-enrobed ganache from the dipping fork on the parchment paper–lined pan to set. (You may use the side of the bowl to lift the coated ganache just a bit off the fork so that is slides off easily onto the parchment paper.)

The chocolates will keep in an airtight container at room temperature for 1 month.

Passion Fruit Pâte de Fruit Layered with Cayenne Ganache

Makes about 32 (1-inch) layered chocolates

We call these vegan layered chocolates "Pure Passion" because the spicy cayenne awakens your senses. Share them with a special friend (wink, wink).

Passion Fruit Pâte de Fruit

1 tablespoon vegetable oil, for the parchment paper

2 cups plus 2 tablespoons cane sugar

1/2 tablespoon apple pectin

2 cups fresh ripe passion fruit, pureed, or 2 cups frozen, thawed store-bought passion fruit puree

2 tablespoons glucose (see Source Guide, page 196)

Cayenne Ganache

30 ounces 70% Cacao Base Chocolate (page 47) or highest-quality store-bought chocolate, coarsely chopped (3 1/4 cups), melted and kept lukewarm

3/4 cup coconut oil, melted and kept warm

1/4 cup invert sugar (see Source Guide, page 196)

2 tablespoons glucose (see Source Guide, page 196)

2/3 cup room temperature water

1/8 teaspoon cayenne pepper

1 pound 70% Cacao Base Chocolate or chocolate bars, coarsely chopped (1 1/2 cups plus 2 tablespoons), melted and tempered (see page 52), for dipping

Passion Fruit Pâte de Fruit: Line a baking sheet or 9 x 12-inch frame (see Source Guide, page 196) with parchment paper, grease it with the vegetable oil, and set aside. Whisk 3 tablespoons of the sugar and the pectin together in a small bowl until well combined and set aside. If using fresh passion fruit, cut each fruit in half, remove the pulp and strain out the seeds. Puree the pulp of the passion fruit in a blender.

Transfer the puree to a large heavy-bottomed saucepan, insert a candy thermometer, and cook over medium-high heat until the temperature reaches 120°F. Add the pectin mixture and whisk continuously until completely smooth and free of lumps. Raise the heat, bring the mixture up to a boil, and boil for 1 full minute. Whisk in the glucose and the remaining 15 tablespoons cane sugar until fully combined. Continue to cook, stirring continuously to prevent burning, until the temperature reaches 223°F.

Carefully pour the hot mixture onto the prepared baking sheet. Set aside to cool for 3 to 4 hours, until the pâte de fruit is firm to the touch.

Make the ganache: Heat the dark chocolate in the top of a double boiler over medium heat just until melted. Remove from the heat. Whisk the coconut oil, invert sugar, and glucose in a small bowl.

Pour the coconut oil mixture into the melted chocolate and whisk slowly and continuously until the ganache is smooth and emulsified. Whisk in the water and cayenne pepper. Set aside to cool at room temperature.

Using an offset spatula, spread the lukewarm ganache on top of the cooled pâte de fruit in an even layer. Set aside to cool for at least 30 minutes at room temperature.

Use a sharp, well-oiled knife to cut the layered ganache into 1-inch squares.

When you're ready to dip the chocolates, line a baking sheet with parchment paper. Working one at a time and using a chocolate dipping fork (or a regular dinner fork with long tines), gently place one piece of layered ganache on the end of the fork tines (don't skewer it) and dunk it into the tempered chocolate, keeping the piece balanced on the end of the fork as you submerge it until it is completely covered in the melted chocolate. Gently bounce the fork a few times so that the piece of layered ganache is well coated in the tempered chocolate. Slowly remove the fork and coated ganache from the chocolate, and gently tap the fork against the side of the bowl to allow any excess chocolate to drip off the layered ganache and back into the bowl. Too much extra chocolate on the layered ganache will form a puddle around the piece as the chocolate sets, and you want to avoid that. Carefully release the piece of chocolate-enrobed ganache from the dipping fork on the parchment paper–lined pan to set. (You may use the side of the bowl to lift the coated ganache just a bit off the fork so that is slides off easily onto the parchment paper.)

The chocolates will keep in an airtight container at room temperature for 1 month.

3.

BAKED, CHILLED & FROZEN DESSERTS

Grandmother Holley's Chocolate Cake with Vanilla Buttercream Frosting

Makes 8 to 10 servings

My grandmother Holley's cake was always moist and delicious. She paid particular attention to icing the cake. If you want to keep cake layers really moist, she explained, brush simple syrup onto each layer before you frost it. Don't use the simple syrup on the top layer; that's reserved for the frosting. This cake tastes decadent iced with either the classic Vanilla Buttercream Frosting recommended below or Chocolate Buttercream Frosting (page 92), so use your favorite. It was always on our holiday table when I was growing up. When I used my own chocolate with a higher percentage of cacao in the icing recipe, I was shocked by the flavor difference. Without the vanilla and soy lecithin contained in the chocolate my grandmother used, this cake has a richer chocolate flavor.

4¼ cups raw cane sugar (turbinado)

1 tablespoon unsalted butter, for greasing the pans

3½ cups all-purpose flour, plus extra for dusting the pans

1½ cups natural (non-alkalized) cocoa powder

4 teaspoons baking soda

2 teaspoons baking powder

2 teaspoons salt

2 cups buttermilk (or substitute 2 scant cups whole milk mixed with 2 tablespoons lemon juice)

1 cup vegetable oil

4 large eggs

2 teaspoons vanilla extract

2 cups hot freshly brewed coffee

1 recipe Vanilla Buttercream Frosting (next page)

To make the simple syrup, combine ¼ cup of the raw cane sugar with ¼ cup water in a small saucepan over medium heat, stirring continuously until the sugar dissolves.

Decant to cool before before brushing on the cake.

To make the cake layers, preheat the oven to 350°F. Butter and flour two 10-inch round cake pans and set aside.

Put the flour, remaining 4 cups raw cane sugar, cocoa powder, baking soda, baking powder, and salt in the bowl of an electric stand mixer fitted with the paddle attachment. Mix on low speed until incorporated.

In a separate, nonreactive bowl, whisk the buttermilk, oil, eggs, and vanilla until combined.

Turn the mixer speed to its lowest setting and add the buttermilk mixture to the dry ingredients, mixing just until combined. (Don't overmix or the cake won't rise as much, and will lose its airiness.) Slowly pour in the hot coffee, mixing just until combined and scraping down the sides of the bowl with a spatula as necessary.

Evenly distribute the batter between the prepared pans. Bake for 45 minutes, rotating the pans three times during baking. The cakes are ready when a wooden toothpick inserted into the center comes out clean.

Let cool on a wire rack for 30 minutes, then invert the pans to remove the cakes.

Flip right side up and let the cakes cool for 2 to 3 hours before filling and frosting. At this stage, the cakes can be stored in the refrigerator, wrapped tightly in plastic wrap, for up to 1 week.

To frost the cake layers, place one of the cooled cake layers on a 10-inch cardboard cake circle. Trim the tops of one layer with a sharp knife to make sure the layers sit evenly. (I use a wire connected to two pencils for this job). Leave the top layer of the cake untrimmed.

After trimming, brush the top of each cake layer with the simple syrup, using all the syrup. There's no need to wait to let the syrup soak in; you can go ahead and frost the cake.

Scoop approximately 2 cups frosting onto the middle of the first cake layer. Use an offset spatula to evenly spread a ¼-inch layer of frosting over the top of the layer. If any frosting falls off the edge, just scrape it back into the bowl.

Carefully center the second layer, bottom trimmed side up, onto the frosted layer.

Scoop enough frosting (about 2 cups) onto the top of the cake to easily spread it to coat the top and down the sides, covering the entire cake as evenly and smoothly as possible, using long back-and-forth strokes with the offset spatula.

Tip: Once the entire cake is completely covered in frosting, you can create different looks and effects. I prefer a smooth, refined surface, which takes some practice to perfect. An easier effect to achieve is an old-fashioned finish with swirls and peaks. The good news is that frosting is somewhat forgiving, so if you don't like the way the frosted cake looks on your first try, you can smooth it over and try again. Do, however, keep in mind that the frosting will begin to dry out after about 10 minutes, so work efficiently, even when you're practicing!

Vanilla Buttercream Frosting
Makes about 8 cups

3½ cups (7 sticks) unsalted butter, softened

8 cups sugar

3 tablespoons heavy cream

1 tablespoon vanilla extract

With an electric mixer fitted with a whisk attachment, beat the butter on medium speed until creamy. Add the sugar gradually, a little at a time, beating on high until all the sugar is until incorporated and the mixure is creamy. While the mixer is running, slowly pour in the heavy cream and the vanilla, scraping the sides of the bowl with a spatula to fully incorporate. Continue beating until the frosting thickens and is fluffy and spreadable.

This frosting can be stored in an airtight container in the refrigerator or freezer for up to 1 week for future use. If frozen, let it come to room temperature and remix it using an electric mixer to achieve a fluffy texture again. As you're mixing, the color of the frosting will lighten a couple of shades.

Rich Chocolate Cake with Chocolate Buttercream Frosting

Makes 8 to 10 servings

This cake gets its rich chocolate flavor from a combination of melted chocolate and cocoa powder. Make sure to choose a high-quality cocoa powder for the best chocolate flavor. Remember, cocoa powder comes from cacao beans, so the powders will have different flavor expressions. They are not all created equal. Try the powder before you use it in this recipe, so you get the flavor combination you prefer. Espresso powder, which is ground expresso beans (you can grind the powder in a coffee grinder yourself) doesn't make the cake taste like coffee, but rather enhances the overall cocoa flavor.

$1^1/_2$ cups (3 sticks) unsalted butter, softened, plus extra for greasing the pan

$1^1/_4$ cup sugar

$1^1/_4$ cups all-purpose flour, plus extra for dusting the pan

4 teaspoons baking soda

2 teaspoons baking powder $1^1/_2$ cups natural (non-alkalized) cocoa powder

2 teaspoons salt

4 large eggs

2 egg yolks

$1/_2$ tablespoon vanilla extract

1 teaspoon instant espresso powder

3 ounces 70% Cacao Base Chocolate (page 47), coarsely chopped (scant $1/_4$ cup) and melted

1 recipe Chocolate Buttercream Frosting (page 92)

Preheat the oven to 350°F. Butter and flour two 10-inch round cake pans and set aside.

Put the butter and sugar in the bowl of a stand mixer fitted with the paddle attachment. Mix on medium speed until light and creamy.

In a separate, nonreactive bowl, whisk the flour, cocoa powder, and salt

Turn the mixer speed to its lowest setting and add the dry ingredients to the creamed butter and sugar, mixing until fully incorporated. Increase the mixer speed to medium and add the eggs and yolks one at a time, scraping down the side of the bowl with a spatula after each addition as needed. Add the vanilla and espresso powder and mix until just combined.

Remove the bowl from the mixer and, using a spatula, fold in the melted chocolate until well combined. The batter will be smooth and even in color.

Distribute the batter evenly between the prepared pans. Bake for 45 minutes, rotating the pans three times during baking. The cakes are ready when a wooden toothpick inserted into the center comes out clean.

Let cool on a wire rack for 30 minutes, then invert the pans to remove the cakes.

Flip right side up and let the cakes cool for 2 to 4 hours before filling and frosting. (At this stage, the cakes can be stored in the refrigerator, wrapped tightly in plastic wrap, for up to 1 week.)

To frost the cake, place one of the cooled layers on a 10-inch cardboard cake circle. Trim the tops of the layers with a sharp knife to make sure the layers sit evenly.

After trimming, brush the top of each cake layer with the simple syrup, using all the syrup. There's no need to wait to let the syrup soak in; you can go ahead and frost the cake.

Scoop approximately 2 cups frosting onto the middle of the first cake layer. Use an offset spatula to evenly spread a ¼-inch layer of frosting over the top of the layer. If any frosting falls off, just scrape it back into the bowl.

Carefully center the second layer, trimmed-side up, onto the frosted layer.

Scoop enough frosting (about 2 cups) onto the top of the cake to easily spread it to coat the top and down the sides, covering the entire cake as evenly and smoothly as possible, using long back-and-forth strokes with the offset spatula. If you want to create special effects, see the tip on page 89.

Chocolate Buttercream Frosting

Makes about 8 cups

1½ cups (3 sticks) unsalted butter, softened

6 cups sugar

½ cup natural (non-alkalized) cocoa powder

¾ cup whole milk

1 tablespoon vanilla extract

½ teaspoon salt

12 ¾ ounces 70% Cacao Base Chocolate (page 47) or highest-quality store-bought chocolate bar, coarsely chopped (a generous 1¼ cups), melted and kept lukewarm

Put the butter, sugar, and cocoa powder in the bowl of an electric stand mixer fitted with the whisk attachment. Mix on medium speed until light and creamy. Add the milk a little at a time until incorporated. Add the vanilla and salt, mixing until well combined and scraping down the sides of the bowl with a spatula as necessary. At this stage, the frosting should look smooth and creamy.

Gradually add the melted chocolate to the bowl, whisking until fully incorporated. The frosting should thicken but still be fluffy and spreadable.

The frosting can be stored in an airtight container in the refrigerator or freezer for up to 2 weeks for future use. If frozen, let it come to room temperature and remix using a mixer to achieve a fluffy texture again. As you're mixing, the color will lighten a couple of shades in color.

Chocolate-Glazed Bourbon Cake
with Blueberry Filling

Makes 12 servings

The flavor combination of blueberries and bourbon and chocolate is a winning trifecta. You don't need to wait for a holiday to make this bourbon-laced dessert, but if you're looking for a recipe to replace those boring holiday bourbon balls or fruitcake, this is the one. Brush the bourbon simple syrup on each layer generously, using the entire cup. This will keep the cake moist for a long while. Also, after you pour the chocolate and let it set, be careful not to touch the surface of the cake because it will show fingerprints (yours!).

$^1/_2$ cup sugar

$^1/_4$ cup bourbon (your brand of choice)

1 recipe Rich Chocolate Cake (page 90), baked into two 10-inch round layers and cooled

1 cup Blueberry-Lavender Confiture (page 184)

1 recipe Chocolate Glaze (page 95)

To make the bourbon simple syrup, combine $^1/_4$ cup water, sugar, and bourbon in small saucepan over medium heat and stir continuously until the sugar dissolves.

Decant to cool before before brushing onto the cooled cake layers.

To assemble the cake, trim the tops of the layers with a sharp knife to make sure the layers sit evenly. Use a pastry brush to spread the bourbon simple syrup over the top of both layers. Repeat until you've used all of the bourbon syrup. There's no need to wait between applications.

Place the bottom layer of the cake on a cake plate and spread all of the blueberry confiture on the top. Run the flat edge of a knife along the edge of the cake to keep it from dripping down the sides.

Place the second cake layer on top of the first one and, using an offset spatula, wipe away any filling that has seeped out.

Once the sides of the sake are free of blueberry jam drips, let it set for 30 to 40 minutes before glazing. When it has set, slowly pour the warm glaze over the top of the cake, using an offset spatula to quickly spread the glaze along the sides of the cake. Let the glazed cake set at room temperature for 1 hour before serving.

Chocolate Glaze

Makes about 3½ cups

Ambient temperature is important to
this glaze. Make sure your cake layers
are cooled to room temperature before
glazing. The glaze should be warm—just
off the stovetop. The more it sits, the
less viscosity it will have. This glaze sets
quickly: You have only about 30 seconds
after you pour it over the top to even out
the glaze on the sides of the cake. After
that, don't touch!

12 ounces 70% Cacao Base Chocolate (page 47) or
highest-quality store-bought chocolate bars, coarsely
chopped (1¼ cups), melted

1¼ cups (2½ sticks) unsalted butter

Melt the butter in a heatproof bowl in the microwave.

Pour the melted chocolate into a large heatproof bowl
or pitcher and then whisk in the melted butter until
combined. Add 1 cup water and whisk to incorporate.

Allow the glaze to cool slightly before using; it should
be warm, as if just off the stovetop. Pour over cakes or
desserts as indicated in the recipe directions.

Pecan Chocolate Tart

Serves 6 to 8

Crust

1/4 cup butter

1 egg yolk

1/4 teaspoon salt

1/3 cup all-purpose flour

1 1/4 tablespoon cocoa powder

1/8 cup powdered sugar

1/4 cup ground pecans

Filling

3/4 cup heavy cream

1/8 cup butter

1 tablespoon cane sugar

2 whole eggs

1 egg yolk

3/4 cup 70% dark chocolate, melted, plus 2 tablespoons for the crust

Whisky Caramel Sauce

1 cup sugar

1/4 teaspoon lemon juice

1/2 cup heavy cream

1/4 cup butter

1/2 tablespoons vanilla

1 teaspoon salt

1 tablespoon whisky, your brand of choice

Garnish

1/2 cup toasted pecans, or more to garnish the tart

1/8 cup whisky caramel sauce

3/4 cup vanilla bean whipped cream

Heat the oven to 350° F.

Make the crust: In a medium bowl, beat the butter with an electric mixer until smooth. Add the egg yolk and salt and beat until blended. With the mixer running on low speed, add the flour, cocoa powder, powdered sugar, and ground pecans and beat just until dough begins to clump together.

On a lightly floured work surface, gather the dough into a ball and flatten it into a disc. Place the disc in a 9-inch tart pan with a removable bottom, and use your hands to press the dough over the bottom and up the sides of the pan. Pierce the crust all over with a fork. Bake for 20 to 25 minutes, until the crust begins to brown.

While the crust is still warm, brush the bottom of the tart lightly with 2 tablespoons melted chocolate.

Make the filling: In a saucepan over medium-low heat, stir the heavy cream, butter, and 1/2 tablespoon sugar until it simmers.

In a bowl, whisk the remaining 1/2 tablespoon sugar, the eggs, and egg yolk. Add the warm cream to the eggs a little at a time, stirring constantly until combined.

Pour the cream and egg mixture into a medium saucepan over low heat and cook, stirring often, until it is thick enough to coat a spoon. Set aside to cool. Strain the mixture into a bowl, and let it cool.

When the cream and egg mixture is cool, stir in the melted chocolate until well combined. Pour the filling into the tart crust and refrigerate for at least 1 hour to allow the tart to set.

Make the Whisky Caramel Sauce: Add the sugar and lemon juice to a medium saucepan and cook over medium heat, stirring constantly, until the sugar caramelized to a medium brown color.

In a separate small saucepan over low heat, stir the cream and butter until the butter is melted, but do not bring to a boil. Stir in the vanilla and salt, then carefully pour the mixture over the caramelized sugar and stir. The sauce will bubble violently for a moment, but continue to stir to combine, then stir in the whisky.

Note: working with caramel can cause serious burns. Be very careful not to let the caramel touch your skin.

Once the tart has set, you may remove it from the pan and transfer to a serving dish or plate. Arrange the whole pecans on the top, 1 or 2 per slice.

To serve, garnish each slice with a dollop of whipped cream, and a drizzle of the Whisky Caramel Sauce, or pass the sauce and whipped cream around the table for guests to serve themselves.

Chocolate Macarons with Ganache Filling

Makes 2 dozen macaron sandwich cookies

A gluten-free delight, the macaron is a popular pastry creation requiring both precision and patience to make. As a lover of this French delicacy, I decided we, too, would embark on the macaron journey and produce the best in Atlanta and beyond. We now make and sell a lot of them. Keep in mind, uniformity comes with practice, but the taste will be undeniably wonderful, no matter what!

Don't try to eyeball the size of the shells. Instead, use a stencil to draw circles on the back of the parchment papers to make the shells precisely the same size. The wait time to let the shells harden is critical—it must be precise! Read the instructions carefully and keep your eye on the clock.

Macarons

2 cups confectioners' sugar

2 cups almond flour

$2^1/_2$ tablespoons natural (non-alkalized) cocoa powder

5 egg whites, at room temperature

$^1/_2$ cup cane sugar

Ganache

4 ounces 70% Cocoa Base Chocolate (page 47) or highest-quality store-bought chocolate, coarsely chopped ($^1/_2$ cup plus 2 tablespoons)

$^1/_2$ cup heavy cream

Make the macarons: Line 2 or 3 baking sheets with parchment paper and set aside. Fit a large pastry bag with a $^1/_2$-inch plain tip and set aside.

Sift together the confectioners' sugar, almond flour, and cocoa powder to aerate them and eliminate any lumps; set aside.

Make a meringue by placing the egg whites in the clean bowl of a stand mixer fitted with a whisk attachment. Beat the egg whites on medium-high speed. When they start getting foamy, gradually add the cane sugar. Beat until all the sugar is incorporated, the peaks are stiff, and the whites are shiny.

Using a spatula, gently fold the sifted dry mixture into the egg whites until the dry ingredients are just combined (do not overmix). The mixture should be smooth and viscous, not runny.

Transfer the batter to the pastry bag. Pipe $1^1/_4$-inch rounds about 1 inch apart onto the prepared baking sheets, about 24 per sheet. Pick up the baking sheets and rap them against a countertop or table to help create the macaron base, or foot. Let the rounds sit at room temperature for precisely 30 minutes to dry the tops and ensure even cooking.

Meanwhile, preheat the oven to 300°F. Bake the macarons for 8 minutes. Rotate the baking sheets between the racks, and cook for 8 minutes more. Using a spatula, check to see if one comes off the tray fairly cleanly. If not, bake a minute or two more. Transfer the sheet to a wire rack to cool completely.

Make the ganache: Put the chopped chocolate in a medium heat-proof bowl.

Warm the cream in a medium saucepan over medium heat until it just starts to boil. Remove the pan from the heat and stir the warm cream into the bowl of chocolate gradually, without creating bubbles. Continue to stir until the chocolate melts. Let sit for 1 minute. Cover the bowl with plastic wrap and chill in the refrigerator until the ganache is thickened, but still spreadable, about 30 minutes.

To assemble the macarons, pair shells of similar size. Remove the ganache from the refrigerator and let it come to room temperature. Fill a piping bag with the ganache and pipe a cherry-sized drop of ganache in the center of each macaron half. Top with another half and press gently, being careful not to crush the shells, until the ganache becomes slightly visible around the edges. Store in an airtight container in the refrigerator for up to 5 days.

Chocolate-Dipped Oatmeal Cream Pies

Makes about 1 dozen sandwich cookies

This cookie pie is one of my guiltiest pleasures and was created to cater to my buttercream indulgence. Fluffy vanilla buttercream is sandwiched between classic oatmeal cookies. For added pleasure, I dip them in melted chocolate. This is not your everyday sandwich cookie!

Cool the assembled sandwich cookies completely before dipping them in the tempered chocolate—I like to dip just half the cookie. You don't want to end up with a thick shell on the cookies, so tap each "pie" on the side of the pot to release any extra chocolate. This will ensure a thin chocolate shell.

Oatmeal Cookies

2 cups all-purpose flour

1 teaspoon baking soda

1 pinch ground cinnamon

$1/2$ teaspoon salt

1 cup (2 sticks) unsalted butter, softened

$1/2$ cup packed brown sugar

$1/2$ cup cane sugar

2 large eggs

1 teaspoon honey

$3^{1}/_{4}$ cups rolled oats

Vanilla Cookie Buttercream

3 cups confectioners' sugar

1 cup (2 sticks) unsalted butter, softened

1 teaspoon vanilla extract

1 tablespoon heavy cream

1 pound 70% Cacao Base Chocolate (page 47) or highest-quality chocolate bars, coarsely chopped ($1^{1}/_{2}$ cups plus 2 tablespoon), melted and tempered, for dipping

Make the cookies: Sift the flour, baking soda, cinnamon, and salt in a medium bowl and set aside.

In a stand mixer with the paddle attachment, cream the butter, both sugars, the eggs, and the honey on low speed until fluffy. Gradually add the flour mixture until just incorporated. Stir in the oats. Remove the bowl from the mixer and transfer to the refrigerator to chill for 15 minutes.

Meanwhile, preheat the oven 325 F and line two baking sheets with parchment paper.

Scoop the chilled dough into 2-tablespoon balls and flatten them with the palm of your hand onto the prepared baking sheets, leaving an inch of space between each cookie. Bake for 5 minutes or until the edges begin to brown. Cool on wire racks for 25 minutes before removing them from baking sheets.

Make the Vanilla Cookie Buttercream: In a stand mixer fitted with a whisk, blend the confectioners' sugar and butter on low speed. Increase the speed to medium and beat for approximately 3 minutes, until smooth. Add the vanilla and cream, and continue to beat on medium speed for 1 minute more until light and fluffy.

To assemble the pies, pair cookies of similar size and turn them so their bottoms face up. Fill a pastry bag fitted with plain tip with the buttercream. Pipe enough buttercream to cover the cookie onto 12 of the oatmeal cookies.

Top the frosted halves with the 12 unfrosted cookies and press gently until the buttercream is slightly visible at the edges.

To dip the finished sandwich cookies in the melted chocolate, follow the dipping instructions on page 58.

Cuppy Cakes with Vanilla Buttercream Cupcake Frosting

Makes 1 dozen miniature cupcakes

Who doesn't like to eat the whole cupcake in one bite? It's pure bliss! In this case, we're talking tiny little bites because these are very small cupcakes. You'll need a mini muffin pan to make them. (Don't try to use this batter to make full-size cupcakes.) To add a nice crunch to these bites, you can decorate the tops with silver sprinkles if you like.

Cuppy Cakes Batter

1/2 cup (1 stick) unsalted butter, softened

1 1/4 cups sugar

2 large eggs

3/4 cup all-purpose flour

1 teaspoon baking powder

1/4 teaspoon salt

1/2 cup cocoa powder

1/2 cup whole milk

1 tablespoon vanilla extract

Vanilla Buttercream Cupcake Frosting

1 cup (2 sticks) unsalted butter, softened

1 cup vegetable shortening

3 cups sugar, plus more as needed

1/4 cup whole milk, plus more as needed

1 tablespoon vanilla extract

Make the Cuppy Cakes: Preheat the oven to 375 F. Line a 24-cup miniature muffin pan with liners.

Beat the butter and sugar in a large bowl with an electric mixer on low speed for 3 minutes until creamy. Add the eggs and mix until combined. In a small bowl, whisk together the flour, baking powder, salt, and cocoa powder. With the mixer on medium speed, gradually add the dry mixture to the butter and sugar mixture, beating until fully incorporated. Blend in the milk and vanilla just until combined.

Divide the batter evenly among the muffin cups. Bake for 15 to 20 minutes, or until a toothpick inserted in the center of a cupcake comes out clean. Let cool in the pan for 5 minutes, then transfer to a wire rack to cool completely before frosting.

Make the Vanilla Buttercream Cupcake Frosting: Beat the butter and shortening with an electric mixer on medium speed until creamy and well combined. Gradually add the sugar, beating on high speed until fully incorporated and the frosting starts to lighten in color and get fluffy. With the mixer set on low speed, blend in the milk and vanilla, adjusting the amount of milk or adding more sugar as needed until a creamy, fluffy, spreadable consistency is reached.

You can make the frosting ahead. It will keep in the refrigerator for up to one week. When you're ready to use it, beat it again until it's creamy, but don't bring it to room temperature.

Spread the frosting onto the cooled cupcakes using a knife or offset spatula. Or, for fancier cuppy cakes, fill a pastry bag fitted with a plain or star tip and pipe the frosting onto the cooled cupcakes.

Devil in My Mouth Cookies

Makes 2 dozen cookies

When I first opened our shop in Atlanta, Christianne Lauterbach, a local food reviewer, came in often. (True fact: I didn't know what she did for a living for a long time, I just knew she liked our chocolate and was great fun to talk to.) One day when she came in, our Cuppy Cakes hadn't risen when we baked them, and I was lamenting about the poor flat things to Christianne. I was ready to throw them out when she suggested we try them. They were so good I added 1 heaping tablespoon of the vanilla buttercream we'd prepared to frost the cupcakes to the middle of each cookie and—voilà!—a devilishly good cookie was born. Lesson learned? A baking mistake might not always be such a bad thing—it's all in how you perceive the results.

Note: Never refrigerate this batter or let it sit before baking; you need to bake the cookies right away. This cookie is thin, crunchy, chewy, and lacelike. If you refrigerate the batter, the cookies will be too soft.

1 recipe Cuppy Cake Batter (page 102)

1 recipe Vanilla Buttercream Cupcake Frosting
(page 89)

Preheat the oven to 375 F while you're mixing the batter. Lightly grease a baking sheet with oil. Immediately drop the room temperature batter in heaping tablespoons onto the cookie sheet, making sure to leave 1 to 2 inches around each cookie as they will spread. Bake for 20 to 22 minutes until the edges of the cookies begin to harden but centers are still soft. (The cookies will develop lacelike holes.) Let cool on the baking sheet for for 5 to 10 minutes before transferring the cookies to a wire rack to cool completely.

If you choose to bake the two cookie sheets at one time, place one sheet in the middle of the oven, and one on the rack just above, and rotate them halfway through the cooking.

Mound 1 heaping tablespoon of the frosting in the middle of each cooled cookie. You are sure to have leftover frosting, so be generous with it.

Crunchy Chocolate Chip Cookies

Makes 2 dozen cookies

This recipe is very particular, so pay attention to the specified times, temperature, and ingredient quantities. These cookies have a wonderful crunchiness, and the secret is in the temperature of the butter. Eat them fresh out of the oven and don' t feel guilty! They are best eaten in the first three hours after baking. I tested the recipe for these with my little daughter and her friends as judges. Word got around the playground and my house became the place to go. The mothers all loved me!

1 cup (2 sticks) unsalted butter, at room temperature

$1\frac{1}{2}$ cups sugar

$\frac{2}{3}$ cup packed light brown sugar

1 large egg

$\frac{1}{2}$ teaspoon vanilla extract

$1\frac{1}{2}$ cups all-purpose flour

$\frac{1}{2}$ teaspoon baking powder

$\frac{1}{4}$ teaspoon baking soda

1 teaspoon salt

17 ounces 70% Cacao Base Chocolate (page 47) or highest-quality chocolate bars, roughly chopped (about $1\frac{2}{3}$ cups)

Preheat the oven to 350 F. Line 2 baking sheets with parchment paper.

Cream the butter and sugars with an electric mixer on low speed for 2 to 3 minutes, until light and fluffy. Add the egg and vanilla and beat for 7 to 8 minutes, scraping down the sides of the mixing bowl with a spatula as needed, until fully incorporated.

In a separate bowl, whisk the flour, baking powder, baking soda, and salt.

Add the dry mixture to the butter and sugar mixture and blend for about 1 minute, just until the dough comes together. (Do not overmix.) Fold in the chocolate pieces to evenly distribute them.

Scoop 1 tablespoon balls of dough onto the prepared baking-sheet, leaving 1 inch of space between each cookie. Bake for 8 to 10 minutes, or until the edges of the cookies begin to brown and harden, but the centers are still soft.

If you choose to bake the two cookie sheets at one time, place one sheet in the middle of the oven, and one on the rack just above, and rotate them halfway through the cooking.

Cool the pan on a wire rack briefly before transferring the cookies to the wire racks to cool completely.

Chocolate Scones

Makes 15 to 20 scones

Use chocolate chunks or shards—the size is up to you. The recipe includes options for additional flavors so you personalize it with what you like—nuts, raisins, dried fruit, lavender, whatever you love. How perfect these are for a coffee break or teatime, especially when they're warm from the oven?

3 pounds (about 9 cups) all-purpose flour, plus more for work surface

12 ounces (about 1¾ cup) sugar

Scant ½ cup baking powder

11 ounces (scant 1½ sticks) cold unsalted butter, cut into cubes

5 large eggs

1 teaspoon vanilla extract

3½ cups heavy cream

1 pound 70% Cacao Base Chocolate (page 47) or highest-quality chocolate bars, broken into shards or coarsely chopped into chunks (1½ cups plus 2 tablespoons)

Optional Mix-Ins (pick one)

1 pound raw pecans, chopped

1 pound dried apricots

1 pound raisins

2 tablespoons dried or fresh lavender

1 pound dried cherries

1 pounds slivered raw almonds

Preheat the oven to 350 F. Line two baking sheets with parchment.

Combine the flour, sugar, and baking powder in the bowl of a mixer fitted with a paddle attachment. Add the cold cubes of butter and mix on low speed until the butter is incorporated and forms pea-sized pieces.

Whisk the eggs and vanilla, and add the cream and mix until just combined.. Fold in the chocolate (and your choice of inclusions).

Dump the dough onto a floured work surface and use your hands to shape it into a long rectangle about 2 inches thick. Use a dough scraper to cut out uniform triangles. Gather any scraps and shape triangles from the remaining dough. You should have 12 triangles

Place the triangles on the parchment-lined baking sheet and bake for 12 minutes, or until the edges just begin to brown. If you choose to bake the two baking sheets at one time, place one sheet in the middle of the oven, and one on the rack just above, and rotate them halfway through the cooking.

These scones are good served warm or at room temperature. They will keep for two days, or frozen for up to a week. If frozen, thaw them and warm again in a 250 F oven.

Chocolate Chip Muffins

Makes 2 dozen muffins

The milk plus lemon juice creates a sort of buttermilk, and the use of brown sugar instead of cane sugar provides more of a molasses flavor to the muffins. They are aromatic, rich muffins you will love.

2 cups all-purpose flour

$2/3$ teaspoon ground cinnamon

$2/3$ teaspoon ground nutmeg

$2/3$ teaspoon baking soda

$2/3$ teaspoon baking powder

$2/3$ teaspoon salt

$1/2$ cup whole milk

$2/3$ teaspoon fresh lemon juice

$1/4$ cup ($1/2$ stick) unsalted butter, melted

2 large eggs

1 cup packed brown sugar

19 ounces 70% Cacao Base Chocolate (page 47) or highest-quality store-bought chocolate, finely chopped (2 cups)

Preheat the oven to 350 F. Line a muffin tin with paper muffin cups.

Sift the flour, cinnamon, nutmeg, baking soda, baking powder, and salt into a mixing bowl.

In a separate mixing bowl, whisk the milk, lemon juice, melted butter, eggs, and brown sugar until well combined.

Fold the dry ingredients into the wet ingredients until just incorporated. Do not overmix.

Gently mix in the chopped chocolate.

Pour the batter into the prepared muffin cups, dividing it evenly. Bake for 12 to 15 minutes, or until a wooden toothpick inserted into the center of a muffin comes out clean. These are good warm or cool. Store cooled muffins in an airtight container.

Dark Chocolate Brownies

Makes 2 dozen brownies

These brownies have a crowd-pleasing texture that's not too fudgy, and not too cake-like. It takes several bowls to mix the batter ingredients for this recipe, but the result is well worth the effort. If you'd prefer a spicy version of this classic, stir in a teaspoon of my Aztec Powder (page 117) before you add the chocolate.

$2/3$ cup (1 stick plus 3 tablespoons) unsalted butter, plus more for the pan

1 cup hot freshly brewed coffee

$2/3$ cup cocoa powder

About $1/2$ cup (5.3 ounces bar chocolate) 70% cacao base chocolate, melted

$2/3$ cup coconut oil

3 large eggs

2 egg yolks

$2^{1}/_{2}$ teaspoons vanilla extract

$2^{3}/_{4}$ cups cane sugar

$2/3$ cup packed brown sugar

$2^{2}/_{3}$ cups all-purpose flour

$1^{1}/_{4}$ teaspoons sea salt

1 teaspoon baking powder

8 ounces 70% Cacao Base Chocolate (page 47) or highest-quality store-bought chocolate, broken into shards or chopped into chunks

Preheat the oven to 350 F. Butter a 12 x 15-inch baking pan and line it with parchment paper.

In a large mixing bowl, whisk the hot coffee, cocoa powder, and melted chocolate. Set aside but keep warm.

In a saucepan over medium heat, add the butter and stir until it starts to turn brown. Add the coconut oil and melt it, stirring to combine. Remove from the heat.

In a second bowl, whisk the whole eggs, egg yolks, and vanilla. Mix the cane and brown sugars in a third bowl. In a fourth bowl, whisk the flour, salt, and baking powder.

Whisk the butter and oil mixture into the coffee and chocolate mixture. (The mixture may look separated.) Add the egg mixture and then the sugars, whisking to incorporate after each addition. Carefully fold in the dry ingredients with a spatula, until just combined. Fold in the chocolate chunks, distributing them evenly.

Pour the batter into the prepared baking pan and bake for 30 minutes, rotating the pan every 10 minutes, until a toothpick inserted into the center comes out clean.

Cool on a wire rack for 10 minutes before removing from pan. Let cool completely before cutting the brownies.

Leftover brownies can be kept in an airtight container for up to a week.

Calino Cookies

Makes 3 to 4 dozen cookies

Named after my best friend and business partner, these are all-butter shortbread cookies. I chop them up and add them to my Chocolate Salami recipe (page 116), but these are a great treat on their own. Dip them in chocolate (page 58) to make finger cookies that pair perfectly with a cup of coffee or sweet wine.

2 cups (4 sticks) unsalted butter, softened

2 cups cane sugar

2 tablespoons brown sugar

2 large eggs

1 tablespoon vanilla extract

4 cups all-purpose flour

1 teaspoon baking powder

1 teaspoon salt

Preheat the oven to 325 F. Line two baking sheets with parchment paper.

Cream the butter and sugars with an electric mixer on medium speed until light and fluffy. Add the eggs and vanilla and mix, scraping the sides of the mixing bowl with a spatula as needed, until fully incorporated.

In a separate bowl, sift the flour, baking powder, and salt.

With the mixer on low speed, gradually add the dry ingredients to the wet ingredients, mixing until just combined.

Scoop 1-tablespoon balls of dough onto the prepared baking sheet, leaving an inch of space between each cookie. If you choose to bake the two cookie sheets at one time, place one sheet in the middle of the oven, and one on the rack just above, and rotate them halfway through the cooking.

Bake for 8 to 10 minutes or until the edges begin to brown. Briefly cool on the baking sheet on a wire rack before transferring the cookies to a rack to cool completely. Store in an airtight container up to 1 week.

Amaretti Biscuits

Makes 2 to 3 dozen bite-sized biscuits

These airy-on-the-inside, golden-on-the-outside breakfast treats or tea cookies are gluten-free. The traditional Italian recipe uses bitter almond paste, but it's hard to find and expensive, so this recipe uses almond flour and almond extract to create a similar flavor. These are used in the chocolate salami recipe, which is why you bake them up in a single pan, then break into miniature biscuits. If you want to enjoy them on their own, just roll the dough into balls and bake them as traditional biscuits. Keep an eye on the cooking time and remove them from the oven when the biscuits rise and are golden brown.

2 cups almond flour

$^1/_2$ cup cane sugar

2 cups confectioners' sugar

5 egg whites

$2^1/_2$ teaspoons almond extract

Preheat the oven to 350 F. Line a baking sheet with parchment paper or a nonstick silicone baking mat.

Whisk together the almond flour, cane sugar, and confectioners sugar in a mixing bowl. In a separate bowl, beat the eggs whites and almond extract with until stiff peaks form. Gently fold the almond flour mixture into the beaten egg whites with a silicone spatula.

Spread the mixture onto the lined baking sheet, using the spatula to smooth out the top. Bake for 15 to 18 minutes, until golden brown and puffed.

Allow to cool completely before breaking into bite-sized biscuits. Serve warm.

Chocolate–Almond Biscotti

Makes about 2 dozen biscotti

These are wonderful dipped in chocolate, but wait a while—at least a day after baking—before you add a chocolate coating (see "How to Dip Truffles and Other Ingredients in Chocolate" page 58). Then, although they may be hard to resist, let the chocolate cool and set before you eat them.

2 cups all-purpose flour

$3/4$ cup natural (non-alkalized) cocoa powder

1 teaspoon baking soda

$1/4$ teaspoon salt

3 large eggs

1 cup sugar

1 teaspoon vanilla extract

$1/8$ teaspoon almond extract

1 cup raw almonds, toasted and coarsely chopped

7 ounces 70% Cacao Base Chocolate (page 47) or highest-quality store-bought chocolate bars, broken into shards or chopped into chunks ($3/4$ cup)

Preheat the oven to 350 F. Line a baking sheet with parchment paper.

Whisk the flour, cocoa powder, baking soda, and salt in a medium bowl.

In a large mixing bowl, use an electric mixer to beat the eggs, sugar, vanilla, and almond extract. Gradually add the dry ingredients, stirring at low speed until combined. Blend in the almonds and chocolate chunks until the dough comes together.

Divide the dough in half. Form each half into a skinny log measuring just 3 inches wide. Transfer the logs to the prepared baking sheet and bake for 25 minutes, until the dough feels firm to the touch.

Remove the baking sheet from the oven and cool for 15 to 20 minutes. (Do not turn off the oven.) Move the logs to a cutting board and cut crosswise, on a diagonal, into $1/2$-inch-thick slices with a serrated knife.

Return the slices, cut sides down, to the baking sheet and bake for another 15 to 30 minutes, rotating the sheet halfway through the baking time. The recommended baking time is 20 minutes, but bake more or less depending on how firm you like your biscotti.

When the biscotti are baked to your liking, remove the baking sheet from the oven and transfer them to a wire rack to cool completely. Biscotti can be kept in an airtight container for up to 3 weeks.

Chocolate Pots de Crème

Makes 8 servings

This classic dessert is one of my favorites, especially when topped with whipped cream! I'm a purist who doesn't like to add other flavors to this creamy, chocolaty custard. You might be so inclined, but I suggest layering instead—with whipped cream, nuts, spices, citrus peel, or lemon curd. Have fun with the flavor-pairing possibilities! If you want a richer, darker dessert, use a base chocolate with a higher percentage of cacao. It will be less sweet.

1 teaspoon gelatin

$1^{3}/_{4}$ cups heavy cream

Yolks of 4 large eggs

3 tablespoon sugar

$1^{1}/_{4}$ teaspoons vanilla extract

13 ounces 70% Cacao Base Chocolate (page 47) or highest-quality store-bought chocolate bars, coarsely chopped (about $1^{1}/_{3}$ cups) and melted

Bloom the gelatin in a bowl of cold water, according to package directions, until soft.

Meanwhile, add one third, about ³/₄ cup, of the of the heavy cream to a mixing bowl and whip with an electric mixer or a whisk until soft peaks form; set aside. In a separate bowl, whisk the yolks, 2 tablespoons of the sugar, and the vanilla.

In a saucepan over medium heat, simmer the remaining two thirds heavy cream and the remaining tablespoon sugar. Temper the cream into the simmering yolk by whisking it gradually into the yolk. Cook over medium heat, stirring continuously, until the mixture thickens enough to coat the back of a spoon.

Remove from heat immediately and stir in the bloomed gelatin and water mixture until dissolved. Stir in the melted chocolate. Gently fold the whipped cream into the chocolate mixture with a silicone spatula until the melted chocolate is evenly distributed.

Pour the custard into ramekins or any type of cup, and refrigerate for at least 30 minutes to set before serving. You can make this the day ahead and refrigerate, but be sure to cover the tops with plastic wrap to prevent a skin from forming.

Chocolate Salami

Makes 10 (4- to 5-inch) logs

This "salami" will delight your guests, and is sure to cause some chuckles when you serve it as dessert. Its rich chocolate flavors incorporates pieces of two of the cookie recipes in this chapter—the Calino Cookies and the Amaretti Biscuits. To make your "salamis" look like authentic Italian salumi, roll them up in parchment paper, then twist and crinkle both ends of the paper. I like to follow this with a layer of butcher's netting (see Source Guide, page 196) and wax paper for added authenticity, although it's up to you if you want to go that far.

8 egg yolks

2 cups (4 sticks) unsalted butter

18 ounces 70% Cacao Base Chocolate (page 47) or highest-quality store-bought chocolate, coarsely chopped (a scant 2 cups) and melted

12 ounces butter biscuits or Calino Cookies (page 110), chopped into $1/4$-inch pieces ($1^1/_2$ cups)

12 ounces Amaretti Biscuits (page 112), crumbled

2 cups confectioners' sugar, for coating

In a large mixing bowl, beat the egg yolks with an electric mixer until pale and creamy; set aside.

Melt the butter in a saucepan over medium heat. Stir in the melted chocolate until well combined. Remove from the heat to cool slightly.

Fold the butter and chocolate mixture into the beaten yolks with a silicone spatula. Add the cookie pieces to the chocolate mixture and stir until there are no more large pools of chocolate between the cookie pieces.

Cut parchment paper into ten 12-inch rectangles. Place $1^1/_2$ to 2 cups of the mixture onto a piece of the parchment paper and roll into a short, squat log. Twist the ends tightly to form a seal. Repeat with the remaining mixture and parchment paper. Refrigerate for 3 hours or until firm.

Unwrap the salamis and roll in confectioners' sugar until well coated. Shake off any excess sugar and package in butcher netting and wax paper, if you like.

Place the chocolate inside a piece of parchment paper.

Roll the chocolate into a firm tube.

Tightly twist the ends of the parchment.

Remove the chocolate from the parchent and roll it in confectioners' sugar to coat.

Insert the roll in the netting, leaving about 2 inches on either end. Use kitchen twine to tie each end tightly, then cut the netting off close to the twine.

Tiramisu with Cocoa Powder

Makes 8 to 12 servings

This is one of my favorite adult desserts: it's textured, sweet, and bitter all at the same time. The coffee in the recipe allows you to enjoy coffee and dessert all in one package. Be wary of sharing this with the children, especially at bedtime!

4 large eggs yolks

3/4 cup sugar

2/3 cup whole milk

1 generous cup heavy cream

1/3 teaspoon vanilla extract

2 cups Vanilla Bean Whipped Cream (page 195)

2 cups mascarpone

1/4 cup brewed coffee, chilled

2 1/4 tablespoons bourbon (your brand of choice)

1 cup lightly crushed Amaretti Biscuits, homemade (page 112) or store-bought (see Source Guide, page 196)

2 tablespoons natural (non-alkalized) cocoa powder

Whisk the yolks and all but 3 tablespoons of the sugar in a mixing bowl.

In a saucepan over medium heat, simmer the milk, cream, vanilla, and remaining sugar, stirring until the sugar dissolves. Temper the yolk and sugar mixture into the simmering milk, gradually stirring the yolk and sugar mixture into the warm pan of milk. Continue to cook over medium heat, stirring constantly, for 3 to 5 minutes, or until the custard thickens enough to coat the back of the spoon. Remove from heat immediately and allow it to cool slightly. Cover tightly and chill in the refrigerator for 1 hour.

When the hour is almost up, prepare the whipped cream.

Remove the custard from the refrigerator and whisk in the mascarpone until smooth.

In another bowl, mix the coffee and bourbon. Add the crushed Amaretti Biscuits and stir so the crumbles soak up the liquid.

You may assemble the tiramisu in an 8 x 8-inch glass dish or in individual serving glasses, dividing the ingredients equally among the servings. Either way, layer the ingredients in the following order: Start by spreading a 1-inch layer of the mascarpone mixture, top with a generous helping of the bourbon-soaked cookie crumbles, scoop on a layer of Vanilla Bean Whipped Cream, and finish with a sprinkling of cocoa powder. Cover with plastic wrap and refrigerate for a minimum of 2 to 3 hours before serving.

Chocolate-Covered Banana Pops

Makes 12 pops

Always popular with kids, these treats on a stick are a healthy dessert that's vegan and gluten free—and can be sugar-free, too, if you use a 100 percent cacao base chocolate. The potassium-rich bananas plus antioxidant-filled chocolate are the closest thing to a totally healthy dessert I can imagine.

6 bananas

1 recipe Chocolate Shell, kept warm (page 124)

$^1/_2$ cup toppings of your choice, such as flaked coconut, slivered almonds, or finely chopped candied fruit

Peel the bananas and halve them lengthwise. Gently insert an ice pop stick into the wide end of each half. Arrange the banana halves in one layer in a zip-tight plastic bag and freeze them overnight.

When you're ready to serve line a cookie sheet with parchment paper. Pour the warm chocolate into a container that is deep enough to fit the banana and narrow enough to have a good depth of chocolate. Working one at a time, dip the frozen bananas into the melted chocolate, all the way down to the stick.

While the chocolate is still warm, sprinkle the toppings of your choice over the banana and transfer to parchment- lined sheet. The chocolate will solidify instantly, so be sure to decorate just one banana at a time.

Serve immediately or store in a zip-tight plastic bag in the freezer for up to 1 week.

Dark Chocolate Gelato

Makes 12 servings

This gelato is so rich and creamy that you'll want to make it year-round, not just in hot summer months. To make Aztec Chocolate Gelato, add 1 tablespoon Aztec Powder (page 177) to the melted chocolate and cocoa powder mixture.

4 egg yolks

1 cup sugar

2 cups whole milk

2 cups heavy cream

9 1/2 ounces 70% Cacao Base Chocolate (page 47) or highest-quality store-bought chocolate bars, coarsely chopped (1 cup), melted

1/2 cup natural (non-alkalized) cocoa powder

In a medium bowl, cream the yolks and sugar until pale and gooey. Set aside.

Warm the milk and cream in the top of double boiler over medium-high heat, stirring constantly. Just before the milk mixture reaches a boil, remove from the heat.

In a small bowl, stir the melted chocolate and cocoa powder until blended. Pour the chocolate mixture into the double boiler and carefully blend it with the hot milk mixture using an electric hand mixer. Let cool slightly, then beat in the egg mixture until fully incorporated.

Pour the gelato mixture into an ice cream maker and process according to the manufacturer's directions until the gelato is thick and holds together.

Transfer to a freezer-safe container and freeze for at least 1 hour before serving. The gelato will keep in an airtight container in the freezer for up to 1 week.

Vanilla Gelato

Makes 12 servings

This gelato tastes great with chocolate cake, so make enough to pair with other recipes for several dessert treats! Don't throw away the vanilla husk after you scrape the seeds into the pot. Instead, place it in a jar of sugar to make aromatic vanilla sugar.

4 egg yolks

1 cup sugar

2 cups whole milk

2 cups heavy cream

1 vanilla bean, halved lengthwise

In a medium bowl, cream the yolks and sugar until pale and gooey. Set aside.

Warm the milk and cream in the top of a double boiler over medium-high heat, stirring constantly. Just before the hot milk mixture reaches a boil, remove from the heat. Scrape the vanilla bean seeds into the pot and save to pods to make vanilla sugar.

Let cool slightly, then beat in the egg mixture until incorporated.

Pour the gelato mixture into an ice cream maker and process according to the manufacturer's directions until the gelato is thick and holds together.

Transfer to a freezer-safe container and freeze for at least 1 hour before serving. The gelato will keep in an airtight container in the freezer for up to 1 week.

Chocolate Shell

Makes 2 cups

This chocolate sauce is perfect as a topping for gelato and as a coating for Chocolate-Covered Banana Pops (page 121), but you can use it for dipping fresh fruits and pouring over other desserts, too. Allow it to set for 30 to 60 seconds to create a hard chocolate shell. This recipe is vegan and, if you substitute a 100 percent cacao base chocolate, sugar-free.

9½ ounces 70% Cacao Base Chocolate (page 47)
or highest-quality chocolate bars, coarsely chopped
(1 cup)

1 cup coconut oil

Melt the chocolate in a small pan fitted with a candy thermometer. Warm over low heat to a temperature no higher than 104 F, stirring until it melts.

Heat the coconut oil in a medium pan over medium heat until just melted. Add the chocolate to the coconut oil and stir just until combined.

Chocolate Shell can be used immediately for dipping or pouring, or it can be stored in an airtight container for up to 1 week. To use, simply rewarm it until melted.

Chocolate–Dipped Waffle Cones

Makes 1 dozen cones

I am guilty of wanting to do everything myself, but I swear, the only way to serve the best waffle cones is to make them yourself! Once you taste these, you'll want to make them all the time. To do so, you'll need a waffle cone–forming tool as well as a basic waffle iron with a 12-inch diameter capacity (see "Source Guide," page 196).

Once you've made your waffle, move quickly and pay attention to technique: the most critical part is to make sure the base of the cone is sealed tightly so the ice cream won't drip out (we've all experienced that, right?). The cones will harden after a minute or two and are then ready for dipping.

3 large eggs

3 egg whites

$1\frac{1}{2}$ cups sugar

$1\frac{1}{2}$ teaspoons salt

6 tablespoons unsalted butter, melted

2 cups all-purpose flour

$9\frac{1}{2}$ ounces 70% Cacao Base Chocolate (page 47) or highest-quality store-bought chocolate bars, coarsely chopped (1 cup), melted and tempered (see page 52), for dipping

Preheat the waffle iron while you make the batter.

In a medium bowl, whisk the eggs, egg whites, sugar, and salt until the sugar is dissolved. Add the melted butter and stir to combine. Whisk in the flour until just combined. The batter should be thick but still pourable.

Open the waffle iron and pour 2 tablespoons batter onto the middle of the preheated surface. Close and secure the lid. Allow the waffle to cook for approximately $1\frac{1}{2}$ minutes (or follow the directions for your waffle iron). Check for doneness soon after the first minute is up. The waffle is done when it appears light golden-brown with white, doughy edges. Use a small offset spatula to remove the waffle from the iron then close the iron to retain the heat.

Working quickly, wrap the waffle around the cone form into the desired shape and size. Allow the waffle to sit in the form for 5 seconds to set.

Remove the cone from the form and carefully place it on a baking sheet to cool completely.

If you want chocolate-dipped cones, you may now dip the tip of the cone into the warm tempered chocolate. Set the cone upside down on a piece of parchment to allow the chocolate to set. Fill with scoops of ice cream or gelato and eat immediately!

Kid–Sized Waffle Cones: To make smaller cones for children (or adults who don't want to overindulge), use half the amount of batter per cone and begin checking to see if the waffle is cooked after 30 seconds. Use a smaller insert to form the cone.

4.

BARK,
FUDGE
& SIMPLE
CONFECTIONS

Chocolate Bark with Cacao Nibs and Almonds

Serves 4

Bark is a chocolate bar made without using a mold—basically a Cacao free-form chocolate bar. Gummy bears, sprinkles, dried blueberries, dried pineapple, cocoa nibs, cinnamon—these are some tasty mix-ins to add to chocolate bark that provide pops of color, fun, and crunch. Be creative and have some fun—or just add healthy ingredients. These recipes for chocolate bark are vegan—unless you decide to mix things up by making the bark out of milk chocolate or adding a mix-in that isn't dairy-free.

Use our master technique for tempering chocolate to create the melted chocolate base, spread it out on a piece of parchment paper, then sprinkle the specified mix-ins onto the still-warm bark. Bark made from an 8-ounce bar of chocolate bar will serve four people. Once it has set, you simply break the bark into four pieces—the pieces won't be symmetrical, but that's part of the charm.

8 ounces 70% Cacao Base Chocolate (page 47) or highest-quality store-bought chocolate bar, coarsely chopped, melted and tempered (see page 52)

$\frac{1}{2}$ cup raw almonds

$\frac{1}{4}$ cup cocoa nibs

Line a baking sheet or serving platter (at least 8 x 8 inches) with parchment paper. Temper the chocolate according to the instructions, then pour an even layer of the melted chocolate onto the prepared pan or platter (see Tip). The shape can be irregular (this is free-form chocolate making!), but keep the thickness as even as possible.

While the chocolate is still warm, sprinkle the almonds and cocoa nibs over the surface and let the bark sit at room temperature for 30 minutes to 1 hour to set.

To serve, either leave it on the platter (or transfer it from the parchment paper to a platter) and pass it around for guests to break off whatever size pieces they want, or break up the bark up yourself into whatever size pieces you prefer. I use a chocolate chipper (see Source Guide, page 196) to break up the chocolate into attractive shards without using my hands.

Tip: I typically make the chocolate bark about $\frac{1}{2}$-inch thick, but you can make the bark as thick or as thin as you want. The desirable thickness depends somewhat upon the platter you intend to serve it on or the container you plan to store it in. If you will be transferring it to a tin for storage or to give as a gift, you may want thinner bark, so you can fit more layers into the container. The photos on pages 131–133 show several different approaches.

Chocolate Bark with Candied Citrus
Prepare the tempered chocolate and spread it out on a parchment-lined baking sheet as described in the recipe above. While the chocolate is still warm, sprinkle $\frac{1}{2}$ cup chopped Candied Citrus Peel (recipe, page 190) and $\frac{1}{4}$ cup dried blueberries over the top. Let it set and break into pieces as described above.

Transfer Tattoos for Bark

1. Spread chocolate onto cocoa butter transfer sheets (see Source Guide, page 196)

2. Sprinkle immediately with your choice of selected toppings.

3. Let it set for 5 to 10 minutes until chocolate is firm.

4. Turn the chocolate over, and carefully peel the transfer sheet off.

Note: If it hasn't transferred, stop peeling and place in the refrigerator for 3 to 5 minutes.

5. Break the bark up and enjoy!

Classic Fudge

Makes 2 pounds

This is a traditional approach to a rich chocolate indulgence. Note that the more you work/stir the fudge, the softer the final texture will be. If you want a more brittle fudge, pour it into the pan as soon as it starts to thicken.

4 tablespoons (½ stick) unsalted butter, melted, plus extra for greasing the pan

1 (14-ounce) can sweetened condensed milk

Scant ⅓ teaspoon salt

12 ounces 70% Cacao Base Chocolate (page 47) or highest-quality store-bought chocolate bars, coarsely chopped (1¼ cups) and melted

Cut a sheet of parchment paper large enough to line a small 5½ x 3-inch loaf pan. Lightly butter the paper before lining the pan with the parchment, taking care to crease the corners evenly.

In a large bowl, mix the melted butter, sweetened condensed milk, and salt until fully incorporated.

Slowly pour in the melted chocolate, a little at a time, stirring after each addition until the chocolate is fully incorporated, making sure there are no streaks remaining. The fudge batter should thicken and become dull as you stir.

Immediately pour the batter into the prepared pan, then smooth the top with an offset spatula. Cover the loaf pan with parchment paper and refrigerate until set, 1 to 2 hours.

Carefully unmold the fudge by flipping it gently onto a platter (or marble slab). Remove the parchment paper and slice the fudge as desired. This fudge will keep in an airtight container in the refrigerator for up to 1 week.

Peanut Butter Chocolate Fudge

Makes about 3 pounds

This fudge features a favorite flavor combination—peanut butter and chocolate—in a sophisticated, not-too-sweet way that appeals to both grown-ups and kids.

$^2/_3$ cup unsalted butter, melted, plus extra for the pan

$3^1/_4$ cups sweetened condensed milk (3 cans)

1 cup Homemade Peanut Butter (page 155) or store-bought

$1^1/_2$ teaspoons salt

2 pounds 6 ounces 70% Cacao Base Chocolate or highest-quality store-bought chocolate bars, coarsely chopped (a generous $4^1/_2$ cups) and melted

Cut a sheet of parchment paper large enough to line two small $5^1/_2$ x 3-inch loaf pans, or one medium loaf pan. Lightly butter the paper before lining the pan with the parchment, taking care to crease the corners evenly.

In a large bowl, combine the melted butter, sweetened condensed milk, peanut butter, and salt. Stir to fully incorporate.

Using a plastic or rubber measuring cup (see Tip), pour the melted chocolate into the sweetened condensed mixture. Stir to fully incorporate the two, making sure there are no streaks remaining. The mixture will thicken and become dull as you stir.

Turn it out onto a marble and "table" it, moving it around quickly for 3 to 5 minutes with a large offset spatula. The tabling process will add elasticity to the texture of the fudge (for more complete instructions, see page 52).

Scoop the tabled fudge up with the spatula and transfer to the prepared pan, smoothing it with a spatula or a gloved hand into a flat, even log. Place the loaf pan in the refrigerator to allow the fudge to set for at least 2 to 3 hours, or overnight.

Unmold the fudge and remove the parchment paper. Use a sharp knife to cut it into $1^1/_2$ inch-thick slices. Serve at room temperature. The fudge will keep in an airtight container wrapped in plastic in the refrigerator for up to 1 week. It tastes terrific cold, straight out of the fridge, or at room temperature.

Tip: When transferring melted chocolate from one vessel to another, I use a plastic or rubber measuring cup. The chocolate can be easily scraped from the sides with a spatula, so you won't lose as much chocolate in the cup.

Rocky Road Fudge

Makes 2 pounds

This fudge sets quickly: When you are in the final phase of making this fudge, make sure you have the marshmallows and toasted nuts for decorating the top of the fudge prepared and nearby.

4 tablespoons (½ stick) unsalted butter, melted, plus extra for greasing the pan

1 (14-ounce) can sweetened condensed milk

Scant ¼ teaspoon salt

⅔ cup mini marshmallows (or about 10 large marshmallows, chopped)

⅓ cup raw almonds, toasted

12 ounces 70% Cacao Base Chocolate (page 47) or highest-quality store-bought chocolate bars, coarsely chopped (1¼ cups) and melted

Cut a sheet of parchment paper large enough to line a small 5½ x 3-inch loaf pan. Lightly butter the paper before lining the pan with the parchment, taking care to crease the corners evenly.

In a large bowl, mix the melted butter, sweetened condensed milk, salt, marshmallows, and toasted almonds. Stir to fully incorporate.

Slowly pour in the melted chocolate, a little at a time, stirring after each addition until the chocolate is fully incorporated, making sure there are no streaks remaining. The fudge batter will thicken and become dull as you stir.

Immediately pour the fudge into the prepared pan and smooth the top with an offset spatula. Cover the loaf pan with parchment paper and refrigerate until set, 1 to 2 hours.

Unmold the fudge, remove the parchment paper, and cut or slice as desired. The fudge will keep in an airtight container in the refrigerator for up to 1 weeks.

Chocolate–Dipped Drunken Cherries

Makes 2 (16-ounce) jars

You can enjoy these cherries as a sweet finish to a light summer meal, or as a topper for Gelato (pages 122–123) or Hot Fudge Sauce (page 194). It's a great way to use seasonal produce when it's at its best.

These also make perfect garnishes for drinks such as the Chocolate-Bourbon Cocktail (page 168). If you don't imbibe or entertain enough to need all these cherries, they make a great gift for anyone at any time.

If you need more convincing to make a batch of these cherries, know that the fluorescent maraschino cherries in the store are made from poorer-quality cherries and full of preservatives. This recipe uses fresh cherries, and the stems are kept on to make it easier to dip them in the chocolate—or pluck them from your drink. Make sure you remove the pit from the side of each cherry. They will keep for months refrigerated in an airtight jar or container.

2 pounds cherries, pitted, stems intact

2 tablespoons fresh lemon juice

4 cups bourbon (your brand of choice)

3 cups sugar

$1\frac{1}{2}$ tablespoons ground cinnamon

$1\frac{1}{2}$ tablespoons vanilla extract

1 teaspoon whole cloves

8 ounces 70% Cacao Base Chocolate (page 47) or highest–quality store–bought chocolate bar, coarsely chopped, (melted and tempered (page 52), for dipping

Pit the cherries from the side, using a cherry pitter, keeping the stems intact.

Combine the cherries with 8 cups water and lemon juice in a large bowl. Allow to soak for 20 minutes, then rinse and drain.

Pour the bourbon into another bowl and stir in the sugar, cinnamon, vanilla, and cloves.

Fill the Mason jars with the bourbon mixture and add the cherries, dividing them equally between the jars. Screw on the lids and, one at a time, flip each jar upside down and gently agitate the cherries. Turn the jars right side up and let them sit overnight at room temperature. (The sugar will dissolve overnight, so don't worry that it didn't break down when you shook the jars.)

The next day, the cherries are ready to be dipped in chocolate. Line a baking sheet with parchment paper. Use tweezer tongs to gently remove the cherries from the jar and drain them on a paper towel for 10 minutes.

Meanwhile, prepare the tempered chocolate and remove it from the heat. One at a time, gently lift the cherries by the stem and dip them into the melted chocolate, submerging the cherries in the chocolate entirely and coating about $\frac{1}{4}$ inch of the stem. Gently remove excess chocolate using the the edge of the bowl and place on the prepared pan, stem sides sticking straight up. Leave at room temperature for 30 to 45 minutes to set before serving. The chocolate–dipped drunken cherries may be kept in the refrigerator in an airtight jar for up to 2 weeks.

Vanilla Marshmallows

Makes about 9 dozen 1-inch marshmallows

Homemade marshmallows have become a very popular gluten-free treat. Forming the marshmallows is easy but cutting them is a messy process. One way to avoid the sticky factor is to oil the knife before cutting. The second method is to sprinkle the marshmallow with cornstarch. Keeping the marshmallows powdered will make it easier to cut them cleanly.

Many marshmallow recipes call for corn syrup, but I prefer to use glucose or invert sugar. Corn syrup is extremely high in sugar, which spikes your glucose levels. Many people are realizing they don't want this heavily processed sweetener in their diets.

1 tablespoon vegetable oil, for oiling the pan and utensils

3 cups confectioners' sugar, or as needed for dusting and coating

1⅓ cups cold water

1 ounce powdered gelatin

½ cup cane sugar

½ cup invert sugar (see Source Guide, page 196)

½ cup glucose (see Source Guide, page 196)

Pinch salt

1¼ teaspoons vanilla extract

Lightly oil a 9 x 13-inch baking pan and dust it with confectioners' sugar, shaking out any excess.

Pour half of the water into the bowl of an electric stand mixer. Slowly pour in the gelatin and immediately whisk it into the water, making sure no lumps are left. Attach the bowl to the mixer fitted with a whisk attachment and set aside.

In a medium-sized heavy-bottomed saucepan, combine the remaining water, the cane sugar, invert sugar, glucose, and salt. Insert a candy thermometer and bring the sugar mixture to a boil over high heat, stirring continuously, until the temperature reaches 240°F.

Immediately remove the pan from the stovetop and turn on the mixer to medium speed. Slowly and carefully pour the hot sugar syrup into the gelatin mixture. Once all of the syrup has been incorporated, increase the mixer speed to high and whip the marshmallow mixture for 13 minutes. It should become very thick and still be slightly warm. Add the vanilla during the last minute of whipping.

When the marshmallow is smooth, glossy, and very thick and stiff (the mixer will feel as if there is a sticky resistance as it beats and the mixture won't pour easily off a spoon), transfer the marshmallow mixture to the prepared pan, using a spatula to scrape the sides of the pan to get all the marshmallow. (Work quickly so it doesn't set.) Gently spread the marshmallow with a lightly oiled spatula, so it is smooth and even across the top.

Set the pan aside, uncovered, until the marshmallow has set and is firm to the touch, but feels like a soft pillow. This could take anywhere from a minimum of 4 hours to overnight

Once set, generously dust the top of the marshmallow with the confectioners' sugar and invert onto a clean cutting board to unmold. Using a lightly oiled pizza cutter or sharp knife, cut the marshmallow into 1-inch squares. Dust the cut sides with more confectioner's sugar, as needed, to prevent them from sticking together. The finished marshmallows will keep in an airtight container at room temperature for up to 1 month.

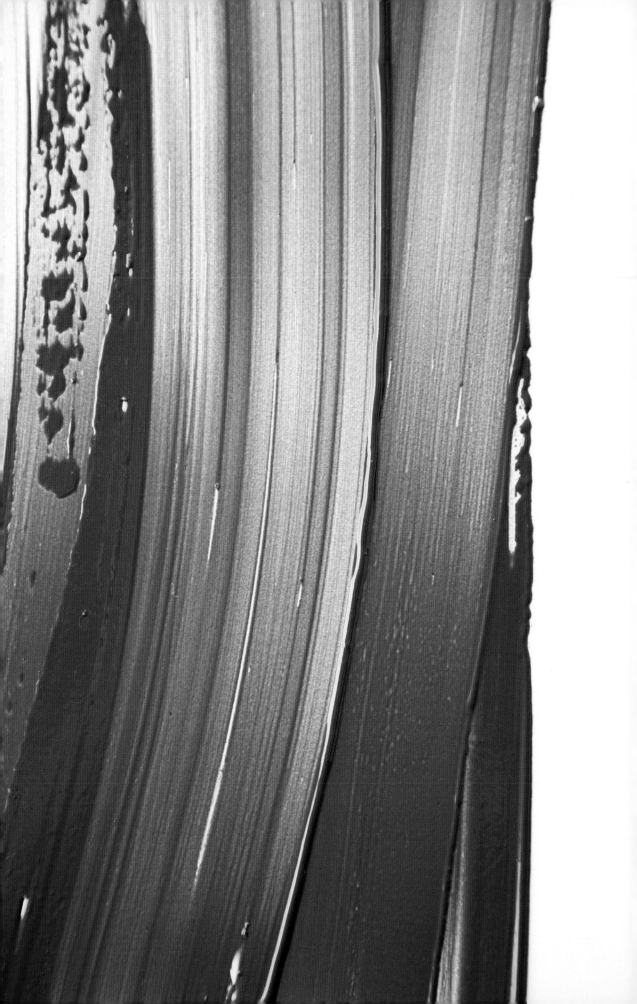

Passion Fruit Marshmallows

Makes about 9 dozen 1-inch marshmallows

Used for sipping chocolate, these confections can be dipped in tempered chocolate for a great treat. The sweetness of the marshmallow, the fruitiness of the passion fruit, and the addition of chocolate make for the ultimate marshmallow. You can also roast these over a fire—have fun with them!

1 tablespoon vegetable oil, for oiling the pan and utensils

3 cups confectioners' sugar, or as needed for dusting and coating

$^3/_4$ cup ($6^1/_2$ ounces) cold passion fruit juice, or puree ($6^1/_2$ ounces)

1 ounce powdered gelatin

$^2/_3$ cup cane sugar

1 cup invert sugar (see Source Guide, page 196)

$^1/_2$ cup glucose (see Source Guide, page 196)

Pinch salt

Lightly oil a 9 x 13-inch baking pan and dust it with confectioners' sugar, shaking out any excess.

Pour the passion fruit juice into the bowl of an electric stand mixer. Slowly pour in the gelatin and immediately whisk it into the juice, making sure no lumps are left. Attach the bowl to the mixer fitted with a whisk attachment and set aside.

In a medium, heavy-bottomed saucepan, combine $^3/_4$ cup water, the cane sugar, invert sugar, glucose, and salt. Insert a candy thermometer and bring the sugar mixture to a boil over high heat, stirring continuously, until the temperature reaches 240°F.

Immediately remove the pan from the stovetop and turn on the mixer to medium speed. Slowly and carefully pour the hot sugar syrup into the gelatin mixture. Once all of the syrup has been incorporated, increase the mixer speed to high and whip the marshmallow mixture for 13 minutes. It should become very thick and still be slightly warm.

When the marshmallow is smooth, glossy, and very thick and stiff (the mixer will feel as if there is a sticky resistance as it beats and the mixture won't pour easily off a spoon), transfer the marshmallow mixture to the prepared pan, using a spatula to scrape the sides of the pan to get all the marshmallow. Work quickly so it doesn't set. Gently spread the marshmallow with a lightly oiled spatula, so it is smooth and even across the top.

Set the pan aside, uncovered, until the marshmallow has set and is firm to the touch, but feels like a soft pillow. This could take anywhere from a minimum of 4 hours to overnight

Once set, generously dust the top of the marshmallow with the confectioners' sugar and invert onto a clean cutting board to unmold. Using a lightly oiled pizza cutter or sharp knife, cut the marshmallow into 1-inch squares. Dust the cut sides with more confectioner's sugar, as needed, to prevent them from sticking together. The finished marshmallows will keep in an airtight container at room temperature for up to 1 month.

To dip marshmallows in chocolate, put 2 cups warm tempered chocolate in a small bowl. Dust as much of the powdered sugar from the marshmallow as you can, then gently hold the marshmallows with your fingers, and dip it partially into the chocolate. Shake the marshmallow to get rid of any excess chocolate, then place on a sheet of parchment, chocolate side down, and let set for 5 to 10 minutes. Once it is set, lift it carefully from the parchment paper. Will keep in an airtight container for up to 2 weeks.

Cinnamon Marshmallows

Makes about 9 dozen 1-inch marshmallows

These are especially tasty in sipping chocolate and also pair nicely with ice cream or gelato. I like to put them on top of my sweet potato casserole at Thanksgiving—pouring the warm marshmallow on top. Cinnamon has the added benefit of lowering blood sugar so all in all, a win!

1 tablespoon vegetable oil, for oiling the pan and utensils

3 cups confectioners' sugar, or as needed for dusting and coating

1$^{1}/_{2}$ cups cold water

1 ounce powdered gelatin

$^{2}/_{3}$ cup cane sugar

$^{3}/_{4}$ cup invert sugar (see Source Guide, page 196)

$^{1}/_{2}$ cup glucose (see Source Guide, page 196)

Pinch salt

2$^{1}/_{2}$ teaspoons ground cinnamon

$^{1}/_{3}$ teaspoon cinnamon oil or extract

1$^{1}/_{4}$ teaspoons vanilla extract

Lightly oil a 9 x 13-inch baking pan and dust it with confectioners' sugar, shaking out any excess.

Pour half of the water into the bowl of an electric stand mixer. Slowly pour in the gelatin and immediately whisk it into the water, making sure no lumps are left. Attach the bowl to the mixer fitted with a whisk attachment and set aside.

In a medium-sized heavy-bottomed saucepan, combine the remaining water, the cane sugar, invert sugar, glucose, and salt. Insert a candy thermometer and bring the sugar mixture to a boil over high heat, stirring continuously, until the temperature reaches 240°F.

Immediately remove the pan from the stovetop and turn on the mixer to medium speed. Add the ground cinnamon and cinnamon oil to the gelatin mixture. Slowly and carefully pour the hot sugar syrup into the gelatin mixture. Once all of the syrup has been incorporated, increase the mixer speed to high and whip the marshmallow mixture for 13 minutes. It should become very thick and still be slightly warm. Add the vanilla during the last minute of whipping.

When the marshmallow is smooth, glossy, and very thick and stiff (the mixer will feel as if there is a sticky resistance as it beats and the mixture won't pour easily off a spoon), transfer the marshmallow mixture to the prepared pan, using a spatula to scrape the sides of the pan to get all the marshmallow. Work quickly so it doesn't set. Gently spread the marshmallow with a lightly oiled spatula, so it is smooth and even across the top.

Set the pan aside, uncovered, until the marshmallow has set and is firm to the touch, but feels like a soft pillow. This could take anywhere from a minimum of 4 hours to overnight

Once set, generously dust the top of the marshmallow with the confectioners' sugar and invert onto a clean cutting board to unmold. Using a lightly oiled pizza cutter or sharp knife, cut the marshmallow into 1-inch squares. Dust the cut sides with more confectioner's sugar, as needed, to prevent them from sticking together. The finished marshmallows will keep in an airtight container at room temperature for up to 1 month.

Ginger Marshmallows

Makes about 9 dozen 1-inch marshmallows

The ginger adds a spicy flavor, and I like to pair it with the Macha Green Tea Sipping Chocolate for a great drink.

1 tablespoon vegetable oil, for oiling the pan and utensils

3 cups confectioners' sugar, or as needed for dusting and coating

$1^2/_3$ cups cold water

1 ounce powdered gelatin

$^2/_3$ cup cane sugar

$^3/_4$ cup invert sugar (see Source Guide, page 196)

$^2/_3$ cup glucose (see Source Guide, page 196)

Pinch salt

$3^1/_4$ teaspoons ground ginger

Lightly oil a 9 x 13-inch baking pan and dust it with confectioners' sugar, shaking out any excess.

Pour half of the water into the bowl of an electric stand mixer. Slowly pour in the gelatin and immediately whisk it into the water, making sure no lumps are left. Attach the bowl to the mixer fitted with a whisk attachment and set aside.

In a medium, heavy-bottomed saucepan, combine the remaining water, the cane sugar, invert sugar, glucose, and salt. Insert a candy thermometer and bring the sugar mixture to a boil over high heat, stirring continuously, until the temperature reaches 240°F.

Immediately remove the pan from the stovetop and turn on the mixer to medium speed. Add the ground ginger to the gelatin mixture. Slowly and carefully pour the hot sugar syrup into the gelatin mixture. Once all of the syrup has been incorporated, increase the mixer speed to high and whip the marshmallow mixture for 13 minutes. It should become very thick and still be slightly warm.

When the marshmallow is smooth, glossy, and very thick and stiff (the mixer will feel as if there is a sticky resistance as it beats and the mixture won't pour easily off a spoon), transfer the marshmallow mixture to the prepared pan, using a spatula to scrape the sides of the pan to get all the marshmallow. Work quickly so it doesn't set. Gently spread the marshmallow with a lightly oiled spatula, so it is smooth and even across the top.

Set the pan aside, uncovered, until the marshmallow has set and is firm to the touch, but feels like a soft pillow. This could take anywhere from a minimum of 4 hours to overnight

Once set, generously dust the top of the marshmallow with the confectioners' sugar and invert onto a clean cutting board to unmold. Using a lightly oiled pizza cutter or sharp knife, cut the marshmallow into 1-inch squares. Dust the cut sides with more confectioner's sugar, as needed, to prevent them from sticking together. The finished marshmallows will keep in an airtight container at room temperature for up to 1 month.

Cashew and Pumpkin Seed Nougatine

Makes about 2 pounds

Nougatine has a glassy texture, like peanut brittle, and is combined with nuts for a delicate textural play. I like to dip pieces into chocolate and add a dash of sea salt for a special treat or a great holiday gift.

1 tablespoon vegetable oil, for oiling the parchment

$1^1/_4$ cups sugar

$^2/_3$ cup glucose (see Source Guide, page 196)

1 cup raw cashew pieces

$^3/_4$ cup whole shelled pumpkin seeds

$2^1/_2$ tablespoons unsalted butter, cut into cubes, at room temperature

$1^1/_2$ teaspoons vanilla extract

$^3/_4$ teaspoon sea salt

Line a 9 x 12-inch baking sheet with parchment paper and use a pastry brush to evenly spread the oil on the paper until it is well coated.

In a large, heavy-bottomed saucepan over medium-high heat, combine the sugar, glucose, and 1 cup water. Stir for 3 to 5 minutes, until the sugar has completely dissolved and the syrup is a dark caramel color.

Immediately remove the pan from the stovetop and carefully fold in the cashews, pumpkin seeds, butter, vanilla, and salt, mixing until well combined and the nuts are evenly distributed.

Pour the nougatine mixture onto the prepared parchment and use an offset spatula to spread and push it around until it is as thick as you want it. I like my nougatine about $^1/_4$ inch thick, but it can be thicker if you prefer.

Set the nougatine aside to cool at room temperture for at least 1 to 2 hours until set. Break it into pieces using your hands or a chocolate chipper (see Source Guide, page 196), and store in an airtight container lined with parchment paper, with parchment between the layers. The nougatine will keep at room temperature for up to 1 month.

Mini Chocolate Lollipops with Sprinkles

Makes 2 dozen miniature lollipops

Notice: These old-fashioned lollipops on a stick are fun and whimsical—for kids of all ages. If you want the lollipops to be the same size, draw circles on a parchment paper using a small cup or shot glass as a stencil. I find the size difficult to eyeball, so I always use a pattern; that way the kids won't argue over who gets the largest lollipop! You can make bigger lollipops, of course, but you may only end up with a dozen of them.

1 cup ($9\frac{1}{2}$ ounces bar chocolate) melted, 70% Cacao Base Chocolate (page 47) or highest-quality store-bought chocolate bars, coarsely chopped and melted, warm but not hot

24 (6-inch) lollipop sticks

$\frac{1}{2}$ cup sprinkles, in the color and size of your choice, for decoration

To make the template, use a pencil to draw six 1-inch diameter circles in a row on a 9 x 12-inch piece of parchment paper, leaving a gap of 1 to 2 inches between each circle. Place the parchment paper upside down on a baking sheet, so the pencil marks won't touch the chocolate, but you can still see the circles.

Add the melted, tempered chocolate to a piping bag (you don't need a tip, just cut off $\frac{1}{4}$ inch of the tip), and pipe 6 circles onto the parchment paper using the template underneath as a guide, then fill in the circles to create 6 round lollipops. Working quickly (the chocolate will set fast), place the tip of a lollipop stick into the middle of each chocolate circle and lay them onto the parchment.

Decorate each lollipop with sprinkles as desired. Refrigerate for 1 hour to harden, then remove from the fridge, lift gently from the parchment, and set aside on a baking sheet. Repeat the process in batches of 6 until all 24 lollipops are made.

The lollipops can be stored in an airtight container at room temperature for up to 3 months using parchment or wax paper to separate the layers.

Ganache Pops on a Stick

Makes 1 dozen pops

These are chocolate ganache pops, dipped in an extra layer of chocolate and coated with sprinkles or your favorite toppings—crushed nuts, shredded coconut, cocoa powder—to make them fun and special.

Ganache Pops

1 cup heavy cream

$^1/_4$ cup raw cane sugar (turbinado)

$^1/_2$ tablespoon invert sugar (see Source Guide, page 196)

$1^1/_3$ cups ($12^1/_2$ ounces bar chocolate) 70% base chocolate, melted and warm

12 (6-inch) lollipop sticks

Chocolate Coating

$9^1/_2$ ounces 70% Cacao Base Chocolate (page 47) or highest-quality store-bought chocolate bars, coarsely chopped (1 cup), melted and tempered (see page 52), for dipping

Your choice of toppings, such as crushed nuts, sea salt, sprinkles, coconut, cocoa powder, or sugar crystals

Heat the cream in small saucepan over medium-high heat. Stir in the raw cane sugar and invert sugar and whisk until dissolved. Remove from the heat and pour into a large heatproof bowl. Add the warm chocolate and whisk continuously, beginning in the middle of the bowl and moving slowly out toward the edges, to emulsify the ganache completely. Let the ganache cool in the bowl until it is firm to the touch but still scoopable.

Use a small ($^1/_3$-ounce) ice cream scoop with a squeeze handle or a melon baller, to make 12 small scoops of ganache and use your hands to form them into 12 smooth balls. Arrange the ganache balls on a baking sheet and push a stick in halfway through the center of each. Refrigerate at least 1 hour, or until firm.

Once the ganache balls are firm, set out your choice of toppings in small ramekins, then temper the chocolate to use for the coating as instructed. Transfer the bowl of warm tempered chocolate from the top of the double boiler to the countertop. Holding the stick[and working quickly and one at a time, dip the chocolate balls into the tempered chocolate, then tap them gently against the side of pot to release any extra chocolate.

Sprinkle the pops with the toppings, or roll them in the toppings in the ramekins to coat, depending on what topping you are working with and how much of it you want to use.

Arrange the coated and sprinkled pops on the baking sheet with the sticks pointing straight up, and let them set at room temperature for 1 hour before serving. The pops will keep in an airtight container in the refrigerator for up to 2 weeks.

Chocolate-and-Caramel-Coated Apples

Makes 1 dozen small candied apples

Choose small apples for this recipe. Their sweeter and tarter taste balances well with the dark chocolate. My favorite apples to use are lady apples because they're so tiny. If not available, use another crisp apple. You can roll the coated apples in nuts or dust them with cinnamon sugar to change it up, if you like. Sprinkles make a fun topping, too.

Be sure to let the caramel harden on the apple before you dip it in melted chocolate, then let the apple drip off any excess on a sheet of parchment. If you use too much chocolate or caramel, you'll end up with too much of a "foot" at the bottom the finished treat.

12 small crisp apples, such as lady apples

1 recipe Caramels (page 156; do not pour and cool)

19 ounces 70% Cacao Base Chocolate (page 47) or highest-quality store-bought chocolate bars, coarsely chopped (2 cups), melted and tempered (see page 52), for coating

2 cups finely chopped nuts, such as peanuts, walnuts, or pecans

12 (6-inch) lollipop sticks

Remove the stems from the apples and insert a lollipop stick into the core of each, pushing the sticks halfway though. Set the apples aside on a parchment-lined baking sheet.

Make the caramel in a medium saucepan as instructed. Allow the caramel to cool for just 30 seconds, then holding the apples by the sticks, dip each one into the caramel to coat. Scrape excess caramel off onto the side of the pot, then place the caramel-coated apples upside down on the parchment, with the sticks pointing upward. The caramel will pool at the bottom of the apple just slightly. If it's pooling too much, let the apple drip a bit more over the pot prior to letting it set.

Once the caramel has set and can be easily lifted from the parchment, about 20 to 30 minutes, prepare the chocolate coating and other toppings.

Put the nuts on a plate with a small lip. Temper the chocolate as instructed, remove it from the heat to the countertop, then dip each apple into the warm chocolate, as deep as you would like to go depending on how you want the finished apple to look (half covered in chocolate, or completely covered). Hold each chocolate-coated apple on the side of the pan for 10 to 15 seconds to allow for excess chocolate to drip back into the pot. Just before the chocolate sets, roll the apples in the nuts and return them, sticks pointing up, to a fresh piece of parchment. Let the coated apples set for several more minutes before serving them.

Peanut Butter Batons

Makes 24 to 30 candies

These are double taste treats for peanut butter lovers because they're made from true peanut butter, and peanut pralines. I like making these with homemade peanut butter (recipe provided below); the roasted peanuts add smokiness to the taste.

If you use your own homemade peanut butter (or a natural peanut butter with a layer of oil on top), make sure you pour off the oil instead of stirring it back into the peanut butter. This helps with the firmness of the batons. You'll probably pour off about ¼ cup extra oil from 3 cups of peanuts.

Peanut Praline

Vegetable oil, for oiling the parchment and utensils

2 cups unsalted roasted peanuts

2¼ cups sugar

1 tablespoon salt

Peanut Butter Batons

4 cups Peanut Praline

2 cups Homemade Peanut Butter (page 155) or store-bought brand of choice

19 ounces 70% Cacao Base Chocolate (page 47) or highest-quality store-bought chocolate bars, coarsely chopped (2 cups), melted and tempered (see page 52), for dipping

Make the peanut praline: Line a baking sheet with parchment. Use a pastry brush to evenly spread 1 tablespoon oil onto the parchment paper until it is well coated.

Grind the peanuts in a food processor set on high speed for 1 minute, or until the mixture is smooth; set aside.

In a large, heavy-bottomed saucepot over medium-high heat, combine the sugar, salt, and ¾ cup water. Insert a candy thermometer and cook, stirring constantly, until the temperature reaches 244 F. Stir in the ground peanuts, mixing until thoroughly incorporated. Immediately remove the pan from the stovetop and carefully pour the mixture onto the prepared parchment. Use an offset or silicone spatula to smooth the praline out to ¼ inch thick. Don't worry about it being an irregular shape, since you'll break it up later.

Allow the praline to cool at room temperate for 20 minutes, or until firm to the touch.

Use your hands to break the praline into pieces. Working in batches in a food processor fitted with the blade attachment, pulse each batch of praline pieces for 30 to 40 seconds, in 10-second intervals, until finely ground. Transfer to a bowl and set aside while you prepare the batons.

Make the batons: Line a baking sheet with parchment paper.

In the bowl of a food processor fitted with the blade attachment, combine the ground peanut praline and the peanut butter. Process on medium speed until the mixture comes together and is the consistency of cookie dough.

Using an offset or silicone spatula, spread the peanut butter mixture onto the prepared baking sheet to form an even layer about ¼ inch thick. Let it harden overnight at room temperature.

The next day, using a lightly oiled pizza cutter or sharp knife, cut 1 x 2-inch batons from the dough to yield 24 to 30 batons total.

Prepare the tempered chocolate according to instructions. Using the technique for dipping (see page 58), lightly balance each baton on a dipping fork and dip it into the pot of melted, tempered chocolate. Tap the fork on the edge of the pot to release the extra chocolate, and place the baton on a clean sheet of parchment to set.

The batons will keep in an airtight container at room temperature for up to 1 month.

Homemade Peanut Butter

Makes 1½ to 2 cups

3 cups raw peanuts

2 teaspoons salt

1 tablespoon vegetable oil

3½ tablespoons honey

In a food processor fitted with the metal blade, pulse 1½ cups of the peanuts for 30 to 50 seconds, in 10-second intervals, or until the nuts are small and grainy. Add the remaining 1½ cups peanuts and continue to pulse to incorporate them. Add the salt and pulse to combine.

With the food processor running on low, add the vegetable oil and honey and mix until the peanut butter comes together evenly to form a dense, grainy paste.

Scrape the peanut butter into an airtight container and store in your pantry, or in the refrigerator, for up to 1 month. Stir before you reuse it to incorporate the oil.

Caramels

Makes about 9 dozen 1-inch squares

This is my basic recipe for caramels. Add sea salt and it becomes Fleur de Sel Caramels. See below for other tempting variations to make.

Vegetable oil, for oiling the parchment and pizza cutter

3 cups cane sugar

2 cups sweetened condensed milk

1 tablespoon vanilla extract

1 cup glucose (see Source Guide, page 196)

1$\frac{1}{2}$ cups invert sugar (see Source Guide, page 196)

1 cup (2 sticks) unsalted butter, cut into cubes, at room temperature

Line a 9 x 12-inch baking pan with a piece of parchment paper large enough to cover the sides of the pan. Use a pastry brush to coat the parchment paper with 1 tablespoon oil until well greased.

In a large, heavy-bottomed saucepan over medium heat, bring the cane sugar, sweetened condensed milk, and vanilla to a boil, stirring constantly. Add the glucose and invert sugar, insert a candy thermometer, and cook over medium heat, scraping the sides down occasionally with a silicone spatula if sugar crystals collect there, until the temperature reaches 220°F. The mixture will still be fairly liquid, not thick enough at this point to coat the back of a spoon. Stir in the butter and continue cooking until the temperature reaches 244°F and thickens enough to coat the back of a spoon. Immediately remove the pan from the stovetop and carefully pour the hot caramel onto the prepared baking pan. Set the caramel aside to cool at room temperature for 2 to 3 hours until firm.

Using a lightly oiled pizza cutter or sharp knife, cut the caramel into 1-inch squares or desired shapes and sizes.

The caramel can be refrigerated in an airtight container lined with waxed or parchment paper (and between the layers), for up to 1 week.

Fleur de Sel Caramels

Sprinkle $\frac{1}{2}$ teaspoon of fleur de sel or other flaky sea salt over the caramel while it is still warm on the baking sheet. Cool and cut as directed.

Hickory–Smoked Caramels

Sprinkle $\frac{1}{2}$ tablespoon hickory-smoked sea salt over the caramel while it is still warm on the baking sheet. Cool and cut as directed.

Espresso Caramels

Sprinkle $\frac{1}{2}$ tablespoon ground espresso over the caramel while it is still warm on the baking sheet. Cool and cut as described.

Rosewater Caramels

Omit the vanilla extract. After adding the butter, cook until the temperature reaches 230°F on the candy thermometer, then stir in 1 tablespoon rosewater (available at many grocery stores or online). Continue to cook and stir the caramel until the temperature reaches 244°F. Pour, cool, and cut as directed.

Salt–Sprinkled Banana Caramels

Add 1 cup plus 2 tablespoons pureed bananas (about 3 bananas) to the pot with the milk and sugar mixture, and proceed as directed. Finish by sprinkling $\frac{1}{2}$ teaspoon of sea salt over the caramel while it is still warm on the baking sheet. Cool and cut as directed.

Chocolate–Dipped Vanilla Caramels

Once the caramels have been cut into squares, dip them in tempered chocolate to coat according to the instructions on page 156. You can chocolate-dip any of the caramel variations described above before the toppings are sprinkled on.

Cocoa Nib Peanut Brittle

Makes 3 to 3½ pounds brittle

This brittle is good dipped in chocolate, too. The cocoa nibs add the nuttiness of cacao, but don't add much of a chocolate taste. I typically give this brittle as a gift, packaged in a decorative, parchment-lined tin.

Vegetable oil, for oiling the parchment paper

4 cups sugar

1⅔ cups glucose (see Source Guide, page 196)

2 cups crushed unsalted peanuts

1 cup cocoa nibs

4 tablespoons (½ stick) unsalted butter, cut into cubes, at room temperature

1¾ teaspoons sea salt

3 teaspoons vanilla extract

3 teaspoons baking soda

Line a large sheet with lightly oiled parchment paper.

In a large saucepan over medium-high heat, combine the sugar with 1½ cups water and stir for 2 to 3 minutes, or until the sugar is completely dissolved. Bring the mixture to a boil, add the glucose, and stir just to combine. Lower the heat to medium, insert a candy thermometer in the saucepan, and continue to cook, stirring often, until the temperature reaches 239°F. The color will be medium brown and the syrup will be thick enough to coat the back of a spoon. Stir in the crushed peanuts and cocoa nibs and continue to cook, stirring constantly, until the temperature reaches to 311°F. The color will be slightly darker, and the texture will be slightly thicker at this point.

Remove from the heat, add the butter, salt, and vanilla, and stir to combine. Add the baking soda and stir quickly to incorporate. The brittle will bubble and turn pale.

Immediately pour the mixture onto the prepared baking sheet. Be careful, it's hot!

Let the brittle cool to room temperature, about 30 minutes, then use your hands to break the brittle into pieces. Store it in an airtight container at room temperature for up to 3 weeks.

Chocolate–Covered Scotch Pecan Toffee

Makes 2 dozen 2-inch pieces

A great gift for men. You can use either a bourbon or a Scotch, depending on how smoky you want the taste to be. Either way, the flavor of the liquor will really come through.

2¼ cups unsalted butter, cut into cubes

2½ cups sugar

½ cup Scotch (I like to use Laphroaig single–malt whisky for its peaty flavor)

½ teaspoon sea salt

2 cups chopped raw pecans

1 pound 70% Cacao Base Chocolate (page 47) or highest-quality store-bought chocolate bars, coarsely chopped (1½ cups plus 2 tablespoons), melted and tempered (see page 52), for dipping

1 tablespoon Atzec Powder (page 177), for dusting

In a medium, heavy-bottomed saucepan with high sides, combine the butter, sugar, Scotch, and salt over medium–high heat. Insert a candy thermometer in the pan and stir until the temperature reaches 300°F. The toffee will be a blond color and thick enough to coat the back of a spoon. Remove from the heat and stir in the pecans.

Immediately pour the hot toffee onto the prepared baking sheet, spread with a rubber spatula to create an even layer, ⅛ to ¼ inch thick. Be careful, it's hot. Let cool to room temperature.
While the toffee is cooling, melt and temper the chocolate.

Once the toffee is cool, use your hands to break it into approximately 2-inch pieces.

When you're ready to dip the toffee, transfer the bowl of warm tempered chocolate from the double boiler to your countertop. Line a baking sheet with parchment paper. Drop a piece of toffee into the chocolate to coat and lift it out using a dipping fork (see Source Guide, page 196). Gently tap the fork on the side of the bowl to remove excess chocolate, and then place the chocolate-covered toffee onto the prepared pan and add a pinch of Aztec Powder. Repeat the process until all the toffee pieces are dipped and dusted. The toffee will keep in an airtight container at room temperature for up to 1 month.

Peppermint Patties

Makes about 2 dozen candies

At Cacao Atlanta Chocolate Company, we were determined to come up with the best peppermint patty, reminiscent of the classic we all know and love. We experimented with different shapes and sizes and found that the circular shape was iconic and allowed for the perfect ratio of peppermint to chocolate. When rolling out the peppermint confection between wax paper, feel free to play around with different shapes and sizes until you find your own personal favorite. You can shape the patties by hand, or cut them out with a cookie cutter of your choice. Just remember, you'll need adequate surface area in order to dip the fondant in the chocolate.

¾ cup sweetened condensed milk

⅓ teaspoon peppermint oil

4 cups confectioners' sugar

1 pound 70% Cacao Base Chocolate (page 47) or highest-quality store-bought chocolate bars, coarsely chopped (1½ cups plus 2 tablespoons), melted and tempered (see page 52), for dipping

In a large bowl, stir the sweetened condensed milk and peppermint extract. Add small amounts of the confectioners' sugar at a time, mixing with a metal spoon or silicone spatula until the dough is firm but not sticky to the touch.

Form the peppermint fondant into 1-inch balls. Using your fingers, flatten the balls between two sheets of wax paper until your desired thickness is achieved.

Allow the patties to dry for 2 hours, turning them halfway through to make sure they dry evenly.

When you're ready to dip the fondant, transfer the bowl of warm tempered chocolate from the double boiler to your countertop. Line a baking sheet with parchment paper. Drop a piece of fondant into the chocolate to coat and lift it out using a dipping fork (see Source Guide, page 196). Gently tap the fork on the side of the bowl to remove excess chocolate, and then place the chocolate-covered patty onto the prepared pan. Repeat the process until all the peppermint patties are coated. The patties will keep in an airtight container at room temperature for up to 3 weeks.

5.

TINCTURES, CORDIALS & SIPPING CHOCOLATES

Master Technique:
How to Make Tinctures

A tincture is a combination of dried herbs infused into an alcohol solution that can be added to an alcoholic beverage or a sipping chocolate for added flavor. Also called an extract (in fact, the same process is used to make real vanilla extract), alcohol tinctures are the most common type and the easiest to make.

First, pick the herbs you plan to use. If you use fresh instead of dried herbs, you will get a stonger flavor. My three favorite tinctures to add to chocolate drinks are lavender-chamomile, peppermint, and rosemary-orange flavored, but you can experiment with other herbs if you like.

1 tablespoon fresh herb, or 1 teaspoon dried herb of choice

Scant $\frac{1}{2}$ cup clear alcohol of your choice (vodka, gin, etc.)

Place the herb of your choice in a 4-ounce jar, filling the jar half full if you are using the leaves only and one third full if you are using the stems with leaves attached (cut the stem to fit the height of the container). Do not pack the herbs down.

Pour enough boiling water into the jar to lightly dampen all of the herbs. (This step is optional, but it helps to draw out the beneficial health properties of the herbs.)

Fill the rest of the jar (or the entire jar if you did not add boiling water) with your choice of high-content alcohol (vodka, gin, or any clear alcohol) and stir with a clean spoon.

Seal the jar and store in a cool, dry place, shaking it daily, for at least 3 weeks or up to 6 months. (I usually allow the herbs to steep in the alcohol for 6 weeks.) Taste the tincture after a week to ensure you like the flavor you chose and its strength. Taste each week thereafter. If the flavor is too strong after one week, remove the herbs. You can add a little more alcohol to dilute the tincture, or just remember to use less of the tincture in the drink recipes than specified in order to flavor them according to your taste preferences.

Strain the tincture through a cheesecloth and discard the herbs. Store the tincture in dark-colored dropper bottles or clean glass jars. They will last for 3 to 6 months.

Lavender-Chamomile Tincture

This is a relaxing formula I call "Inner Calm." Use it to flavor truffles, chocolates, or a sipping chocolate. For this tincture, you may use dried lavender flowers or fresh lavender, and dried chamomile flowers; choose a culinary grade in both cases. If using fresh lavender, you can use the stems or the flowers. Use an equal amount of chamomile and lavender.

Peppermint Tincture

Fresh whole leaves or dried mint leaves work for this. As with any of the tincture recipes, taste it along the way to test how strong the flavor will be. It should taste fragrant in your mouth and that fragrance will end up in your drink. If you can't taste the fragrance, use more mint. If the mint isn't strong enough after 3 weeks, double the amount of mint and leave for 2 days, then strain and enjoy.

Rosemary-Orange Tincture

Purchase or clip fresh stems of rosemary and cut them to fit in the jar. For the orange, use $\frac{1}{4}$ cup whole candied citrus peel (see Candied Citrus recipe, page 190) to fill the jar one third full. Test after 1 week; if you want a stronger orange flavor, add a couple of drops of orange essential oil to the tincture.

Chocolate–Bourbon Cocktail

Makes 1 cocktail

If you haven't premade your sipping chocolate, this cocktail is a bit time-consuming to prepare. So, I suggest you make a basic sipping chocolate when you have the time (you can leave it in the refrigerator for up to a week), then you'll be ready to whip up this cocktail whenever friends stop by. We make this drink for every party we have—and our guests love it. It also tastes good with the Maple-Candied Bacon (page 189) as an accent.

2 ounces (5 tablespoons) Dark Sipping Chocolate (page 174), cooled

1 ounce bourbon, your brand of choice (I like Bulleit Bourbon)

Sprinkling of Aztec Powder (optional; page 177), for serving

Fill a cocktail shaker with crushed ice. Pour the sipping chocolate and bourbon over the ice and shake for 30 seconds.

Strain into a cocktail glass and add 1 ice cube. Garnish with Aztec Powder to add some spice, if you like. Serve immediately.

Chocolate Bitters

Makes about 2 pints

Colorful decorative bottles of these bitters make a great gift. Use the recipient's favorite booze as a base. Feel free to play with different types of cacao nibs, which will yield different flavors. African nibs have more of a cacao flavor, while those from Venezuelan are nutty, and the Peruvian nibs are fruity.

$\frac{1}{2}$ cup cacao nibs

16 ounces liquor of your choice (vodka, bourbon, rum)

2 to 3 tablespoons Vanilla Simple Syrup (below)

Combine all the ingredients in a 1-quart glass jar, screw on the lid, and let sit at room temperature for a minimum of 1 day, or up to 1 week before using. (The flavor builds over time.) Strain out the nibs, transfer the bitters to two 1-pint bottles, and store at room temperature for up to 1 month.

Vanilla Simple Syrup

Makes about 3 cups

2 cups sugar

$\frac{1}{2}$ vanilla bean, seeds scraped

In a saucepan over medium heat, combine the sugar, 1 cup water, and the vanilla bean seeds and pod. Stir constantly until the sugar is dissolved. Remove from the heat and let cool, then strain. Pour the simple syrup into glass jar, screw on the lid, and keep in the refrigerator for up to 1 month.

Chocolate Syrup

Makes 2 quarts

Use this syrup to make chocolate milk for kids (or for yourself, if you're like me). Or add it to hot or iced coffee to make a mocha drink. It's way better than store-bought chocolate syrup because there are no preservatives added, but it will keep in the refrigerator for 2 weeks in a sealed container. (It doesn't thicken with age, so there's no need to thin it.) Just stir 1 tablespoonful into 1 cup milk for a single serving.

3 cups sugar

2 tablespoons vanilla extract

$3\frac{1}{2}$ cups natural (non-alkalized) cocoa powder

Heat 5 cups water, the sugar, and vanilla in a large saucepan over medium-high heat, whisking for 2 to 3 minutes, until the sugar has fully dissolved.

Bring the mixture to a simmer and add the cocoa powder, whisking vigorously to get rid of any clumps. Continue to stir until the mixture begins to thicken into a syrup.

Remove the pot from the heat and use immediately as you like, in coffee, chocolate milk, over ice cream, etc. Let the rest cool to room temperature, then transfer to an airtight container. The syrup will keep, in a glass or plastic container, in the refrigerator for up to 2 weeks.

Chocolate Rum Punch

Makes 1 drink

The fruit and spices in this cold rum punch give it a Caribbean flavor. If you want to prepare a big punch bowl of this for a party, you can easily scale up the recipe. Just remember, if you make the punch the day before plan to serve it, decrease the quantity of rum; the longer the rum sits, the stronger the drinks will be!

2 ounces rum (your brand of choice)

1 ounce lime juice

$^{1}/_{2}$ ounce simple syrup

$^{1}/_{4}$ ounce allspice liqueur

1 teaspoon Vanilla Simple Syrup (page 170)

1 teaspoon Chocolate Bitters (page 170)

1 thin orange slice, for garnish

Put all the ingredients into a cocktail shaker and shake for 30 seconds, or until the mixture has a bit of froth. Pour into a tall glass filled with crushed ice and garnish with a slice of orange.

Dark Sipping Chocolate

Make 5 (1-cup) servings

Sipping chocolates must be made hot, but can then be refrigerated and enjoyed cold—it's your choice to serve them cold or hot. Instead of coffee, have one of these drinks in the morning for an amazing start to your day. Or you can use sipping chocolate in smoothies or cocktails, such as the Chocolate Bourbon Cocktail (page 186). Mix this basic recipe using a whisk, or an immersion blender. If you choose to use an immersion blender, be sure not to beat this elixir for too long—the drinkable chocolate will quickly turn into pudding. The sipping chocolate is ready to drink when it thickens enough to coat the back of a spoon.

3 cups whole milk

¾ cup half-and-half

9½ ounces 70% Cacao Base Chocolate (page 47) or highest-quality store-bought chocolate, coarsely chopped (1 cup)

⅓ cup sugar

To whisk by hand, combine the milk and half-and-half in a medium saucepan over high heat. Heat until the mixture almost boils, then whisk in the chocolate until melted and well incorporated. Remove from the heat, add the sugar, and whisk for 2 to 3 minutes until the sugar dissolves and the sipping chocolate will be just thick enough to coat a spoon.

For faster results, use an immersion blender to blend for 30 seconds. (Be careful not to use the immersion blender for too long as it will thicken the recipe too much.)

Serve the sipping chocolate hot.

The sipping chocolate may be stored in a tightly sealed container in the refrigerator for up to 1 week.

Vegan Dark Sipping Chocolate

For a nondairy version, simply substitute 3¾ cups nondairy milk (almond/soy/coconut) for the whole milk and omit the half-and-half.

Matcha Green Tea Sipping Chocolate

Matcha is a finely ground green tea powder made from shade-grown plants and is known for its calming properties. Choose a good-quality tea–lesser-quality matcha is very bitter. Simply prepare the Dark Sipping Chocolate according to the instructions, adding 1 teaspoon matcha green tea powder along with the milk and half-and-half, stirring until the powder dissolves.

Malted Sipping Chocolate

Malted milk powder was originally created as a malt- and wheat-based nutritional supplement for babies, trademarked in 1887. In 1922, a creative soda jerk put the malted milk powder into a chocolate milkshake and the malt was invented. To make a grown-up version of a chocolate malt, prepare the Dark Sipping Chocolate according to the instructions, adding 1 to 2 teaspoons malt powder (see Source Guide, page 196) along with the milk and half-and-half, stirring until the powder dissolves.

Aztec Sipping Chocolate

Makes 7 (1-cup) servings

This chocolate gives you an energy lift because of the chiles and spices it contains, and the caffeine gives you a boost, too. At our store, we've historically called this drink Aztec Aphrodisiac, a nickname it earned after customers kept telling us it had a romantic effect! This drink is served hot, topped with whipped cream for a sensuous finish.

2 cups heavy whipping cream

1 tablespoon Vanilla Simple Syrup (page 170)

1 recipe Dark Sipping Chocolate (page 170)

2 teaspoons Aztec Powder

To make the whipped cream, pour the heavy cream and Vanilla Simple Syrup into a stainless steel mixing bowl and whip with an electric mixer or a whisk until soft peaks form.

Reheat the sipping chocolate if necessary. Pour the chocolate into cups, top each serving with a mound of whipped cream, and sprinkle with Aztec Powder. Serve immediately.

Aztec Powder

Makes 7 tablespoons (scant ½ cup)

1 tablespoon crushed red pepper powder, available at most groceries

1 tablespoon chili powder

½ teaspoon ground nutmeg

2 teaspoons ground cinnamon

2 tablespoon smoked paprika

¼ teaspoon allspice

Put all the ingredients in an airtight plastic or glass container and shake to mix. Give it a good 30 seconds of shaking. Store in your pantry at room temperature for up to 1 year.

6.

PÂTE DE FRUIT, ACCENTS & FLOURISHES

PÂTE DE FRUIT

These jewel-like candies are composed of fruit mixed with sugar pulp and apple pectin. I share three versions here, made with mayhaw, passion fruit, and strawberries. The fruit content is more than 50 percent of the total content. These sweet fruit squares are lovely to eat on their own, but they may also be layered with ganache to create elegant, double-layered truffles (page 78). Chocolate and fruit is, of course, always a tasty combination, especially when you use seasonal berries. Both milk and dark chocolate pair well with pâte de fruit.

Mayhaw Pâte de Fruit

Makes 32 (1-inch) chocolates

Wild mayhaw berries grow in the swamps of the American South, and are gathered in boats with nets and scoops. The delicate, wild Mayhaw berries resemble a pink cranberry, although their colors range from pink to red. Mayhaw jelly became popular in the late 1800s as a sauce or jelly served with wild game. If you plan to make chocolate-layered pâte de fruit, prepare the pâte de fruit a day ahead so it has ample time to set.

1 tablespoon vegetable oil, plus more for oiling the knife

2 cups plus 3 tablespoons sugar (see Tip), plus ½ cup for coating

½ tablespoon apple pectin (see Source Guide, page 196)

2 cups pureed mayhaw berries

2 tablespoons glucose (see Source Guide, page 196)

Line a baking sheet or 9 x 12-inch frame (see Source Guide, page 196) with parchment paper. Grease the parchment and set aside.

Whisk 3 tablespoons of the sugar and the pectin in a small bowl until well combined; set aside.

Place the fruit puree in a large, heavy-bottomed saucepan on the stovetop. Insert a candy thermometer and cook over medium-high heat until the temperature reaches 120°F. Add the sugar and pectin mixture, whisking continuously until the mixture is completely smooth and free of lumps. Bring to a boil and boil for 1 full minute, then add the glucose and remaining 2 cups sugar and whisk until fully combined. Continue to cook, stirring continuously to prevent burning, until the temperature reaches 223°F.

Remove the pan from the stovetop and carefully pour the hot fruit mixture into the prepared frame. Set aside to cool for at least 2 to 3 hours at room temperature, or in the refrigerator for 2 hours, until set.

When the pâte de fruit has set, use an oiled knife to cut 1-inch squares. Transfer the pieces to a lidded plastic container, add the remaining ½ cup sugar, and shake to coat. Store at room temperature in an airtight container with parchment between the layers for up to 1 month. If, after a couple of days, the sugar has been absorbed, you can sprinkle with more sugar.

Tip: For a more consistent look and feel, you may use sanding sugar in place of the granulated sugar.

Passion Fruit Pâte de Fruit

Follow the recipe above, substituting 2 cups pureed passion fruit (from about 12 medium fruits) for the mayhaw. If you can't find fresh passion fruit, you may substitute store-bought passion fruit puree from the freezer section of your grocery store.

Strawberry Pâte de Fruit

Follow the recipe above, substituting 2 cups pureed fresh strawberries for the mayhaw.

Blueberry Pâte de Fruit

Follow the recipe above, adding 3 tablespoons fresh lemon juice along with the sugar and pectin and substituting 2 cups pureed fresh blueberries for the mayhaw.

Blueberry–Lavender Confiture

Makes about 12 (8-ounce) jars

This jam is luscious in my Chocolate-Glazed Bourbon Cake with Blueberry Filling (page 93). Either cultivated or wild blueberries will work in this recipe, but if you can get wild blueberries, they are more flavorful, especially the small ones. This is because the blueberry flavor is derived more from the shell than the pulp; the shell of wild berries is thicker, and the smaller berry has more surface area than pulp. The yield can easily be halved, but why not stock up when blueberries are in season so you can share some jars with friends?

5 pounds fresh blueberries, stems removed

3 tablespoons fresh lemon juice

$3^3/_4$ tablespoons pectin (see Source Guide, page 196)

$6^1/_2$ cups sugar

$1/_4$ cup fresh or dried buds lavender buds

In a large saucepan, combine the blueberries, $1/_2$ cup water, and the lemon juice. Mash the berries with a whisk and begin to heat them over medium–high heat.

Add the pectin and whisk to completely dissolve any lumps. Add the sugar and stir to incorporate. Cook for 25 minutes, stirring occasionally, until [describe texture/break down of blueberries], and then stir in the lavender buds, until the blueberries begin to break down and become a sauce,

Remove from the heat and immediately pour into sterilized Mason jars. Cool to room temperature and screw on the lids. The confiture will keep in the jars in the refrigerator for up to 1 month.

Mayhaw Jelly

Makes 12 to 14 (10-ounce) jars

Mayhaw berries are a delicious Southern fruit that have almost disappeared from the region. Considered to be an heirloom fruit, regional chefs, in increasing numbers, are cooking and using them in beverages to try to preserve the berries to keep them from going completely extinct. I like mayhaw jelly served cold with Calino Cookies (page 110) for breakfast, and as a topping on Dark Chocolate Gelato (page 122) for a fruity dessert.

8 cups mayhaw juice (see Source Guide, page 196)

$^1\!/_3$ cup pectin (see Source Guide, page 196))

10 cups sugar

Pour the mayhaw juice into a large saucepan, insert a candy thermometer, and heat the juice over medium-high heat until the temperature reaches 120°F. Whisk in the pectin to dissolve any lumps, then bring the mixture to a boil and boil for 3 minutes. Stir in the sugar and whisk until dissolved. Return the jelly to a boil for 1 minute. Remove the saucepan from the heat and pour into Mason jars that have been sterilized in a hot dishwasher. Cool to room temperature and screw on the lids. The jelly will keep in the jars in the refrigerator for up to 1 month.

Hot Pepper Jelly

Makes four 12-ounce jars

I like to use this jelly in the traditional Southern snack manner: over cream cheese on crackers. Use your favorite chile peppers—jalapeños, red or green bell peppers, or a mix of sweet and spicy peppers. Just be aware that some chiles are hotter than others.

8 ounces bell peppers (2 to 3 bell peppers)

4 ounces chile peppers (4 to 6 chiles, depending on their size)

$3^1/_4$ cups sugar

$^3/_4$ cup cider vinegar

5 tablespoons pectin (see page 196)

Cut the tops off the bell peppers and chiles and scrape out the seeds and membranes. In a food processor with the metal blade, chop the peppers into very fine pieces.

In a large pot, heat the peppers, sugar, and vinegar over medium-high heat until the sugar dissolves, stirring constantly. Insert a candy thermometer into the mixture, bring it to a boil, and add the pectin, carefully whisking to dissolve any lumps. Continue to cook the jelly, stirring constantly, until the temperature reaches 222 F. Remove from the heat and pour immediately into sterilized glass jars. Cool to room temperature and screw on the lids. The jelly will keep in the jars in the refrigerator for up to 1 month.

Raspberry-Thyme Jam

Makes about 2 dozen 12-ounces jars

This jam can be mixed into a chocolate ganache, with Chocolate Scones (page 107), Amaretti Biscuits (page 112), or between layers of the Chocolate-Glazed Bourbon Cake (page 93). Fresh thyme stands up best to the fragrance of the raspberries, so I don't recommend substituting dried thyme. This recipe is best to make during raspberry season, especially if you have the opportunity to pick your own. The yield can easily be halved or even quartered.

$4^1/_2$ pounds fresh raspberries

4 pounds (about 9 cups) sugar

$^1/_4$ cup loosely packed fresh thyme leaves

3 tablespoons plus 1 teaspoon pectin (see Source Guide, page 196)

Pour the raspberries into a large pot and then add the sugar. Over medium-low heat, use a wooden spoon or spatula to mash the berries, stirring to dissolve the sugar in the berry juice. After about 3 to 5 minutes, when the mixture has become more liquid, increase the heat to medium-high, bring the jam to a boil, and add the pectin, carefully whisking to dissolve any lumps, and cook for 15 minutes, stirring frequently, until it is thick enough to coat the back of a spoon.

Pour the hot jam into sterilized glass jars and divide the fresh thyme leaves between the 12 jars, stirring the leaves into the jam before screwing on the lid. The jam will keep in the jars in the refrigerator for up to 1 month.

Lemon Curd

Makes one 16-ounce jar

This rich, tangy preserve is useful to have on hand as a filling for cakes or to spread on scones (page 107). To make a very special confiture, layer this lemon curd with Blueberry-Lavender Confiture (page 184) in jars. Put the blueberry preserves on the bottom of the jar and let it cool in the refrigerator, then add the lemon curd layer. This way, when you dig your spoon into the jar, you'll get to enjoy the sweet/tart taste combination.

15 egg yolks

3 cups sugar

1 cup fresh lemon juice, plus the zest

$1\frac{1}{2}$ cups (3 sticks) unsalted butter, chilled and cut into cubes

Add one inch of water to a medium saucepan. Bring to a boil and then reduce to a simmer over medium-high heat.

Meanwhile, combine the egg yolks and sugar in a medium heatproof bowl and whisk for about 1 minute until smooth. Add the lemon juice and zest and whisk until smooth.

When the water reaches a simmer, reduce the heat to low and place the bowl on top of the saucepan. Whisk until the egg yolk mixture becomes light yellow and thickens enough to coat the back of a spoon, about 8 minutes.

Remove promptly from the heat and stir in the butter, one piece at a time, allowing each piece to melt before adding the next.

Pour lemon curd into a sterilized jar or a clean, plastic container with a lid. Let it cool to room temperature before you cover. If you use a plastic container, cover the curd with a layer of plastic wrap placed directly on the surface of the curd so it won't develop a skin. Refrigerate immediately. The lemon curd will keep in the refrigerator for up to 2 weeks.

Maple-Candied Bacon

Makes ¾ cup candied bacon pieces

These days, bacon has become a popular flavor to add to chocolate bark. I candy mine in maple syrup because the maple flavor pairs so well with bacon—it's rich, salty, and sweet. Be sure to cook the bacon until it's very crisp. Cool it on a wire rack after you dip it in the syrup, which will allow the excess syrup to drip off the bacon as it dries. Once the bacon is candied and dry, you can use it as an accent in drinks, such as the Chocolate-Bourbon Cocktail (page 168).

Ground candied maple bacon can be sprinkled on bars, bark, and ice cream.

4 slices thick center-cut bacon

2½ tablespoons maple syrup (a dark-colored syrup will turn the candy darker)

Preheat a cast-iron skillet over medium-high heat. Add the bacon slices and cook until crisp, flipping halfway through cooking, then remove to paper towels to drain. Pour off the grease from the skillet and return it to medium-high heat.

Add the maple syrup and ½ cup hot water to the hot skillet, stirring to combine. Return the bacon to the skillet, tossing the slices until they are completely covered in the syrup mixture. Cook for 1 minute, then remove the bacon to a wire rack to cool.

Let the candied bacon cool, then break it into ¼-inch pieces. (Use a knife if the job's too sticky). Store in an airtight container in the refrigerator for up to 1 week.

Candied Citrus Peels

Makes 2 cups

You don't need to buy candied oranges or lemons at the grocery store. Here is the basic process for making them at home. Stored in an airtight container, they will keep for a couple of months in the pantry. Chop them up and use them to add flavor and color to chocolate barks (pages 130–133) or Chocolate-Almond Biscotti (page 113)—or enjoy them out of the jar as little sweet and tangy treats.

Choose the most fragrant lemons for this recipe: just rub your finger on the outside of a lemon to check the strength of their scent. Meyer lemons are the best choice because they have the thickest rinds. As a variation, you can substitute limes in this recipe.

Try different varieties of oranges for candied orange peels. The candying process dehydrates them, so look for an orange with a thick, fragrant peel. When you cut the oranges open, cut crosswise in half, slice the halves into triangles, then lift out the pulp. This makes it easier to remove the peel.

Peels of 6 oranges

Peels of 6 lemons, preferably Meyer lemons

$2\frac{1}{2}$ cups sugar, plus 1 cup for dusting

Use a Y-shaped potato peeler to peel the fruit. Cut the peels into $1\frac{1}{2}$ x $\frac{3}{4}$-inch strips. Combine the sugar and $1\frac{1}{4}$ cups water in a medium saucepan over high heat and stir until the sugar dissolves, about 1 minute. Add a candy thermometer to the pot and bring the sugar-water mixture to a boil, then add the citrus peels and continue to cook until the mixture reaches 230°F, or until the peels are translucent. Remove from the heat, strain the peels, and set them aside to cool completely.

Line a baking sheet with parchment paper. When the peels are cool, arrange them in a single layer on the prepared pan and dust with the remaining 1 cup sugar. Shake the pan to coat the undersides of the peels with sugar.

Store in an airtight container in the refrigerator for up to 1 week.

Chocolate-Dipped Candied Citrus Peels

To coat one batch of Candied Citrus Peels, temper 8 ounces 70% Cacao Base Chocolate (page 47) according to the master instructions on page 52. Remove the bowl of warm melted chocolate from the top of the double boiler and dip the candied peels in the chocolate according to the instructions on page 58. Once the chocolate is set, transfer to an airtight container, with parchment paper between the layers, and store in the refrigerator for up to 1 week.

Candied Mint Leaves

Makes 48 candied leaves

You can use these leaves, chopped up, in a bark, or on Peppermint Patties (page 163). For candying, use smaller mint leaves, which maintain their shape better.

1 teaspoon vegetable oil, for oiling the parchment

1/2 cup egg whites (from about 3 large eggs), or storebought pasteurized egg whites

2 tablespoons fresh lemon juice

2 cups sugar

48 small mint leaves

Cut a sheet of parchment paper large enough to hold the mint leaves in a single layer. Lightly oil it.

Lightly beat the egg whites and lemon juice in a medium bowl. Put the sugar in a separate bowl. Use tweezer tongs to carefully dip the mint leaves, one at a time, into the egg white mixture; shake excess liquid off. Toss the dipped leaves in the bowl of sugar until evenly coated, then place the sugar-coated leaves on the prepared parchment paper. Let dry overnight. Layer the dried candied leaves in an airtight container with parchment paper between the layers and store in the refrigerator for up to 1 month.

Hot Fudge Sauce

Makes 10 (10-ounce) jars

Fudge sauce is one of those things you can put on or swirl into anything—from a decadent coffee drink to mocha ice cream—or simply eat it out of the jar. Like all of our recipes, this fudge sauce is preservative-free, so don't fear if your sauce separates. A little work with a whisk will bring it back together.

The yield can be halved easily, but this chocolate sauce makes wonderful gifts, so why not make a full batch?

5 cups sugar

1 cup glucose (see Source Guide, page 196)

$7^1/_2$ cups heavy cream

$2^1/_2$ cups (5 sticks) unsalted butter

15 ounces 70% Cacao Base Chocolate or highest-quality store- bought chocolate bars, coarsely chopped (about $1^1/_2$ cups) and melted

$3^1/_2$ tablespoons vanilla extract

$^1/_2$ teaspoon salt

In a large saucepan over medium-low heat, mix the sugar, glucose, and $1^1/_4$ cups water, stirring continuously for 3 to 5 minutes until the sugar has caramelized and the syrup is smooth and light amber in color. Remove the pan from the heat and whisk in the cream, followed by the butter, until smooth. Stir in the melted chocolate, vanilla, and salt until fully incorporated. (An immersion blender can be used to help fully incorporate the ingredients.)

Pour into clean glass jars, twist on the lids, and refrigerate for up to 2 weeks. When you're ready to use the fudge sauce, pour what you need into a microwave-safe bowl or measuring cup and microwave for 10 seconds, then stir. If the fudge sauce is not completely hot and melted, microwave for another 10 seconds before serving it.

Vanilla Bean Whipped Cream

Scoop this vanilla-scented whipped cream on ice cream topped with our Whisky Caramel Sauce (page 195), in our Tiramisu (page 120), or on any dessert you choose!

1 cup heavy cream

2 tablespoons sugar

$1/4$ vanilla bean, seeds scraped

In a chilled mixing bowl, whip the cream, sugar, and vanilla bean seeds with an electric mixer or a whisk until firm peaks form. Use immediately, or cover and refrigerate for up to 2 hours before using.

Whisky Caramel Sauce

Makes a scant 1½ cups

For a thoroughly grown-up treat, I serve this sauce over ice cream or gelato—Vanilla, Dark Chocolate, or Aztec Chocolate (pages 122–123), take your pick!

1 cup sugar

$1/4$ teaspoon fresh lemon juice

$1/2$ cup heavy cream

4 tablespoons ($1/2$ stick) unsalted butter

$1/2$ tablespoon vanilla extract

1 teaspoon salt

1 tablespoon whisky (your brand of choice)

Combine the sugar and lemon juice in a medium saucepan over medium heat and cook, stirring constantly, until the sugar caramelizes, about 5 to 7 minutes.

Meanwhile, in a separate saucepan, warm the cream and butter over low heat (do not let it boil). Stir in the vanilla and the salt and carefully pour the cream over the caramelized sugar, stirring to create a thick sauce. Remove the sauce from the heat and serve warm. Or let the sauce cool and store in an airtight container for up to 1 month. Warm over low heat low before serving.

SOURCE GUIDE

Cocoa Beans
Chocolate Alchemy
shop.chocolatealchemy.com

Casa Fransceschi
casafranceschi.com

Cocoa Nibs
shop.chocolatealchemy.com

Amaretti Biscuits
Amaretti Virginia
amarettivirginia.com

Bacon
Pine Street Market
pinestreetmarket.com

Peanuts
Healthy Hollow Farms
Contact: Connie Hayes
(912) 823-3563

Butter
Banner Butter
bannerbutter.com

Oats
Bob's Red Mill
bobsredmill.com

Ginger
Verdant Ginger
verdantkitchen.com

Salts
Beautiful Briny Sea
etsy.com/shop/BrinySeaDryGoods

Pure and simple salts:
The Meadow
themeadow.com

Glucose
Caullet
frenchfoodexports.com
divinespecialties. com

Organic Brown Rice Syrup
Lundberg Farms
lundberg.com

Malt Powder
Hoosier Hill Farm
hoosierhillfarm.com

Mayhaw Jelly
Springhill Jelly
providencefoods.mysimplestore.com

Lavender Buds
Mountain Rose Herbs
mountainroseherbs.com

Cane Sugar
Wholesome
wholesomesweet.com

Ganache Frame
pastrychef.com

Cinnamon Oil
Mountain Rose Herbs
mountainroseherbs.com

Cinnamon Extract
Oregon's Wild Harvest
oregonswildharvest.com

Invert Sugar (Nevuline)
Gourmet Food World
gourmetfoodworld.com

Gelatin Powder
Vital Proteins
vitalproteins.com

Non-Alkalized Cocoa Powder
Now Real Foods
nowfoods.com

Chocolate Chipper
Cuisipro
surlatable.com

Stone Countertop and Alternatives
Williams Sonoma
Williams-sonoma.com

Lakeland
lakeland.co.uk

Chocolate Molds
Chef Rubber
shop.chefrubber.com

Kerekes
bakedeco.com

Tabletop Chocolate Grinder
Cocoatown
cocoatown.com

Chocolate Alchemy
shop.chocolatealchemy.com

Heat Gun
Porter Cable
portercable.com

Waffle Cone Maker
Chef's Choice
Williams-sonoma.com

Candy Thermometer
Taylor
webstaurantstore.com

Heat Resistant Spatula
Williams Sonoma
williams-sonoma.com

Macaron Mat
Williams Sonoma
williams-sonoma.com

Double Boiler
All Clad
williams-sonoma.com

ACKNOWLEDGMENTS

Thank you to God for my faith, which has always guided me from the start.

Thank you to my father, who built me as an independent woman who has a fearlessness for conquering anything in life, and to my mother, who believed in my vision enough to help me fund the opening of my first factory.

Thank you to my partner, Caline, for trusting my intuition from day one and believing in me and my crazy visions of the chocolate future enough to get on board with me and stand by my side through thick and thin. Thank you, Caline, for becoming who I needed you to become, so that I could birth a child as a single parent and be a mother while running a business. Thank you, Caline, for accepting the CEO as well as the artist side of me, and always fostering the artist side whenever and however was needed. Thank you for answering the phone at 2 a.m. to hear about my chocolate visions and for taking notes, knowing I would not remember what I had said the next day. Thank you for always taking notes when it came to the important stuff, and for knowing it was important stuff. Thank you for trusting I would be okay every time I jumped on an airplane to fly to distant countries, knowing I would be in situations that may not be so safe. Thank you for allowing me to even go back after I got stuck on the side of the road by myself for 24 hours in Peru while I was pregnant. You have protected me and my overtrusting mentality and defended me when needed. You have been my light when I couldn't see. I am thankful for all of the choices we have made together, right and wrong, and for always choosing our partnership and commitment over money or growth. Chocolate has been the path, but the journey has been learning to navigate the world through the business, keeping our fundamental pillars at the core.

Thank you, Numan, for your support, guidance, and for loaning your wife to me all of these years.

Thank you to Stefano for my discovery of cacao and for allowing me to exercise all of my chocolate experiments on the boat.

Thank you to my sister Kim for believing in me from the beginning and loving my chocolates, even though that meant that she was eating them all the time and depleting my inventory.

Thank you to my sister Catherine who told me at an early age that you can do anything in life that you want, and I believed her.

Thank you, Bill Addison, for being fearless enough to travel with me–waking up at the crack of dawn to drive to the abandoned cacao farms and getting stuck in the Jeep on the side of a cliff–and for believing in me enough to wake up the next day and do it again.

Thank you, Lauren Gosnell, for your desire to work with me years ago, even though I did not have the money to pay you, and for becoming my right hand for years to come.

Thank you, Katie Moorman, for your diligence and quiet resilience through the years. You made every package perfect.

Thank you, Nadine, for always being there. You have been an amazing friend and have always made it work when we needed you. We have walked a path together from the very beginning, and through comings and goings, we always find our way back. Let's face it, maybe it was meant to be.

Thank you, Eddie Russell, for being my biggest fan and for all that is to come in our creativity together. We make a great team when we allow it.

Thank you, Peter, for believing in me and my vision. Thank you for pushing me just hard enough.

Thank you to the talented cacao growers who have persevered through my persistent view on quality and who have been determined enough to meet me there.

Thank you to the writers and other influencers for being interested enough in what we were doing to tell our story.

Thank you, most of all, to the customers, fans, and followers of CACAO; I am humbled by their support and encouragement. I set out on this path of chocolate to transform people from the inside out, attempting to awaken their senses by offering something that was of quality and consciousness and, in fact, my customers have transformed me, showing me that dreams can come true.

Thank you to Fig House Vintage for supplying for such great props. Thank you, Chia and Libby, for the beautiful works of art you created. I don't think I really knew the beauty of the cacao creations until I saw them through your eyes in your photos.

Thanks to Annette Joseph for introducing us to Janice Shay.

Thank you, Janice, for making this book a reality. You are a dream come true. This book would have never come to fruition without you. You knew exactly how to push me while helping me maintain confidence that I could do it. It has been a long road and you holding my hand made it possible. I am speechless when I think of all the hard work you put into this book. You balanced me in every possible way.

Thank you, Rizzoli, for choosing us to put inside these bindings. You are truly an amazing publisher. Thank you, Chris and Martynka, for your perseverance and guidance.

The Briefcase

Carry what matters the most...

Rajan Gupta, MD

Published by: Gurucool Academy

The Briefcase Life…. Carry what matters the most

Dr. Rajan Gupta, MD

Do not take your life so **SERIOUSLY**

And

SERIOUSLY never ever take your life

Contents

Dedication

This book is dedicated to

my parents, **Omvati and Suresh**, and

my two beautiful daughters,

Meera and Ria

Without their unconditional love,

this book would not have materialised.

Special Dedication and Thanks to all those people who have helped shape my past, present, and future

I also dedicate this book to my brother **Sanjay** and sisters **Meena** and **Anju**.

Many of my friends from my childhood **Alka**, **Hera**, **Poochi**, **Juli**, **Bittoo**, **Girish**, **Vijay**, **Rajiv**, **Anita**, **Pratima**,

My maternal and paternal cousins: **Anni**, **Guddi**, **Kapil**, **Muniya**, **Nidhi**, **Manoj**, **Guddu**, **Priti**, **Saransh**, **Dimpi**, **Ashu**, **Ruchi**, **Surabhi**, **Pappe**, **Bhushan**, **Rajat**, **Neha Pawan**, **Bhola**, **Anil**, **Kusum**, **Naveen**, **Kalpana**, **Seema**, **Rajni**, **Kammo**, **Sudesh**, **Dipak**, **Ravi**, **Babita**, **Chanchal**.

My maternal and paternal uncles **Ramesh Tauji**, **Sri Tauji**, **Mahendra chachaji**, **Subash chachaji**, **Vinod chachaji**, **Ratan mamaji**, **Omi mamaji**, **Subash mamaji**, **Suresh mamaji**, **Mahesh mamaji**, **Mohan mamaji**, **Mohan Lal mausaji**.

My maternal and paternal aunts: **Devi bhuaji**, **Prem bhuaji**, **Kiran taiji**, **Pushpa bhuaji**, **Shakunt bhuaji**, **Geeta bhuaji**, **Vijay bhuaji**, **Saroj mausaiji**, **Sarla mamji**, **Prem mamiji**, **Renu mamiji**, **Usha mamiji**, **Madhu Mamiji**.

My College Friends: **Anju malik**, **JB**, **Pandey**, **Ashvini**, **Bakul**, **Anukul**, **Sabiha**, **Sameer**, **Sabyasachi**, **Sashi**, **Smita**, **Amrita**, **Vandana**, **Manoj**, **Roma**.

All my teachers including **Umashankar**, **Dr. Billimoria**, **Dr. Johnson** **and many more.**

My friends during residency and fellowship: **Saquib, Anu, Manju-nath, Aparna, Naveen, Mohana.**

Some of my very special friends: **Ainaa, Asna, Manish, Aisha, Sunil, Kajol, Shivani, Manju, Kim, Anita, Nadia, Sonali, Danny, Anurag, Nadia, Raani, Farrah, and famous artist Paul SEQUENCE Ferguson.**

I may have forgotten many names who have been in the past, very close to me and helped shape my future. I thank each of them for making me who I am now.

Purpose

Everyone wants to live the best life possible. Thus, I did it from birth, we live in **three-dimensional life** made up of *Physical, Emotional and Spiritual* aspects. These dimensions define the purpose of our life. We believe that more we will get, better our life will be. But when things happen against our will, we feel pain and suffering.

Just like everyone else does or tries to do, I got good education, had a comfortable and loving childhood, came to the United States for further training, which many people dream of , married a good person, had two beautiful children, had many amazing friends, had also gathered many physical comforts, including many properties, money in the bank, good and abundant food, expensive clothing, and was also spiritually connected to God. I planned to grow bigger and bigger as everyone else does.

But after 14 years of marriage when I faced my lengthy, very expensive, emotionally traumatizing divorce, the actual meaning of life and relationship changed for me. I was disheartened. I even thought of ending my life. I came to realizations with many things. I learned many lessons. I read many new books and scriptures, learned, and experimented with teachings from those in my personal life.

In the end, the three most important lessons were clear to me:

- **nothing belongs to you**
- **change is the only constant and**
- **you cannot plan or predict your life; you can only adapt to it.**

We are the by-product of our beliefs. Our thoughts make us. There are many books written on how we can change our lives by changing our thoughts. Our lives are what we perceive it to be.

"Your perception is your reality." This is the central law of this book which I will explain later.

The only purpose of me writing this book was to simplify life and to get rid of suffering. I believe that we unnecessarily make our lives complex. The whole concept of this book is geared toward making things simple. Not knowing too many things. I have attempted to present the complexity of life in the simplest form possible.

"Look for simplicity in this complex life
Not for complexity in this simple life."

— Raj

I have tried to dissect life through my own experiences. **I understood that there are certain universal laws, life is governed by. These laws are like lenses. We are our thoughts. Whether it is happiness or pain and suffering, it is just our thoughts. So, when we are suffering, it is just a cloud of thoughts. If we can filter our cloud of thoughts through these lenses, we can see our lives without suffering.** Everything looks clear, and we become successful and happy. We can make our lives as complex or as simple as we want. It all depends on how we perceive our life.

My Divorce was the reason for me to go through these sufferings of life. That was just one reason like many other reasons people go through. I had the realization of certain facts about life which I am presenting in this book. I will be giving examples of things that happened in my life which led me to develop these laws and create an amazing understanding of life. During the development of this book, I have talked to many people about the concept of this book and literally everyone could relate to these.

What I went through, was nothing new or different than so many people go through on a daily basis. In my other upcoming book, "7 Ways in 7 Days to change your life" I have put together 7 important ways which can be learned in just 7 days and can amazingly change your life forever. These techniques will give you the tools to be successful and happy by preventing the sufferings.

One primary way to simplify life is to carry in life what matters the most. This book is an awesome effort to look at life through the magnifying lens and identifying the amazing universal laws that can help us not carry the suitcase full of suffering but to carry what matters the most…. "The Briefcase of happiness".

I found out that making this book simple, was the hardest part and took me the longest time to do. I hope all my efforts will be able to change lives of many people.

Being a doctor, I look at things or problems in two ways. One, how can I treat them, and second how can I prevent them. This book kind of does both. When you apply the laws during the state of suffering, the clouds of negative thoughts filter away. Also, when you are in a good state and remember these laws, they can help prevent the thoughts from building up that would lead to suffering in the end.

Acknowledgement

Dec 13, 2013, was the day when my life changed forever. I am very thankful to my ex for creating the circumstances that led me to experience amazing things in my life. Living life was so hard before that as if there was a burden on my body, mind, and soul. What came next was more than four years of unnecessary, expensive legal battle that emotionally traumatized me. They say you must go through fire and water to achieve something big. I feel the same way. **I wouldn't have been the person I am now if I wouldn't have gone through that experience. Number 13 usually being the unlucky number, had always been lucky for me.**

I learned a lot from Gita, the Indian holy scripture. I believe that all the secrets of life are in this fantastic book. I am sure other holy scriptures also have similar teachings. In fact, one time when I was talking about the laws of this book in Florida amongst American people I noticed that the majority of the personal improvement books had taken some or all the teachings from this book.

One other book which has been the key to transforming my thinking is Dale Carnegie's "How to Win Friends and Influence People." I think it is such an amazing and necessary book that teaches us lessons of humanity.

A few other books that have helped shape my mind are "millionaire course" by Marc Allen, "Four Agreements" by Miguel Ruiz, "One Thing" by Gary Keller, "Where will you be five years from now" by Dan Zadra.

There are many personalities, whose ideas and thinking left a long-lasting impression on my mind. **Gautam Buddha and his teachings have made most of the framework of my book.** Albert Einstein's theory of relativity is one of the most important concepts that helped me understand that your perception is relative and is your reality. Another person in my early childhood who made me understand the same concept was my 2nd-grade classmate Rajaram, about whom I will discuss in the perception chapter.

Sri Sri Ravi Shankar of the Art of Living emphasizes on breath and meditation to achieve happiness. Steven Covey's saying "begin with the end in mind", my father's writing on mantelpiece "Ishwar aur maut ko mat bhulo" means never forget God and death, and my Subash uncle's saying "read one book, read it over and over again, till its language becomes your language", all of these important life lessons have affected me deeply. As I have been writing this book for a while, I came across many other inspirational books like "Obstacle is the way" by Ryan Holiday which has provided me a different perspective of life.

From the beginning of our lives, we come in contact with so many things and so many people. Every single thing has its impact in shaping us. I am really thankful to all the people and all the things, whether my perception of them was good or bad, who came in contact with me that has shaped me, who I am today.

Introduction

Statistically, divorce is the second most stressful situation in one's life, first being the death of their child. It changes your life. It sure did mine. During my lengthy divorce, I learned many crucial life lessons. I learned the secrets of life. I felt as though I had achieved Nirvana (enlightenment), just like Gautama Buddha felt after months of meditation.

Based on the unpredictability of life I learned a very important lesson.

My divorce inspired me to put together my thoughts into this book. I hope it will guide others who are going through similar chaotic situations in their lives. This book is not about saying that divorce is a right or wrong thing, it's not even about me having a painful divorce after 14 years of marriage. It's not even about my perception of my ex being bad or her father being destructor of our family with two beautiful daughters. Once again what I felt was only my perception at that time. As I previously mentioned that I am really thankful to my ex and her family for making me go through this tough period of time which has changed my life forever.

*"Life can never be planned
It can only be adapted"*

– Raj

This book is not about me crying about my divorce-related sufferings. <u>**It's about the lessons that I learned in finding the real purpose of life.....**</u>

This book will help us understand life, to identify the causes of suffering, finding our purpose in life and ways to achieve that purpose. *For the most part, actually discovering what life is all about.* **This book is not merely a book to read but a *discipline* to follow.**

Even if the inspiration of this book is from Hinduism and teachings of Buddha it embraces the concepts of spirituality and ideology of the eastern and western religions.

During an overseas trip. I was packing for a journey that was only three to four days long. I packed so many things, thinking that everything I brought was necessary. I feared that if I needed to go to a party or dance, that I would need many accounterment or look unprepared. I packed many pieces of clothing, a few pairs of shoes and many other items. My bags were heavy; in fact, I even got hurt while carrying them during my trip. When I reached my destination, I realized that I needed only a couple of outfits and a few accessories. I felt silly for carrying so much unnecessary stuff.

> *"Not to carry a suitcase of sufferings but to carry what matters the most...the briefcase of happiness."*
>
> – Raj

I thought, are we not doing the same in our lives too? We are carrying unnecessary baggage with us which is the cause of suffering whether these burdens are physical or emotional.

I am a physician by profession. I've enjoyed abundant respect and earned considerable money and respect during my ten years of a professional career and my 14 years of marriage. I had purchased multiple properties, established few businesses, and accumulated a decent amount of money. I worked very hard in developing myself and giving my family an elite lifestyle. I had plans to do many things. During the divorce process, I lost most of my wealth. It shattered many of my dreams. Besides losing the property, I also lost the respect my kids had for me. Just like my ex they also treated me as if I was a failure in my life, a cheater, and a jerk. Furthermore, it was very stressful. **I learned a crucial lesson that there are no certainties in life.**

Let's learn what this life is all about and how we can get rid of our sufferings and be happy.

This book is comprised of 9 chapters. Each chapter has its significance. The first chapter is about understanding life, sufferings, and the purpose of life. Next 7 chapters are the 7 universal laws which have been taught to us all our life one way or the other. These laws are amazingly powerful and can clear the clouds of suffering. These are laws because it happens every time you follow it. These laws are not new. These are based on the lessons I have learned through my divorce process. Even though there are many similar teachings we learn in our lives, but I kept it limited to only 7 laws to keep it simple for us to remember and follow. I think there is something about 7. The colors in the rainbow are 7. The days in a week are 7. The notes in music are 7. And we also know 7 is a lucky number. Sometimes I even believe that there are only 7 real planets in our solar system…lol. The last chapter is about understanding how we can apply these 7 laws and become free of suffering. Once we learn these laws and apply them, we can carry the briefcase of happiness.

All the laws in this book are timed tested by me and hold true. They have changed my life and I believe if they are followed properly and consistently, they can help you get rid of suffering from your life too. You will not only become successful, be happy but most importantly you will feel at peace.

I am not saying that after following them you will become a millionaire, or you will never feel sad. But if you follow them you will the feel minimal impact of the problems in your life and you will be able to rebound back pretty fast.

In this book, I have put only my beliefs, my observation, my analysis of life. My beliefs have been influenced by many personalities, and literature but still they are my own interpretations. It may be totally different from someone else's reality, but this is what I believe in. Just like Gautam Buddha always talked about his own experiences rather than what was written in the scriptures I also wrote this book based on my own personal experiences.

I wish everyone good luck...

Suitcase

of

Sufferings

CHAPTER 1

LIFE

The Suitcase of Sufferings

My Own Story

Let me share my background, I was born in New Delhi, India. My childhood was amazing. I always used to be a positive child. I enjoyed my primary education at Ramjas School no.2. I made many friends. I may have made a few enemies also. I had good times and bad times. Sad times, happy times. My father was from a village called Hodal (in Haryana) and my mother was from the capital of India, New Delhi. My grandfather was a very famous person in Hodal. He and all his sons owned big Kirana (spices etc.) business. My mother was from an educated family where we had doctors and engineers. I remember going with my family during summer vacation and spending time, one month in Hodal with my father's business side of the family and one month in Delhi at my mother's education side of the family. We were extremely fortunate that we learned both aspects of life and became very successful doctors. After finishing my medical school and the dermatology training at B J Medical College of Ahmedabad, Gujarat I came to USA in 1996. I really did not want to come to USA but it seemed that my brother was having a tough time so I thought coming here would help him, plus he always used to say a doctor's life is better in USA so I thought let's try it. My first year was very painful when I was in Detroit. I had a good friend from Pakistan Waseem who helped me tremendously during my time in Detroit. We both used to study at Kaplan Institute and were preparing for our USMLE exams. After the exams, I got into a residency in Pittsburgh where my search for a life partner began. Met my ex through the online matrimonial site and got married in 1999. Life was beautiful in the beginning, had two beautiful kids. Later I noticed the diminished love and a dragging married life. Also went to Vanderbilt University for a fellowship program which was a wonderful experience academically but was painful for my relationship. Number 13 plays an important role in my life. I do not think it is bad for me but in fact, it brings special luck to me. During my childhood most of the time my roll number was 13 and I always did well education-wise. My life changed forever on December 13th, 2013 when a major break in our marriage took place.

Then began the most difficult 4-year journey of my life from 2013 till 2017, from the beginning of my divorce till the end of my divorce. In the beginning, I was happy that I would be away from a miserable life I was living, but soon after I realized that whatever that life was, it was not too bad. If we really think about it, there is not really a perfect life as I believe *perfection is only defined by our own perceptions*. I realized quite early after the initial break and tried to fix the broken relationship. My attempts to fix the marriage were not remarkably successful. *Later I realized that in a relationship with one person wanting something, would not work till the other person wants the same thing.* So, I dropped the idea of fixing the marriage and just focused on ending the divorce. My feeling was that not everything in life works out. If you really are not compatible, then it is better to move on. Many things during the divorce process happened. I believe almost everyone who is getting a divorce goes through what I went through. My kids were instilled with hatred for me, there was no communication with my ex, my in-laws had taken over my house as soon as I moved out of the house, my practice was affected because of my recent move, on top of that was my attorney's enormous expense. **My suitcase of suffering was more than full**. Sufferings were overflowing from my suitcase. I felt every pain I could feel at that moment.

I started feeling that life was not worth living. Why me? Why do I have to go through this? I have always done well (at least that is what I thought) so why is this happening to me. Obviously, if you would ask my ex, she may have a huge list of reasons which she had been collecting for the last 10 years in her diary to explain that.

Since that time, I have observed people closely. I met many people. *I noticed that almost everyone seems to be carrying a HUGE suitcase full of suffering.* Everyone has their own story of life suffering. Everyone wants to write their own book. Facebook is full of people's lives and their sufferings. Millions of people will put out the status everyday how they are suffering. Everyone is looking for a perfect life. We imagine life without suffering. Even Buddha left his palace in search of life secrets to end suffering.

Suitcase Life: As I mentioned previously about my trip when I packed a suitcase full of things the majority of which I did not even use. I think we do exactly this in our personal lives too. We complicate our lives with unneeded baggage.

These burdens consist of our physical and emotional attachments. We all are carrying a big suitcase that harms us along the way.

Everyone is carrying their suitcases intentionally or unintentionally. I see multiple posts on Facebook from people preaching great things about life, high-flown ideas that they want to spread. Everyone seems to be unhappy. I think we all are searching for a short cut, a formula for life which can solve all the problems. **We fail to realize that life is simple**. It may not be easy, but it is simple. It is as simple as we want to make it. God has made it beautiful, but we make it complicated.

It is a fact of life that everyone who is born will die one day. It is also true that we came with nothing and will go with nothing. Nevertheless, we fail to comprehend the true purpose of life. Our aim or goals are based on the three dimensions we live in.

Suffering: What is it?

Definition: the state of undergoing pain, distress, or hardship.

When I was going through my divorce, I suffered for many reasons. Primary causes were that I was losing a lot of things like money, time, sleep and I was not able to get the love of my kids, was not able to grow my business and was not able to get peace of mind.

A friend of mine was suffering as he lost everything in his business and had to restart again.

Another person I came across was suffering because he was not able to achieve high scores in his exam.

Losing a child, or a family member caused people to suffer.

Being in a bad relationship was the cause of many people's suffering.

The point I am trying to make here is that almost everyone seems to be suffering for one reason or the other. Agree?

Why Do We Suffer?

The Cause Of Suffering:

Ancient teaching that comes from the Hindu philosophy, Vedanta, in India describes five causes of suffering called the five Klashas, a Buddhist term for the five afflictions.

- The first cause of suffering is **not knowing the true nature of reality.**
- The second is **grasping and holding onto what is illusory or insubstantial**.
- The third is an **aversion to or a fear of something that is unsubstantial.**
- The fourth is **identification with the false self or ego**. This constricts and limits our consciousness.
- The fifth cause of suffering is the **fear of death.**

As you can see, these causes of suffering are contained in the first one which does not know the true nature of reality. *Not knowing the true nature of reality is thinking and seeing things in distorted ways.*

Buddha taught that desire causes suffering. When we do not have what we want, we long for it, and this causes a burning in our being until it is satisfied. **If we withdraw our attention from the object of our desire, then we cease to suffer.** Buddha taught this to his disciples 500 years before Jesus came.

Commonly if we see there are 5 D's which are causes of suffering. Those include **desire, detachment, disease, divorce, and death.**

Sadhguru says suffering is due to **a change** we are not ready for.

But if you really observe my divorce story or someone else's, causes of suffering, you will find that there are primary two reasons to suffer.

*One **when we are not able to achieve** what we love which can be satisfaction (power, money, & sex), peace, love &happiness, and other is **when we lose** the things we love like satisfaction (power, money, & sex), peace, love &happiness*

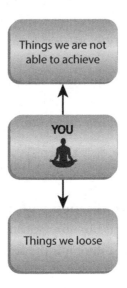

Impact of Suffering

Have you ever suffered in your life? I have. So, I remember an incident when I was doing a meeting in my office with about 5-6 people and I asked everyone a question. This was during the time when I was having a tough time during my divorce. The question was... **who has thought of killing themselves** in their lifetime should raise their hand? I was shocked to see that everyone raised their hands. Then I asked another question. Who have thought of killing themselves more than once to raise their hands? I was AMAZED by the same response. Everyone again raised their hand. So, one thing became absolutely clear to me that everyone feels that they are suffering and suffering bigtime to the point they have thought of ending their life. Everyone is carrying the suitcase of suffering which is making their life miserable. I was not alone in this miserable thing called…. life.

It's very common to think about ending your life. We know that ending your life is not good and in fact against the law but having thought of ending your life is not uncommon. Our day to day sufferings in many ways make us feel that our life is not worth living and we sometimes feel it is better to end it. It all depends on how our mind is trained. How are we perceiving information? For one person a problem while for others it could be a solution. For example, if you have a lot of old furniture in the house, for you it is a problem as you do not have much space and want to throw it out. So, having unused stuff in the house is a problem but at the same time, that old furniture is something a person who sells old furniture would love to have. Someone's trash is another person's gold. It's all about perspective.

Pain & Suffering Is Inevitable

Gautam Buddha said that suffering will stay with us till death.

I say just like suffering happiness stay with us till we die too. It's all about our perspective on how we look at a situation. I learned a lot from my divorce about suffering. For me, the end of divorce never meant the end of suffering. With new relationships comes a new set of suffering. It is just part of life.

"Suffering and happiness both are habits.

Either one can be mastered.

You just need the right practice"

— Raj

Living in this world and having some needs are in itself cause for suffering.

Life: What Is It?

Life

Yes I was born
With a cry
Nothing I brought
With me
But only my breath
That made me cry
The purpose was to grow
From birth to death
In size and thoughts
My life became
Interplay of
Love and hate
I had friends and enemies
Many known and many
UNKNOWN
I learned ALWAYS
From my mistakes
And realized
In the END
Nothing I took
Only my SOUL
With my experiences....

– Raj

Life Is An Absolute Miracle

It is a gift given to us by God. I believe that we all are part of God. When we are born, we are given a beautiful body, an amazing heart, an incredible mind, and our breath to achieve anything we want. Our life is an interplay between our needs, wants, our genes, our circumstances, and our destiny.

The following topics about understanding life may appear to be weird and boring. Once again, it's my understanding and if it makes sense then take it otherwise leave it…

> "*Life is a journey between birth and death.*
> *We came with absolutely nothing in our hands.*
> *We will take absolutely nothing with us.*
> *All we take with us will be the experiences of our lives".*
>
> – Raj

Anatomy and Physiology of Life

The universe is made up of two things. Physical structure and spiritual structure. With every structure, there is a soul connection and with every soul, there is a structure connected. The unit of the physical structure is an atom and the unit of spiritual structure is a soul (in Hindi "Atma" sounds kind of similar. Every soul is made up of Mind, Spirit, and Heart. Every atom is made up of electron, neutron, and proton. There is a body assigned to each soul that is intermingled with the mind.

Do we only live once "YOLO" or are we born again? I am not sure. Is life a straight line or is it a circle? Some religions believe that we only live once while some do believe in rebirth. I would think if we only live once then life would be a straight line with a beginning and the end while if life is a circle then it will be a continuous circle with the beginning being the end or vice versa.

I believe life is a circle. Death is the beginning of life somewhere, for someone and in some form. There had been many instances in history that some people remembered their past lives. *Whatever be the case one thing is for sure that we are born with a body that ends after some time.*

Path of Life

If we really look at life, it is *the time period between our birth and death.* I believe we live our lives in a predetermined path which could be based on our previous life Karmas and may be influenced by current Karmas. The shorter the circle, the shorter you live, and the longer the circle longer you live.

My Three Lane Concepts

I also believe that our lives circular path is a 3-lane path. The inner circle is the shortest but slowest, while the outermost circle is the longest but fastest. The reason for that assumption is the time taken to complete a period of life must remain constant. Someone who understands physics will understand this concept easily. *I believe shifting from inner to outer circle or vice versa is the only thing in our control. With our mind we can push ourselves outwards and drive on a faster satisfactory lane or with our heart we can pull ourselves to inwards and attain a slow and happy time. When we attain a balance between mind and heart, our soul which is neutral will drive on a middle lane which is like a perfect path of peace including happiness and satisfaction.*

Theory of Simplicity

Since the beginning of time scientists have tried to explain life, universe, and God. There had been attempts to understand it through something simple, like a simple equation, or theory of everything. My theory of simplicity is **my attempt to explain the simplicity of this life. I believe that the origin of our world around us is simple.** *Everything is made from the same template* **whether it is the whole universe or structure of an atom or a soul, all have similar design and components.**

The template I am putting forth in my theory of simplicity is made up of three major forces. These three forces are **negative, positive, and neutral.**

For example, ATOM which is considered as indivisible unit is made up of a core (nucleus) which consists of NEUTRONS and PRO-TONS. Around that core is the set of ELECTRONS revolving. As it has been explained by scientists that electrons are in pairs and spinning in opposite directions.

Structure of Soul "ATMA"   Structure of ATOM

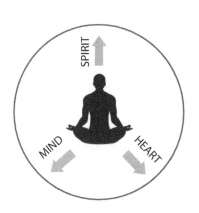
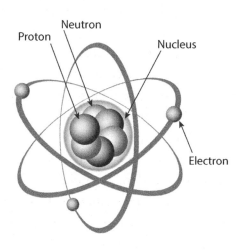

In a similar way in any living body, we have Soul (ATMA) which has also three components with a core (nucleus) of SPIRIT (neutron) and a HEART (proton) and a revolving MIND (electron). We can reproduce the same template in this universe. There must be a central core consisting of a black hole with neutral and positive and all these planets, galaxies around that are electrons spinning.

"Atom is a structural unit for living and nonliving while Atma (sounds similar) is a spiritual unit of life for living and nonliving"

– Raj

Law of Coexistence the theory of simplicity describes the template we are all made up of. I have observed that things are always present in three forms. So, I have formulated a law to make my point. I think this law can explain many things. It can explain the behavior of why something happens, the way it does. According to this law

> **"At any given time, three forces (negative, positive and neutral) coexists in anything and everything and they are present in three forms"**

Those three forces are **Negative, Neutral, and Positive**. These three components of forms must coexist in life in any structure whether it's an atom, element, person, society, or literally anything. Just like in atom there are electrons which are negatively charged, and neutron is neutral, and a proton is positively charged, in the same way in a living thing there exists Mind (negative), Spirit (neutral) and Heart (positive). There is one more assumption about the electron and the mind. We have come to know that electron is in pair and the pair spins in the opposite direction. The same way the mind is in pairs and has two parts which spin in two different directions. Mind also has good and bad components which makes conscience.

Double slit experiment in quantum physics very well demonstrated the dual wave-particle form of anything. In my opinion, there are three forms, one of which is a transitional form.

These forces also exist in three forms at any given time. Understanding this concept may clarify the conflict between conventional physics and quantum physics. These forms **are the particle form, transition form, and a wave form. Interestingly, we all exist in three forms**. What are these three forms of life? **Particle form, wave form, and transitional form**. Particle form which we are as human, a neutral form which is the combination of the transition phase in between particle and wave form and third a wave form which is the form of God. When we convert totally into a wave form, we become supreme.

Particle form-Transitional form-Wave form

Which form we exist at any given time is observer-dependent. Someone's, or ourselves perception will decide what we are, who we are. What people perceive is dependent on what forms they are using. Some people may just perceive a particle form of you, or some people may perceive the wave form of you. I believe the existence in wave form could be the explanation behind terms like telepathy.

I hope I did a good job of making my theory and the law clear. It may raise questions, but I believe understanding it properly can find many answers about this life.

Mind Is the Source of Suffering and Happiness

Practically what we think, we are. Our mind creates our life. It is the master and we follow. The mind and body are connected. The mind has the potential to do anything it believes in. There had been processes like bio kinesis when with the power of mind someone can even change the color of their eyes. The mind has an amazing feature called **plasticity**. That means it can conform to our requirements. It has the power to become what is needed. It just needs proper training. It's a scientific fact that we only use less than 10% of our mind at any given time.

The role of the mind is to perceive, store, and respond. Perception is done through many anatomical structures of the body. Often, we think the mind is the same as the brain. It would be incorrect to assume that. The brain is just an anatomical structure through which the mind operates. Perception, about which we will read more in the 5th chapter "Your Perception is your reality" is done through special senses like eyes, ear, ear, nose, tongue, and skin. All the information obtained through these senses is processed in the brain and stored. A proper response is created after it is processed. This whole process is unbelievably fast.

The mind is very powerful but often critical. I correlate the mind with electrons in an atom. Just like an electron is negatively charged mind is also negative. But I believe there is a purpose in that negativity. Our mind wants to ensure that we are complete, and we are provided every comfort and we are completely safe. So, it scans constantly and tells us what is lacking in our life. The mind is there to fulfill our every need. Unfortunately, we commonly focus on that negativity alone and forget our positive heart.

The mind is constantly at work. When we have a stressful situation, it creates multiple permutations and combinations of negative thoughts of what bad may happen and create fear and anxiety. That fear and anxiety creates a cloud of thoughts that lead to suffering.

In upcoming chapters, you will read more about Raj's different universal laws and how to apply them in those stressful situations and clear those cloud of thoughts of suffering.

With a positive mind, anything can be created which is the basis of my third law "anything is possible if you believe in it".

Purpose of Life

That is a very interesting question. We are born and then we later die. Why? What is the purpose of this process? Why do we even have a life? These questions have divine meanings and are very hard to explain. But during our life, we live in three dimensions. For some purpose could be to get a new house, an excellent job, to find a great relationship, to take care of parents or kids, do good things for others and so on. I will try to explain the three dimensions in the following paragraph, so it is a little clearer.

The Three Dimensions

We live our lives primarily in three dimensions. These dimensions are physical, emotional, and spiritual dimensions. Every dimension is very critical and is expressed in a different capacity at various times of life. Also, each dimension is controlled by one of the major forces of life.

The physical dimension is primarily related to our body and bodily needs. This dimension is set by two components of our, the mind and the body. Our mind and the body are intertwined. Our mind is the force to fulfill our bodily needs. All the bodily needs are satisfied in this dimension. Here we set purpose to achieve and fulfill our physical needs like food, clothing, shelter, sex, money, and possessions in other words everything like money or what money can buy. I believe that the fulfillment of the physical dimension **is timed and destined.** There are many people who work very hard and smart but don't have much money. At the same time, we have seen many people in life who don't do anything, but they have an enormous amount of money. This is the common purpose we focus our lives on . Unfortunately satisfying this dimension only can give us success and satisfaction. It doesn't give us peace of happiness. Our misconception is that if we fulfill this dimension, we will also get peace and happiness but that doesn't happen. What we get seems like happiness, is pleasure, bodily pleasure but not happiness.

The emotional dimension on the other hand is controlled by the force of the heart. The heart tries to fulfill our emotional needs. Here we set the purpose like love, beautiful relationships, connecting with others. When the purpose is fulfilled from this dimension, we feel happy. Interestingly when we are loved and love others, we feel happy. When we feel happy then we may also feel satisfied and successful but not the other way around.

The physical dimension and emotional dimension are constantly trying to create a perfect balance between each other. When that balance is achieved, we enter the spiritual dimension where our spirit is.

"Life has three dimensions: Physical Emotional & Spiritual.
They all need to be fulfilled and that fulfillment defines our life's purpose"

– Raj

The third dimension is controlled by the neutral force, our spirit. This is fulfilled when our spiritual needs are met. Spiritual needs are met when we do good for others or connect to God. This is one of the most important dimensions and when it is fulfilled, we feel peace. When we feel peace, we feel happy and satisfied.

In my personal opinion, our ultimate purpose is to be free. I think that's what we are longing for. Freedom of mind, heart, and spirit leads to eventual freedom of the soul.

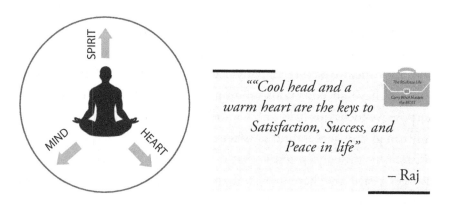

""Cool head and a warm heart are the keys to Satisfaction, Success, and Peace in life"

– Raj

Freedom

I believe this is the ultimate goal of everyone. In spite of driving pleasure from attaching to other things in life, our inner desire is to be free.

Karma

The law of cause and effect is known as **karma.** It is the action. It is a choice. It decides what happens to us. What path our life takes. Gita says there is no right or wrong. We should just keep doing our karma. Nothing ever happens to us unless we deserve it. We receive exactly what we earn, whether it is good or bad. We are the way we are now; due to the things we have done in the past. Our thoughts and actions determine the kind of life we can have. If we do good things, in the future good things will happen to us. If we do bad things, in the future bad things will happen to us. Every moment we create new karma, by what we say, do, and think. If we understand this, we do not need to

> *"Karma is like an automation God has set. So, He does not have to watch us closely."*
>
> – Raj

fear karma. One of the three teachings of buddha tells us how and what type of karma we should do. He says "Dhammam Sharnam Gachami" where he talks about doing the RIGHT things and doing no harm.

What I have learnt after dissecting my life is that just like three forces, there are three aspects of life. One which we have full control over, second we have no control on and third is our way of looking at these two aspects. The middle aspect is the neutral, and most powerful aspect of our life, perception. I have given a lot of emphasis on this neutral aspect.

The first aspect of our life is where we have full control over it. I have given 3 laws to understand it. One is to counteract our fear, second to give importance to ourselves and third is to be able to achieve anything we want.

The second aspect is the NO control aspect where I believe is controlled by GOD or superpower we all believe in. I have given three laws to understand that. One that defines that loss of control, second to understand unpredictability due to the change, and third is to understand destiny.

The third aspect is the perception, how we perceive things in our lives.

We as human beings are attached to sufferings all our lives. It seems like they will never go away. In the next 7 chapters, I will explain those amazing laws which if used properly are able to get rid of your sufferings. These laws are nothing but suggestions or formulas when applied to one particular situation, give a different perspective about the situation, and removes its cloud of suffering.

I have attempted to make it simple and brief....

LAW 1

Don't Worry: Everything Will be Fine
Whatever happens, happens
for a good reason

CHAPTER 2

Law 1

Don't Worry: Everything Will Be Fine Whatever Happens, Happens For A Good Reason

This is the first and foremost law. It primarily is based on the fact, that there is God or a supreme power who is protecting us. It is the first law because it removes Fear which is the biggest factor restricting us from doing so many incredible things, we are able to do.

Our parents and old people have always told us this law, since childhood whenever we feel we are in trouble. Some will say, don't worry, belief in God, he will take care of everything. And we know in the end everything does get better. *Anything and everything happens for a good reason.*

If we look back in time, we will realize that what we were fearing at the time was not that great of a problem. If we are surviving to look back in time, that means everything went well.

Interesting saying by Winston Churchill *"When I look back on all these worries, I remember the story of the old man who said on his deathbed that he had a lot of trouble in his life, most of which never happened"*.

I am not saying that, what we call bad things, don't happen to people. It happens all the time, but what I am saying is that Everything happens for a good reason even if it appears bad and, in the end, everything will be fine.

Unpredictable Life

Am I gonna pass this exam? Will I be able to catch this flight? Will my girlfriend say yes? Will my pain ever go away? What if I die tomorrow? Would I ever be successful? These are the common questions that occur in our minds all the time.

Our lives are highly unpredictable. Nobody knows what is going to happen next second, a minute, or a year from now. History is the proof of that unpredictability. People who were rich turned into poor, and vise versa. A young healthy-looking person can succumb to death in a moment while a frail, comatose person can come back to life.

One time I was traveling to San Francisco. I was driving to the airport parking and when I reached there, I saw right at the entrance of that parking, a motorcyclist laying on the road with blood gushing from his head. He was not moving and people around him were just standing watching him. I got the impression that he must be dead. I thought at that time, what must be going through this motor cyclist's mind 5 minutes before the accident. He never would have been thinking that he will die in the next few minutes. *That's how unpredictable life is. We don't know what the next moment can bring us.*

Another incident when I was attending an art of living course in Boone, North Carolina. There was a task given to us to tell another person in the group about your life in less than 5 minutes. One person in the group who was from California he started telling his story. He said he came from India. Many years back he was enjoying his life with his one brother, one sister, and parents. They were well off and his father had a good job. All the kids including him were in school. They used to talk about their plans for the future, of buying a new house, a new car, etc. One day when he came back from school, he found out that his father has passed away suddenly. *His life changed forever in a moment.* He had to do jobs after school to support his family as he was the oldest of them. Whatever plans they had, were buried in the cruelty, of this unpredictable life. But now he was a successful person and working in California.

Personally, if I talk about my life, I had moved from my office on King's highway to an independent building on Berlin road in September 2013. I was very excited as the building had good signage and I was really looking forward to increasing my business and reaching out, too many people who were suffering from pain. I was developing so many plans to do so many things in my life. I thought my life was going according to my plan. Four months later when my ex filed for divorce everything changed for me.

From all these incidences and my personal experiences, the most important lessons I learned was

> *"Life can never be planned,*
> *It can only be adapted".*
>
> – Raj

Fear

Is an unpleasant emotion caused by the belief that someone or something is dangerous, likely to cause pain or a threat?

In our lives, we develop Fear because of the unpredictability of the Future. Fear creates worries.

It's interesting that fear is an inbuilt phenomenon. Even the child is afraid. What are we afraid of? If fear is a built-in phenomenon, so did God give us fear for a good reason. One way if we look at it, fear is designed to protect you. It is designed so you can assess your surroundings. It is there so you can learn from the past mistakes and don't repeat them.

I believe everything in this life originates from energy and it has a purpose. Even fear has a purpose.

Fear is a two-fold process. One is the thought of fear and second is the interpretation of that fear. I believe the first part is important and protective of

> "Fear is a built-in phenomenon; it is there to protect us. Interpretation of the fear which turns into worry is where the problem lies... So be worry free."
>
> – Raj

our lives. The second part which is very individualized creates the main issues. In the second part are all the perceptions of that fear takes place and the reactions of everyone are different. Generally, response to the fear is Worry. So if we really think about fear, it is a positive phenomenon and a protective one. If we control our reactions without worries it will lead to a positive outcome.

My personal life was a roller coaster at the beginning of my divorce. I had recently moved my office to a new location and that change was a little traumatic on the growth of my business. It was not only growth being a concern but the decline in the business that made me worried. On top of that, expenses of the divorce were making me worried about my financial stability. I was anxious, depressed, and often found myself with the thought that I wouldn't be able to make it. Everybody told me, please do not worry, everything will be fine. I was questioning the credibility of this sentence. Fear was creeping up constantly and kept getting intense. For the next 4 years, my revenues from the practice and my resources of money kept declining. I thought of filing bankruptcy and even consulted with one of the bankruptcy attorneys. Also, my kids were living with their mother, and I did not even have their love and affection for the amount I wanted to as a father. I attempted to distract myself to avoid fear. I went on many trips and started exploring myself.

After 4 years of unwanted struggle, I realized that whatever I was fearing was useless and in the end, everything turns out to be fine. ... I also feel if I had not feared and worried I may have made better decisions.

Concept of God

I am not sure if God exists. Some scientists believe that God does exist. There was even a recent experiment where scientists were looking for "God's Particle". In the vast world, we live which is so well organized and has perfect conditions that force us to believe there has to be a mind behind it, a power behind it, which we can call God. Is God a physical being, I am not sure. I believe God primarily exists in Wave form but has a capacity to get converted into physical form. We and anything on this planet on the other hand are present in primarily physical form but have a capacity to convert into wave form. So one way we are part of God or just a different form of that divine energy. And if we are part of that energy which cannot be created or destroyed then I believe **"No one can harm you and you cannot harm anyone"**.

We Are What We Think We Are

The world we live in is created by our minds. We discussed in the previous chapter, that the power of the mind is amazing. The reality we feel is created by our minds. I will be discussing this further in my chapter "Your perception is your reality."

There is a great book by Psychologist Carol Silver where she says that our thoughts are so powerful that it can even make genetic changes.

Everything happens for a good reason

What is good in bad things that happen to us?

When I was suffering from divorce-related sufferings, I asked myself, if everything happens for good, what good is in it as I was suffering. I could not find any good that at that moment.

I have tried to tell many people that everything happens for a good reason and I always get a tough reaction from them. One of my good friends lost a newborn child soon after his birth. When I told her that everything happens for a good reason and she was very upset and asked me what was good in me losing a child.

It is very hard to explain to anybody when those things happen to them. One thing I have seen when I go through tough times in my life I become stronger. I observed this fact in my divorce case also. I learned so much through this process which I had not learned all my life. So now when I look back through my 4 years of suffering I actually feel thankful to my ex for creating the circumstances that lead to the divorce, because who I am now is an amazing person and I would not have become without going through that period.

What you will have or not is your shear destiny. As our seventh law states that attachment and detachments are timed and destined. This universe and God has amazing powers and have designed something for us.

Destiny

Commonly we ask ourselves that I think positive, I believe in everything but still, I don't achieve what I really want. Why so many people work so hard but are still poor and while some people don't do much at all and have the luxuries of life. If everyone has the same power, energy and potential then why not everyone has everything they want. I think this is beyond our comprehension and control of what we get in life. That's where Destiny plays a role. That's where God plays a role.

Learning Is The Key

Life is a simple path from birth to death. Unpredictability makes it a complex one. It also leads to fear and worries. Whether we live or die is not in our hands. This is a divine task only in God's control. The journey from birth to death is called life. The unpredictability makes us learn how we react to the situations that come. One of my dear friend Farrah from New York always says that "learning never ends".

Our mind has the power to design our life. Our mind if full of negative emotions, fear, and worries, will lead to a life full of suffering while a mind full of positive thoughts of love, passion, and content can lead to a beautiful, happy life.

How Did I Come Up With This Law?

When my divorce started, everything started to go downhill. There was financial, and emotional loss I was dealing with on a daily basis. My practice suffered a lot from this. When I noticed that in spite of having a hard time throughout the divorce process, in the end, I survived. Whatever has happened, happened for a good reason. One way or the other, things turned out to be good. Even after losing a tremendous amount of money, losing peaceful nights, In fact, this process made me tough and gave me so many great ideas to not only sustain myself well but to flourish. It made me capable of tolerating anything that comes in my way now. I feel that this was an MBA, a very expensive one, from the amazing school of life.

People commit suicide for very trivial reasons. Some students do it for anticipated failure in an exam, some adults do it for many types of difficulties in their lives, some do it for failure in love relationships. If you really look back on those reasons, they definitely are not worth ending your life. Someone else's problem may always be bigger than what you are going through. In life, everything is relative and related.

There was a fascinating quote from the movie "Three Idiots" in which Aamir Khan says "**All is well**" in every situation.

We all know the saying from the Engine "**I think I can**". So the main concept of this law is that you are all part of God, and nothing can go wrong. Just keep doing your job, and He is there to protect us all.

Who doesn't know the term **"acuna matata"** means no worry. It goes very well for our lives, that we should not worry about anything. Life will pass.

Everything happens for a good reason. Nothing happens by chance or using good luck. Illness, injury, love, lost moments of true greatness, and sheer stupidity all occur to test the limits of your soul. Without the small tests, whatever they may be, life would be like a smoothly paved, straight flat road to nowhere. It would be safe and comfortable, but dull and utterly pointless.

Always remember that God is there to protect you always." Don't worry everything will be fine. Whatever happens, happens for a good reason."

At a certain time In the next chapter you will be introduced to the second law that emphasizes the importance of you.

LAW 2

You Are It.
You are the most important person
in your life, and you have right
to be happy

CHAPTER 3

Law 2: You Are It

You Are The Most Important Person In Your Life, And You Have The Right To Be Happy

You And Others

If we look at life there are only two things that exist, You and others. Both have to coexist together. Budha says in his teachings "Sangham Sharnam Gacchami" means to surrender to the others. It means in this world we have others that we have to live with and we should do good to others. Live and let live.

We Are All Same

Everyone else is exactly the same, just like you. We all come with the same capabilities. Physically we may not appear to be the same but what we can do mentally is amazing. Some people may say oh there is always a difference between one and the other like some are born painters, singers, musicians etc. Someone may have a very high IQ while some are dumb. In my opinion, we may appear different, but we all are capable of learning things to become whatever and whenever we want. This you will learn more in the capabilities of the brain in the next chapter where we will introduce you to the third law "Anything is possible if you believe in it".

Influence Of Others

We live with others. We influence others and vice versa. We learn from observation. We perceive the world around us and that becomes our reality. When certain things are told to someone, over and over again, that becomes a part of them. *Like in a marriage or in any relationship, if one person keeps telling the other person that he or she is dumb, and is incapable of doing anything good, then that becomes the part of them and they start believing that's what they are.* Although there may not be any truth, to what the other person is saying, we still make it our reality.

The impact of what others feel or say to us is very strong and affects us deeply. Just like in a double-slit experiment in quantum physics electron changes its form from wave to particle form because of mere observation by the cameras. In other words, our reality also is dependent on other observations.

Others play an integral part in our life. *Facebook has proven this fact over and over again. When we post something we want it to be liked and loved.*

We literally cannot do many things, if not all, without

> *"Facebook has proven this fact over and over again A basic human nature that, we all want to be liked and loved"*
>
> – Raj

> *"Do No Harm, there is nothing we can do without being dependent on something or someone one way or others So, let's respect things and people around us"*
>
> – Raj

someone or something else. Even for breathing, we have to depend on plants to provide us oxygen.

World Is A Mirror Of You

Majority of the times we see us through other's eyes. Same thing others do too. This is an important concept to understand. Sometimes we think another person is not behaving well or is in a bad mood. If we observe ourselves we may find that other people is just reacting to our bad energy. Reflecting our own self. So remember when you feel that way, just give a smile and notice how others give you smile back. This is true majority of the time. Don't worry if it doesn't happen a few times, some people are just in a bad mood..lol.

Even if others are important for your existence always remember don't make them responsible for your sadness or happiness. Don't give others control of your life.

> *"Don't make others responsible for your sadness or happiness.*
> *People in your life may change or appear to change but you are the most important person in your life."*
>
> – Raj

Self Love Is An Inherent Quality

There is literally no one in this world or maybe universe who doesn't love themselves. Even if someone says they don't, I doubt it to be true. *We all have an inherent quality to protect us, and do good for us.*

Since birth, every task we do is to benefit us. When a baby is crying for milk he or she is thinking about the hunger which will benefit him or her. All the competition during school comes from self-love.

Even if we do anything for others like helping others, donating any money or something of that sort, that also has some benefit attached to us

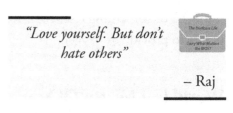

"Love yourself. But don't hate others"

– Raj

like, we will get blessings of God, or we will go to heaven, which again is doing something to benefit us only. Self love is important but we need to remember not to hurt others in what we do.

Focus On You

At the beginning of my divorce process my kids were taught to use words like a cheap, jerk, to torture me. This was very painful and insulting to me. I thought my relationship with my children was broken. I tried to win that relationship back by taking them on many vacations, spending money to give them what they wanted. Later I found out that it was fruitless. In spite of me doing so many things for them, they were still misbehaving with me. You cannot buy love in a relationship. One day during a walk with one of my dear friends, **Manju,** she advised me to let things go. "Focus on you," she said.

I started doing that. I know after that my kids may not have gotten what they wanted but at least I was not hurt. This is how I thought of the second law. Put yourself first. You have the right to be happy.

"Focus on you and all problems will disappear"

– Raj

Criticism

I have written more in detail on this topic in my other upcoming book "3SSS in a SUCCESSFUL Relationship". Here I would mention briefly that in our life we are dealing with two important relationships.

One is with others and the second one is with ourselves. The second relationship is the most important relationship for us.

Criticism is a negative force that pushes people away. Some people call "constructive criticism". In my opinion, criticism can never be constructive, and the term constructive criticism is just a BS. We have talked earlier that we create our reality based on others' criticism and start to believe in it. We may overcome other criticism in our lives, but it is literally impossible to overcome our own criticism to yourself. We are generally our own enemies in most of the situations which stop us from doing something. So, I would say, do not criticize others and more importantly, never ever criticize yourself.

"Few moments of criticism Leaves lifetime full of emotional scars."

– Raj

You Have the Right to Be Happy

Every single human being or even animal or creature has the right to live. You have a right to be happy. You deserve to be happy, and the universe responds to this happiness.

When we are happy, there is a tremendous shift in our energies. We are vibrant. We are more alive and alert. We take on challenges with optimism. We are more flexible, and we seek possibilities. When we are happy, we relate to others differently. Happiness creates happiness; it is as though it is contagious.

How Did I Come Up With My Second Law?

As the learnings that I have put together in this book originated from my divorce process I will tell you how I was feeling and how did I come up with this law. During the divorce, I felt my kids do not love me, in fact, they hate me. There was anger in them, along with some type of hate that was instilled in them. I will take them for movies, vacations, shopping but I was still getting hate in return. Each time I went out with them I kept feeling that was trying to buy their love. I felt as if no one was with me at that moment of stress. The only thing I had was my family and friends which was a huge support. Without them, I think I may have done something to myself for sure. One time when I was doing an evening walk with my friend Manju, she advised me, that what the kids were doing was normal as they were probably trying to adjust to their lives, but I need to make sure that I put my life on top. It was hard but then I started spending time with myself. I went to different places alone, did things for myself, including going on a sky-dive, which was an amazing experience. The result was, I felt good, and I felt happiness and peace. One thing is important to understand in this law, that you should not harm others to be on top. It's about creating self-love.

My divorce is over now, and my kids are growing fast and are in school. I think they still have that feeling of hate which has been in-stilled in them from the beginning, and I am hoping one day when they are mature enough to think of their own, they may realize that I was not as bad as they thought of me. I have and would have missed many many years with them by then, but, in the end, it is you alone. You have to keep moving. I still love them and keep wishing them the best. It is not their fault in any way. It is just how my life is written. My seventh law is "attachment and detachments are timed and destined" which can be applied here explaining their time with me.

As I said, I suffered for a long time before I made and followed this law in my personal life. I started putting myself first. It never meant to cause harm to others. I gave my time to my kids as much as I could, or they allowed but did not let them insult me or use me. It is to put your-self first. Next, we are going to learn my third law "anything is possible if you believe in it".

LAW 3

Anything Is Possible
If You Believe In It.

CHAPTER 4

Law 3

Anything Is Possible If You Believe In It

This is the 3rd law. *It's a law just like all other laws because it happens every time we follow it.* We have examples over examples to prove this in history. When we are not able to achieve something we suffer and ask God, why am I not able to achieve something? This is the incredible law that says if you **BELIEVE** in what you want, it has to happen. There was a famous dialogue from an Indian movie acted by ShahRukh Khan "Kehte hain .. Agar kisi cheez ko shiddat se chaho to puri kayanate usey tumse milaney ki koshish me lag jati hai" means "it is said... *if you really love something with great passion then the universe makes every effort to make it happen for you*". **I believe it holds true, 100% true.**

If it is destined for you, you will get it. No doubt about it. But you have to create a want.

Often Life Seems Impossible

When I was going through tough times during my divorce I questioned myself almost everyday , and every moment "is my life going to be better"

Ever? My divorce was prolonged for almost 4 years. I believed it was dragged for unnecessary reasons but according to my 5th law, I really didn't have any control what kept coming to me. I kept playing along as if I had no choice. During the whole time, I was making decisions based on fear, anger, and disgust. My beliefs were negative, and I felt frustrated, hopeless, and more andworse kept happening to me besides drainage of hundred of thousands of dollars, worsening of my business and affect my health.

I am not alone in these types of doubtful thinking. Almost everyone goes through similar thinking in similar situations. There is an unlimited number of incidences in people's life which will make you feel that you will not be able to achieve something whether it is success, love, money, promotion, health, passing an exam, or anything that creates a roadblock in your life.

When I came to USA in 1996, as a physician I had to take the USMLE exam which was a board exam all the foreign medical graduates had to take to become equivalent to US graduates. I had taken one of that exam while I was in India by going to Thailand and Singapore. Interestingly I failed that exam twice with just one percentile. I was disheartened by my two failures and passing the exam seemed impossible. I could not understand why I keep failing. I joined a coaching institute in USA after coming and discovered that my approach to studying for the exam and applying that knowledge was faulty. I was studying with an Indian subjective style while USA had an objective style. I discovered effective exam-taking skills and along with my positive belief, I was not only able to pass the exams but did extraordinarily well. Afterward, I also went on to teach that secret to many students in that institute so they could apply and become successful.

One important lesson I learned by reading books and exploring my own life that *our*

> *"Your belief drives the outcome*
> *Whether it's good or bad."*
>
> – Raj

own thinking affects our outcome. When we think positively, the outcome is positive, and if we think negatively, the outcome is also negative. Your belief drives the outcome.

History of Possibilities

If we look in our past or present, we can find millions of people who have achieved things we cannot even imagine that we can achieve. At the same time, we know they all are normal people like us.

Who would have thought that a person of African descent would run for the presidency and will change history forever? It never ever happened before and the task was impossible but the man **Barak Obama** proved that anything is possible.

A chai wala "person selling tea" at the train station became prime minister of India and a very successful one. Who doesn't know **Narendra Modi** and his achievements? He has been selected as prime minister of India second time now, changing India for good.

In 2011, **Arunima Sinha**, twenty-four years old girl, was thrown off a moving train because she refused to give her gold chain to a thug. She lost her left leg when the train went over it. Later she decided to climb Mount Everest, the highest mountain in the world and made the impossible possible.

Shahrukh Khan, an average boy from New Delhi, whose parents did not have enough money to take him to movies has become the "King Khan", one of the richest stars in Indian movies. He saw endless struggles in his lifehe slept on the streets, lost his parents at an early age, due to which his sister became mentally ill. He single handedly showed the world that anything is possible.

Who doesn't know about **Steve Jobs** who has literally changed this world with his amazing products? What he had gone through in his life was incredible.

Naveen Jain who is a billionaire had a very poor background. His father who used to be a civil engineer refused to take bribes due to which he had to face many transfers in rural areas. They had no life, even no food sometimes. Later he went on to study engineering and came to USA with 5 dollars in his pocket. He has become successful with his many amazing companies.

Dashrath Manjhi also known as Mountain Man was a poor labourer in Gehlaur village of India, who carved a path of 110 meters long through a hillock using only a hammer and chisel. He was married to Falguni Devi. One day while bringing him lunch she slipped continuously and seriously injured herself and died. Manjhi was deeply disturbed and decided to carve a path through the hill so people can get access to the city for medical attention. It took him 22 years to build that path.

Jim Carrey came from a very rough phase. When his father lost his job, they had to go through a financial crisis and had to move into a van on a relative's lawn. Going through multiple struggles and failures of life he became one of the biggest stars of Hollywood.

Who doesn't know **Oprah Winfrey**? She went through a terrible childhood. She was a victim of sexual abuse who was molested by her cousin, uncle, and a family friend repeatedly. She got pregnant at the age of 14 and gave birth to a child who died after 2 weeks. She never gave up and proved that anything is possible even if you are of a minority race.

Jan Koum a Ukrainian American, founder of an app "WhatsApp" which he designed while having tea with his friend. When he moved with his mother to California he was living in a two bedroom apartment under a social support program. In the beginning, he was working as a cleaner in a grocery store. After years of struggle but with a positive attitude he made impossible possible and he is worth almost $9.7 billion currently.

Who is not aware of internet sensation **Mark Zuckerberg** who has changed the world by his famous app "Facebook". He dropped out of

Harvard to develop this app. Currently his worth almost $69.3 billion last I checked.

There is a boy from New Jersey I would like to mention here, a child prodigy, **Sparsh Shah** who is a wheelchair bound, physically disabled due to a medical condition osteogenesis imperfecta, *but is more able than so many others kids* and has become, an amazing writer, musician, singer. He has changed the meaning of impossible to IMPOSSIBLE.

Paul "Sequence" Ferguson, a great man who has beaten death multiple times. He has achieved immense success as an amazing keyboardist, guitarist, and martial artist. Best of all is his achievement of helping so many veterans through his charitable foundation "www.Yes We Care.net".

These are examples of well known people who had gone through many struggles in life but they proved again and again that anything is possible. There are unlimited examples like that where people have done amazing things in their life which appears to be impossible but with their belief, it was made possible.

We come across so many examples of so many people in our lives where they have made changes which in the beginning felt impossible. Like we all know how hard it is to lose weight. My nephew OJ was trying to lose weight for years. Recently he lost 37 lbs proving that anything is possible if you believe in it.

- I planned while going through the divorce that I will create a successful pain practice. I believed in it and I did make it happen. That's how I came up with this law that if you believe in it, it will happen.

E=Mc2: Enormous Potential We Have

Are we physically capable of doing anything? How much energy and power we have. *The energy in us is huge.* If we just look at the world famous equation given by Einstein E=MC2 (where E is the energy which could be converted from a Mass and C being the speed of light) we can get some idea how much energy each individual has theoretically.

There is a lot of energy condensed into the matter. As per the equation, 1 kg of "stuff" contains around 9x10^16 joules. That is almost equal to 40 megatons of TNT. Practically it is the amount of energy that would come out of a 1 gigawatt plant, big enough to run 10 million homes for atleast 30 years. A 100 kg person, therefore has enough energy *locked up inside* them to run that many homes for 300 years. That's a lot of energy. So practically we have an enormous amount of power and energy to achieve anything.

Now if we know that we have that much amount of energy locked up inside us then why are we not able to achieve what we want in life. Why only a few people are successful in getting what they want. This can easily be explained by a secret called "law of attraction".

Law of Attraction

The term law of attraction appeared in print for the first time in 1877 in a book written by Russian occultist Helena Blavatsky

Later in the 19th century, it was being used by new thought authors such as Prentice Mulford and Ralph Waldo Trine. In the 20th century, it really became famous when it was being used by books like Think and Grow Rich by Napoleon Hill and You Can Heal Your Life by Louise Hay. In 2006 the movie and the book "secret" caught widespread attention in the media and made this law a household term.

New thought authors believe that the law of attraction is always in operation and that it brings to each person the conditions and experiences that they predominantly think about or which they desire or expect. *It is the belief that by focusing on the positive or negative thoughts people can bring positive or negative experiences into their life.*

Power of Mind: Power of Belief

In the first chapter, we described theory of simplicity according to which mind and body are one unit. The mind has the task to design the body the way it wants. The body is the slave of our mind, not vice versa. In fact, if we have to say as per quantum physics body is the physical form while the mind is the energy or wave form.

Eric R. Kandel, a Nobel prize winner, has shown how *thoughts can turn on or off certain genes to bring structural changes in the neurons.* Many scientists including Bruce Lipton, Norman Doidge, have shown the remarkable power of the thoughts to change the brain.

There is a fantastic book written by Dr. Caroline Leaf "**Switch on your brain**" which beautifully describes the power of your mind. The mind is plastic. It is moldable. It conforms to your requirement. *She states that thinking changes our DNA.* Your mind is the most powerful thing in the universe after God.

Neuroplasticity is the ability of the brain to change throughout an individual's life. We have commonly seen that happening after brain injury and strokes. But the power of thoughts to bring neuroplastic change is also visible in so many examples we come across on a daily basis.

If you have not read a book called "The Obstacle Is The Way" by Ryan Holiday, I would highly recommend it. He phrases the beauty of mind and ways to achieve success through the opportunity which looked like a problem before.

"Our life is what our thoughts make it"

– Marcus Aurelius

Power of Imagination

With the simple power of imagination, we can achieve anything. In my upcoming book 7ways in 7 days to change our life I will write more about success but briefly, I would like to share a mnemonic which is very important for achieving success.

"ABCD" where I say in order to achieve the success you need to Accept your situations or circumstances as is. Most of the people accept the situations but they don't really believe in it. I suggest you have to Believe in it. Later you have to create goals that you want to achieve and finally, you have to Dream about your creations.

Viktor Emil Frankl was an Austrian psychologist as well as a Holocaust survivor. Frankl was the founder of logotherapy, the will to meaning and is most notable for the best-selling book Man's Search for Meaning. While he was in Nazis camp, he practiced playing golf every single day in his imagination and always hit a perfect score. When he came out and played golf in spite of never touching a club, he hit the perfect score. That's how is the power of imagination.

Success

Is different for different people. I say "success is only defined by you". What do we really mean by achievement? Having lots of money in the bank is success? That is commonly a misconception people have. An amazing billionaire Naveen Jain talks about success as *changing the lives of other people positively.*

I call myself successful not because I am very rich, but because I have peace of mind. I am contained. I am happy with what I have. I always say I just need to continue having peace.

I have worked a lot about success, in the book 7 ways in 7 days to change your life. It's all about being successful.

We Are Byproducts Of Our Beliefs

Our life is designed by our thought process. If we believe in positive thoughts our life will be full of positive experiences and if we believe in negative thoughts our life will be full of negative experiences. Our beliefs attract what we are thinking according to the Law of Attraction.

You are a work in progress, on a never ending journey. What's important is to keep moving forward, ensuring you're heading in the right direction.

One of the common themes that runs through my writing is that if you believe in yourself, anything is possible, as long as you work hard enough to achieve your dreams, having the determination and persistence to never give up no matter how many times you get knocked down or take a wrong turn. Without a belief in your potential and abilities, you are doomed to failure.

Are you living the life of your dreams? Or do you have unfulfilled dreams and now you feel that it's too late to pursue them?

I tell you that it's never too late to make all your dreams come true.

The only thing that matters is what you think of yourself and what you believe you can achieve. So yes if you've given up all hope of ever achieving your dreams, you're right, you won't achieve them. On the other hand, if you believe that anything is possible, then again, you will be right. In as much as you believe it, it becomes your personal truth.

I'm talking about trusting your gut, listening to your heart as well as your mind, and visualizing achieving your dream. The minute you start to believe in yourself anything is possible because a person who believes in himself will not be afraid to push himself to the next level and to risk the possibility of failure. They also know failure is only temporary, and sometimes it's only a stop on the journey to success.

Every Olympian believes in themselves, and it is their belief that carries them past obstacles, keeps them committed to their training program and prepared to make the sacrifices they have to make to achieve their dreams. They are the greatest example that if you believe in yourself, anything is possible.

Your beliefs hold great power. Start believing that you can do anything you put your mind to.

"All our dreams can come true if we have the courage to pursue them."

You have the power to reach for your dreams and achieve your heart's desires. If you believe in yourself, anything is possible. You just have

> *"Transform your thoughts and transform your life"*
>
> – Raj

to have faith in your abilities and always strive for your best!

It's essential to better our lives and reach our dreams, to develop a strong positive belief in ourselves and our abilities. Every one of you has your individual strengths, talents, and passions. Well, isn't it time you allowed these to define you and your life?

The beliefs we have about ourselves are responsible for who we ultimately become and what we eventually achieve in life. Indeed, a positive self-belief is a prerequisite for achieving anything and everything in life.

You can do anything you put your mind to. You just need to focus, do your best and everything else will follow.

Today I'm telling you that if you believe in yourself, anything is possible. You must learn to believe in yourself. Your beliefs hold great power. I

> *"Life grows on the tree of thoughts."*
>
> – Raj

want you to start believing that you can do anything you truly put your mind to. If you believe you can, you will go to great lengths to prove yourself right. And isn't it great being right?

"If you believe in yourself and have dedication and pride – and never quit, you'll be a winner. The price of victory is high but so are the rewards."

– Paul Bryant

Self talk is the only talk that matters. When we tell ourself everyday, how good we are, we can achieve anything in this life, there is nothing can hold us down.

How Did I Come Up With My Third Law?

My divorce years 2013-2017, there was in the beginning, a period of decline in my life, in everything and in every way. Money, love, peace, my health, my medical practice, and literally everything was going down. I was fortunate that I had amazing books with me and my parents and friends who kept me floating. I thought of bankruptcy many times also. I had the idea of setting up a practice that can increase awareness for pain and make people avail of excellent pain management. That idea was flourishing with my belief slowly. I kept believing that I can survive and do very well. At the end of 2016 I established Pain Instacare, a new dimension in pain, and fulfilled my dream. It could happen with my belief and I thought YES, anything is possible if you believe in it.

Success, failure, happiness, and suffering, are all a matter of our perspective. Let us learn more about the perspective in our next chapter of the 4th law "Your perception is your reality".

LAW 4

Your Perception Is Your Reality

CHAPTER 5

Law 4: Law of Perception

Your Perception Is Your Reality

This is the central law of the universe and my book. Everything revolves around this law. Perception leads to action.

per·cep·tion definition

/par'sepSH(a)n/

noun

the ability to see, hear, or become aware of something through the senses

Perception Defines Your Reality

In this world, as we said before there are three types of forces that exist in every form, positive, negative, and neutral. When we look at something or someone, we are trying to perceive them or that thing as one of that force. The perception becomes our reality. We make an opinion about that thing or that person based on perception. Also based on that perception our actions are decided. Who and what they are, are only our observations, not their reality but it is our reality only.

For example, when you meet someone for the first time, and they started lying to you about things that you very well know, You will immediately perceive that person as a liar and that will become your opinion. You will decide to take any action which may be to stay away from that person, or with a reaction of telling that person that he or she is lying. Now in this situation whatever you perceived is your reality. That person may be saying the entire truth from his or her knowledge. That does not mean if that person is a liar.

This type of situation we come across all the time. Let's take the situation of a couple who is having problems in their marriage. Each person blames the other, saying something bad about the other person. Obviously, families are polarized on what they are saying but we do not come to know who is right, and who is wrong. In fact, most of the time they both are right and may have valid issues. What each person thinks is their reality.

We fight onreligious issues all the time. Recently India made Kashmir as an independent territory and central government ruling started to take place on it. I have so many Facebook friends from Pakistan who are living in USA. I personally had no clue what was going on in Kashmir (Indian part) but apparently some of my Pakistani friends in USA knew exactly what was happening in Indian part of the Kashmir, in spite of literally zero communication from Kashmir due to governmental restrictions on the internet, etc. That led to hatred among them for India which you could see from their Facebook posts. I am not saying they are wrong or right, but I am just trying to prove here that it is just our perception of the facts or opinions which becomes our reality.

Who doesn't remember the conflict on the color of a dress all over the internet? The fact that a single image could polarize the entire Internet into two aggressive camps is, let's face it, just another day. But for many months, people across social media had been arguing about whether a picture depicted a perfectly nice bodycon dress as blue with black lace fringe or white with gold lace fringe. And neither side will budge. This fight was about more than just social media—it was about primal biology and the way human eyes and brains have evolved to see color in a sunlit world. So, it was a blue dress, but different people perceived it differently.

In a story I tell later in this chapter, when five blind men were perceiving different parts of an elephant, they thought different things for different parts of the elephant body. Perception depends upon how much blind we are to the information.

Tools of Perception

In any living being primarily there are two basic functions that take place, perception and reaction. From a single cell to the biggest animal, whale, at least these two functions are provided. Perception is a multifold process. It is not just sensing something. The process of perception is primarily the observation and processing of that observation.

Perception = Observation and Processing.

In the majority of the animals there is an additional part of the perception which is the memory where the observed or processed information is saved which in fact can trigger future reactions by itself without any external stimulus.

As human beings, we are given many tools for perception. Our external sources like **skin, ears, eyes, tongue, and smell** provide us with information that our mind processes and converts into thoughts. Often, we don't even need any external stimuli to perceive something as our memory plays an amazing role in it. We are blessed with an amazing mind which can create thoughts based on our previous experiences, or even dreams. Also, one very important sense which is commonly used is the 6th sense. That is the sense of intuitions.

What Are We Perceiving?

Physically what we see, hear, feel, smell, taste can be perceived by all the five major senses. With the sixth sense, in my opinion, we can sense the wave form (as discussed in the first chapter) of anything. This is a sense of intuition.

As I mentioned in my theory of simplicity that everything exists in three forms, physical, transitional, and wave form, and there are 3 major forces found in any existence, negative, neutral, and positive.

Physical forms are something we can touch, smell, hear, taste, and see while wave forms are something we just feel. I would say ghosts may be considered in this category. ... lol. Believe me, I do think ghosts exist, but I do not think they are bad. In my opinion, whatever exists in matter form also exist in wave and transitional form at the same time. We may not see every form. Some form we can see, and touch, and some form we just feel and sense. Therefore, we can even feel someone's presence from distance or even communicate with them called telepathy.

Whatever we perceive is perceived as three forces of negative, neutral, or positive. For example, if we taste something, we say it's good, bad or it is ok. If we see someone or something, we havea similar response. Even the 6th sense intuition about someone or something is considered as one of those.

Law of Coexistence

Interestingly just like three forms are present in everything and everyone so is the three forces present in everything and everyone at any given point. How do we classify someone or something that is all based on our perception? Whatever we perceive becomes our reality. So, let me expand on it a little bit. In every situation there is happiness and sadness, beginning and the end, loss and the win, good and the bad, what we feel it all depends on our perception, which further becomes your reality.

Existence of Anything And Everything Is <u>Observer</u> Dependent: Quantum Physics

How you see something will completely depend on who is observing it. According to my law of coexistence, everything is present in everyone and it only depends on the observer how much and what they see. That observer could be someone else or you.

If you know the famous double slit experiment you will realize how an electron changed its existence from wave to particle based on the observation.

In the basic version of this experiment, a coherent light source, such as a laser beam, illuminates a plate pierced by two parallel slits, and the light passing through the slits is observed on a screen behind the plate. The wave nature of light causes the light waves passing through the two slits to interfere, producing bright and dark bands on the screen – a result that would not be expected if light consisted of classical particles. However, the light is always found to be absorbed in the screen at discrete points, as individual particles (not waves), the interference pattern appearing via the varying density of these particle hits on the screen. Furthermore, versions of the experiment that include detectors at the slits find that each detected photon passes through one slit (as would a classical particle), and not through both slits (as would a wave). However, such experiments demonstrate that particles do not form the interference pattern if one detects which slit they pass through. These results demonstrate the principle of wave–particle duality.

This type of duality coexists in everything. Which form something is present at any given point, is observer dependent. In my opinion, there are actually three forms in which a transitional form also exists which is the major component.

5 Elephants And Blind Men Story

Almost everyone has heard this story. Here it goes. A group of blind men heard that a strange animal, called an elephant, had been brought to the town, but none of them were aware of its shape and form. Out of curiosity, they said: "We must inspect and know it by touch, of which we are capable". So, they sought it out, and when they found it, they groped about it. In the case of the first person, whose hand landed on the trunk, said "This being is like a thick snake". For another one whose hand reached its ear, it seemed like a kind of fan. As for another person, whose hand was upon its leg, said, the elephant is a pillar-like a tree-trunk. The blind man who placed his hand upon its side said, "elephant is a wall". Another who felt its tail described it as a rope. The last felt its tusk, stating the elephant is that which is hard, smooth, and like a spear. In this story, we can easily see how one's perception twists the reality for them.

Rajaram The Bad Guy

When I was in 3rd grade, I remember having a classmate name Rajaram. He always will take lunch boxes from the other students' bags. He will also often curse. So, I thought he was a bad guy as most of the other kids thought so too. I noticed that Rajaram had very few friends who were helping in his bad tasks. These friends were always found together doing something wrong. They really loved Rajaram and thought he was a great guy.

I was thinking if Rajaram was a bad guy whatI and so many others classmate felt, how come he has friends who really loved him. Then I realized the perception of someone is only relative. It was just a perception. Rajaram's perception for some was good and some were bad.

So, there are many Rajaram's in our lives who are perceived differently. They may be good for a few and bad for others. But by no means have that proved if Rajaram is a good or bad guy.

13th Floor Perception: Modified Perception

So, I noticed in most of the buildings they don't put 13th floor. The elevator doesn't show the 13th floor mark either. It is interesting how by not putting that 13th number, our mind feels relieved. But, the 14th floor is the actual 13th floor. So, we can see how mind perception can play a role.

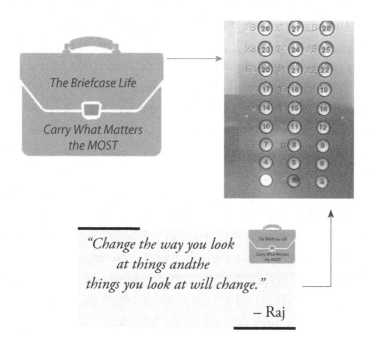

"Change the way you look at things andthe things you look at will change."

– Raj

Your Perception Is Your Reality

The way people view you and the way you present yourself is the impression you will leave behind. As you go about the business of carrying out your life people will make judgments about your appearance, personality, and capabilities.

If you don't like the way your life is playing out, you can always take charge of your perception of reality. You are in control of your story. Not everyone in life is a top performer, but they all have the ability to give off that impression.

Perception = Projection

Things are not always what they seem, and marketers and artists rely on this to make you see things the way they want you to see them. You can meet someone, and they can tell you everything you want to hear without any hint of truth. Anyone can give off any perception they want. The world we see is a reflection of who we are and what we believe.

The self-fulfilling prophecy lays at the foundation of this concept; a statement that alters actions and therefore becomes true. Someone who thinks their night is going to play out terribly will subconsciously change their actions so that their actions fulfil this prediction. Often the way we perceive reality is coloured by how we want it rather than simply the way it is.

Perception drives people's behaviors every day. Take a look at the movies "Romy & Michelle's High School Reunion" and "The Girl Next Door." Upon receiving word of a 10-year high school reunion, Romy and Michelle realise their lives are not as impressive as they wish they were. So when the time comes to attend the reunion they show up in an expensive car dressed in business suits, equipped with cell phones, and bring along a huge fictitious success story.

Romy tries to convince everyone that she invented the post-it notes while Michele tries to convince everyone she created a type of glue. In "The Girl Next Door" the teenagers all pay porn stars to pose as their prom dates in hopes of giving off a cooler vibe.

"When lies and misinformation blur truth, perception becomes a reality, and all is lost."

What people perceive is usually what they believe, and this is based on what they hear, see and think. Most of the time we cannot control what happens, but we can always control our reactions.

Important point here is what you see, is just your reality not mine.

In Life, Everything Is Relative and Related

I always talk about this example when I am talking about perception. Let's think about the story of a girl who is walking down the street. You found out that girl killed a guy on the street. If you were to think who the culprit will be, you will obviously think it is the girl. But if I add a piece of information that the girl was attacked by this man for rape and in self-defence, she killed this man. Your perception will change. You may not consider this girl as the culprit. Once again reality is defined by how we perceive things and how blind or aware we are to the information.

Einstein had given us a great theory of relativity. Depending upon how fast we are traveling we can change the time and space. The similar way our mind is constantly perceiving things. One person can perceive the same thing in a different way if the frame of observation is different for that person.

Everything in life is related. We all are part of the earth. One way or the other there is a relation between each of us. We may all breathe the same way; we may all live in similar houses or so many other things.

Life Is outcome Of Your Own Observation

There is no absolute right or wrong. There is no absolute left or right. Everything is relative to something. Good is defined as good when compared to bad. Up is defined as up when compared to down. If you are rich there are richer people than you. If you are poor there are poorer people than you. One person is smart but there are others who are smarter.

> *"There are only two ways to live your life. One is as though nothing is a miracle. The other is as though everything is a miracle."*
>
> – Albert Einstein

Einstein's theory applies to almost everything in life. Similar way when you are in an argument one side has its own story based on their perception. Just like in divorce husband says wife and her relatives are the cause for divorce and the wife says husband and his relatives are responsible. She says, he did bad things and he says she did the bad thing. The point I am trying to make here is everything is relative. Often times we really don't know the truth. So, when you are in a dispute always try to put yourself in other shoes and give the benefit of the doubt.

Just like in my previous example, even I perceived that my ex and her father were responsible for our divorce. She probably had her theories to prove me wrong. After some time, I stopped looking for reasons and accepted the fact that the relationship broke. My life is how I see it. So, I started looking for life through a different frame of mind. This is how my 4th law came about. I started believing that she may not be right or wrong, it was just her perspective, her perception.

Glass Half Full vs. Glass Half Empty

Who doesn't know the concept of glass being half full or half empty? It is the same scenario for two types of people who are perceiving it in two different ways, one negative and one positive.

Interestingly one thing for one person could be a cause of suffering while for other a cause of happiness. Someone who is poor who walks miles to a place when he gets a bicycle as a gift is very happy while someone who is rich may react sadly on getting a bicycle.

What You Don't Perceive, Doesn't Mean Is Not Real: Ability To Perceive

A bat can hear much more frequency than a human being can hear. An eagle can see much farther than a human being can see. It doesn't mean that if we are not able to see something it is not real. It is just we are not able to see it. Every person has a different level of perception. You may have heard, 10 doctors looking at a patient may have 10 different diagnoses. It is not one doctor is better, but it is because everyone is different in their perceptions.

Perfection Is Only Defined By Your Perception

What is perfect? There is no scale to define perfect. Perfection is only defined by us. If we are satisfied, then wherever we are, and however we are perfect but if we are not satisfied than wherever we are or however we are, we will never consider ourselves as perfect. This concept is commonly seen in schools when kids are trying to be perfect, whether it is peer pressure or pressure from their parents. Kids even commit suicides from this pressure as they are not able to be perfect as defined by others or themselves. In my opinion, perfection is your perception. Feel every day, that if you are alive, you are perfect. Whatever situation you are in, it is perfect. Whichever relationship you are in is perfect.

Suffering and Happiness Are Only Perceived Reality

Suffering is the gateway to happiness as long as you are able to see it. People who have suffered are the people who are successful and happy. They are two sides of the same coin. Only thing is that we are not able to see the other side when we are facing one.

The world around you is the mirror of you

What we are we see the same. This concept is critical to understand when we are talking about perception. When you are angry, almost everybody will seem angry with you. When you are fearful, you seem to see fear everywhere. The way you act people seems to react in the same way. Sometimes if you see the other people are not behaving with you, try to watch your behaviour, and you may find the cause of others' misbehaviour. Just like when someone yells at you, you will have a tendency to yell back at him or her.

In this world, we have to deal with others. We feel like people are close to us or far from us. In reality, nobody is ever close to you or very far from you, it is only your perception. God has given us powers to be connected to anyone and everyone in the way we want.

Change Your Perception, Change Your Life

Every time we perceive something it becomes part of our reality. How we perceive something becomes our reality. It all depends on how we program our minds. Some people look at everything in a negative way while others do it in a positive way. Steven covey in his book says that it's all about our perspective. If we want to change our lives, we should change our perspective.

> *"When the sun doesn't shine on you, go and stand in front of the sun."*
>
> – Raj

Recently in a Sadh guru event in New York City, I learned that in order to perceive better in life, we must enhance our perception.

In the next three chapters you will read about the laws which will help you with suffering related to the loss. The loss can be of any type from poor health to death, or loss of a relationship, or money. Remember one thing while understanding these laws that once again the central law is our perception is our reality as what we are considering as a loss may not really be a big loss.

Also understand that each incident in our life is like a picture, not a movie, while life in itself is a movie that is made up of all these pictures. So when you are looking at life, look it like a movie.. just like in the movie Om Shanti Om, Shahrukh Khan says "picture abhi baki hai mere dost" means the story is not finished, my friend.

LAW 5

Law of Control

You Have 0% Control On What Comes To You, But 100% Control How You React To It.

CHAPTER 6

Law 5: Law of Control
You Have 0% Control On What Comes To You, But 100% Control On How You React To It

Because this book originated from my divorce process-related sufferings, the laws and teachings in this book were my solutions or ways to justify the things that happened. Later when I looked at different aspects of my life, I realized that the principles and the laws hold for every painful situation of my life whether it was in the past or happening currently. **Even after my divorce was finalized, sufferings didn't say goodbye to me.** Occasionally they came in abundance and much harder than my divorce did, but how I reacted was different which made me stronger and I was able to take those blows of life with less suffering.

Many things happened during my divorce process that I didn't have any control. In the beginning, I attempted to reconcile, but it didn't work. Later, I tried many times to negotiate the terms, but it didn't work. One time we even signed an agreement, but later she decided to change her mind. We lost almost ½ million dollars in this battle to the attorneys, but I couldn't do anything about it. In the beginning, for a couple of years, I used to react to these situations by getting frustrated, angry and wanted to do harmful things to me, but it wouldn't have been right. Later I realized that I don't have any control over anything that is coming to me, but I can choose the way I react to them. And I did. I changed the way and I positively responded to things. My life is much better now. This is how comes the law of control.

Why do I say 0% control? Some people say that they can plan their lives. They can predict the outcome. That is true but whatever happens, never happens exactly how you planned.

When I was a kid in 4th grade, I received news that I got a scholarship. That made me very happy.

I was a bright student in my medical school. I wanted to stay in India but due to family influence, I decided to come to the USA. For me to practice in the USA, I would have to take boards, we called USMLE. We could go and take those exams in Singapore or Thailand. I studied hard for it and took the exam twice but failed both times with a small margin.

One fine morning in Dec 2013 we were planning to go to India and suddenly argument started and that led to filing for divorce.

What comes to you may be good or bad but having control over it, is just not possible. Gautam Buddha's teachings focus a lot on the reaction. He taught us to stay in the middle lane. Do not be too happy when there is happy news and do not be too sad when there is sad news.

Unpredictable Life

Since my birth, there have been many instances that I wanted to do something, but I end up doing something else. Things didn't go the way I wanted them to. For example, I could not get my first love as my life partner, I could not get into medical school on the first attempt, I could not pass my USMLE exam in the first attempt, and so on. Even Gita in the following quote says that man has only control over his actions or Karma but not the results.

> *"Karmanyevaadhikaaraste maa phaleshu kadaachana;*
> *Maa karmaphalahetur bhoor maa te sango'stwakarmani."*

In chapter 2, I have talked more about the unpredictability of life. The story when I was traveling to San Francisco. I was driving to the airport parking and when I reached there, I saw right at the entrance of that parking, a motorcyclist laying on the road with blood gushing from his head. He was not moving and people around him were just standing watching him. I got the impression that he must be dead. I thought at that time, what must be going through this motor cyclist's mind 5 minutes before the accident. He never would have been thinking that he will die in the next few minutes. *That's how unpredictable life is. We don't know what the next moment can bring us.*

"Life cannot be planned It can only be adapted"

– Raj

In life, attitude is everything; it is what shapes our beliefs and our desires. Harsh times will occur throughout our lives, but how we interpret them is our responsibility. We are always in control of our emotions despite any given situation.

Many people blame their circumstances for their shortcomings and as a result, accept the harsh reality of their situation. These people believe an event is equivalent to its outcome; however, for the remarkable person, adversity is where they thrive.

"Every time I feel I have control I realize that I am fooled"

– Raj

What comes to you is not always negative of course. Many things happen in our lives which are positive too. For example, winning a lottery, finding true love, getting into a position, surprise gifts, etc. So, in life, everything happens by surprise and that surprise could be positive or negative.

Having no control is not a bad thing though. It gives us a feeling of adventure. You know it is like playing a video game with many levels.

Reaction Is The Key

It is true that whatever happens to us, we have 0% control. **How we react to it is what defines our destiny.**

In another book that I am working on "7 ways in 7 days to change your life", I have talked in detail about the reaction. One of the 7 ways to succeed is "Pause, Breathe and Respond". I believe that if we act upon something or react to something, we should take at least a single long breath before we make a decision. One single breath can change the outcome of your decisions.

One single breath only takes about 7 seconds. We act on many things on impulse of lesser time. Usually, the decisions made impulsively have a negative outcome. Many people commit suicide based on a less than 7-second impulse. I wish I could have reacted slowly in my past life.

> "*Most of the mistakes happen when the response time is less.*
> *Pause, Breathe, and Respond. A single long breath can change your life*"
>
> – Raj

Often in relationships, we respond or want to respond very quickly. We want to tell rather than listen. Most of the time our ego drives our conversations. We feel that if we do not respond quickly then we will be considered as dumb. I feel that it is better to be dumb than later feeling sorry about it.

"It's better to be dumb than sorry"

– Raj

I have discussed with many divorced people and each one of them has mentioned that life with their ex was not that bad and it could have been better if we would not have reacted in that way. I am not saying divorce is a bad thing. It is totally fine if you think it is the right thing to do but we should always try to think from a cool mind because once the damage is done, it is a slippery slope. And if it comes in the hands of attorneys then the communication stops, and it becomes an ongoing financial and emotional trauma.

The reaction in the success world is also very important. I have discussed and interviewed many successful people for my "The Centerspread" show and have found the way to react to the problems is what makes them successful.

What allows these people to succeed? They realize it is not what has happened to them in their lives, but the manner in which they react to these events. The way a person decides to respond to individual occurrences is what will shape his or her feelings, actions, and results. It all lies within ourselves to be successful in life or not.

We can choose to live the life we want, no matter how tough it can get. It is all a matter of mentality; only we will prevent ourselves from achieving greatness. The rest are just small detours before we reach our destinations.

"I am responsible. Although I may not be able to prevent the worst from happening, I am responsible for my attitude toward the inevitable misfortunes that darken life. Bad things do happen; how I respond to them defines my character and the quality of my life. I can choose to sit in perpetual sadness, immobilized by the gravity of my loss, or I can decide to rise from the pain and treasure the most precious gift I have: life itself."

– Walter Anderson

Adversity is something that everyone faces at some point in his or her life. These difficult and trying times, however, are not what define us, but the way in which we react to them is what reveals our true character. Anyone can be defeated when life does not go as planned, but the strong survivors are the people who can overcome such hardships.

Knowledge comes from everything we do and everything that happens to us. We learn valuable lessons over the course of time-based on our experiences and the ways in which we react to them. Every hardship presents an opportunity; we just need to recognize that instead of letting it defeat us. Your thoughts and attitude change your experiences and shape your life.

You have a choice when it comes to reactions, and although at the moment, you want to get angry, you need to remind yourself why that is so detrimental.

> "The longer I live, the more I realize the impact of attitude on life. Attitude, to me, is more important than facts. It is more important than the past, the education, the money, than circumstances, than failure, than successes, than what other people think or say or do. It is more important than appearance, giftedness, or skill.
>
> It will make or break a company, a church, a home. The remarkable thing is we have a choice every day regarding the attitude we will embrace for that day. We cannot change our past we cannot change the fact that people will act in a certain way. We cannot change the inevitable. The only thing we can do is play on the one string we have, and that is our attitude. I am convinced that life is 10% what happens to me and 90% of how I react to it. And so, it is with you we are in charge of our Attitudes."

The only environment we have control of is our internal one, so the way we interpret situations is the only control we have over them. Each day we are presented with a variety of situations, and it is up to us on the way we react. Too many times we rush into decisions during difficult times, only to regret them later on. At that moment, our responses are clouded, and our judgment is askew.

Our Reactions Pave The Way To Our Future

Logic is thrown out the window while we let our emotions take control. We don't think things through because when tough times occur, we become angry and frustrated. These are two overwhelming emotions that do not allow our intelligence to reach the forefront of our minds.

The truth is that the way in which we react to everything that happens around us determines the quality of our lives. There are things in the world we can control and things that we cannot. First and foremost, it is essential to accept the fact that not everything is in our control. Only then can you realise the impact your attitude has on your experiences. As soon as this is recognized, you will start to feel a greater sense of control in your life.

The real things haven't changed. It is still best, to be honest, and truthful; to make the most of what we have; to be happy with simple pleasures, and have courage when things go wrong."

You always have a choice of how you are going to respond to what the world offers you. Do not let something dictate the way you react to things. You need to look within yourself and realise that you have the power to make things happen. We are a sum of all of our life's experiences, so use these past lessons to help better your present situation.

In the next chapter, we will learn about the changes in life. The unpredictability of life brings so many changes. Ups and downs of life make it an adventurous one. Life cannot be static, otherwise, we will be dead. Change is the only constant. Each and everything, every situation is changing constantly.

Reactions are like making a turn while driving. Each turn will decide where will you end up. So be careful when you are reacting, otherwise you will end up somewhere you may not want to go.

LAW 6

Law of Change

Change Is Inevitable
Don't Fear It, Learn From It.

CHAPTER 7

─◦⌢◦◦⌢◦─

Law 6: Law of Change

Change Is Inevitable.
Don't Fear It, Learn From It.

We are born and we die. In between birth and death is what we call life. Our lives are lived in three dimensions as we discussed earlier in the first chapter. The three dimensions are physical, emotional, and spiritual ones. Have you noticed that a newborn is only worried about his or her physical being? Is he getting milk or food on time? There is no concept of the emotional and spiritual aspects. As the child grows up you can see the emotions. Later life there are more spiritual components.

Why Change Is A Problem

Most of the problems and frustrations we have in our life come as a result of our attitude towards change. The cycle is that usually some change happens; we become upset about the things we lost in the change, and we develop an aversion towards some of the new things that have come about as a result of the change. Then, usually after some drama and a fair amount of time, we come to let go of what we have lost, we come to accept our new inconveniences, and we even begin to discover some new good things in our changed environment. Just when we get comfortable and happy with our new situation, some new change will come about and the whole cycle starts over again. This cycle occurs with basically everything: our friends, our jobs, our kids, our surroundings, our enjoyments, etc.

We do not really expect a change, and that's why when it comes, it disturbs us.

The impact of change is due to the unpredictability of the situation. That brings fear. We have talked about unpredictability and fear in the second chapter.

"Change is not accepted When it is not expected"

– Raj

Change in Every Dimension

In our lives, change comes in almost every dimension of life. A change could be positive, or it could be negative. A change could be more in one dimension than the other. It could be slow or fast. Everything in life changes. This is a fact of life, whether we accept/like it or not. Some people use all of their energy trying to resist this inevitable change. They do everything they can to keep everything the same. When we approach life this way, we begin to fear everything, view everything as a threat, and we increasingly ensconce ourselves in an artificially static world. It eventually grows harder and harder to hold back the tide of change, our mental strain grows and grows, we become increasingly grumpy, dissatisfied and picky.

We get stuck in our habits and can't imagine life any other way. The radius of our world gets smaller and smaller, the information and new perspectives we become exposed to narrower and narrower until eventually, we find ourselves in a single chair in an informational echo chamber of things confirming what we already believe. We become completely stuck, enmeshed in what is for all practical purposes a karmic straight jacket. To do anything out of our normal routines becomes inconceivably hard. But even then, like it or not, change comes – and for us, it becomes all the more traumatic and wrenching. This is no way to live!

How Came The Law?

As the sufferings which I am referring to here are related to my divorce time, the law came from the events related to that. I realized that since I got married everything in our relationship changed. Some for better and some for worse. The change was there. Our finances changed, as we got richer. Our emotions changed as our kids were growing bigger and bigger. The way we were perceiving each other changed also.

How my ex reacted during the time of divorce, felt like a totally different person, all because of that change. During the divorce, my financial situation changed as I started losing money. I almost got bankrupt. The love of my kids towards me changed. Literally everything had changed over time. This law came due to the realization of all those changes in my life. This just didn't happen in my life with my ex only, but it is happening now and will keep happening in future relationships. It is bound to happen in your life. Generally, permanency is what we seek but is not possible.

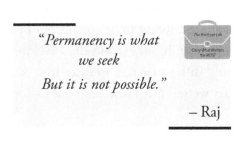

"Permanency is what we seek

But it is not possible."

– Raj

If someone loves us, we want that love to remain the same. If we are rich, we want that money to stay forever. Interestingly if we are poor, we feel that we will remain poor. But no one can avoid change in life. Therefore, I say,

Change is the only constant in life.

If we look at our Universe we see billions of galaxies moving steadily, billions of solar system moving around galaxies, planets in solar systems constantly moving, earth revolving on its axis constantly, every single moment things are changing, we take birth and grow old, rich becoming poor, poor becoming rich, without any control by us. I believe change is the only true constant in our lives.

Embracing Changes: Don't Fear it, Learn from it

Since change is inevitable, instead of resisting it, we need to learn to embrace and adapt to it. We should view each major change in our life as if we have died and been reborn in a new life. We take from our old life the lessons we have learned, and we enter our new life with a mind eager to discover what is around the corner. Each new change will force us to grow in some way, to change ourselves, to learn how to be equally happy in any and all circumstances. The reality is all worlds; all lives are equally empty.

Therefore, no matter what new world or situation we find ourselves in, we have an entirely equal chance of being perfectly happy. This is simply a fact. Our job as a *Kadampa* in this ever-changing world is to gain the ability to be equally happy everywhere. Each new world is an opportunity to expand the envelope of our capacity to transform new and different circumstances into something we consider to be "ideal." As we tell our kids, "every situation is equally good, just in a variety of ways."

It will sometimes be hard, it will sometimes take longer than we would like, but through embracing this task of learning to be equally happy in every new situation we find ourselves in, we will develop the ability always to be happy. From this, enormous confidence comes which knows we will be able to take this knowledge with us in life afterlife. It is not enough to just be happy in this life; we need to learn how to be satisfied in every life, life afterlife. Learning to embrace and adapt to change is, therefore, not only the key to happiness in this life but to happiness in all our future endeavors.

I was surprised by the fact that my ex asked for a divorce after 14 years of marriage. I wouldn't call my marriage as perfect, or flawless. My ideas about a relationship changed. My perception of marriage changed. Anything can happen anytime. Things in this Universe change in a blink of an eye. We must accept that fact and keep moving in our lives.

Are We Responsible For The Change?

Today is the result of yesterday. If you want a better tomorrow, make a better today.

> *"Your today is the outcome of yesterday*
> *If you want a better tomorrow*
> *You need to have a better today"*
>
> – Raj

We are the one who make life complex. Often, we are confused how we should do certain things and that is the cause of complexity also. As I previously said that life is like driving. Each action we will take is like taking a turn. If we take a turn, we need to make sure we are ready for the consequences on the way.

> *Complexity keeps creeping up in my simple life*
> *And I am fully responsible for it*
>
> – Raj

Impulse is very dangerous. We commonly make decisions in impulse due to anger. Majority of the time if we look back, the decisions made with the impulse were wrong. Like In my own life when things

> *"Anger is an instant gratification which is followed by years of pain"*
>
> – Raj

were not going right, I decided to leave the house. I feel now, that was the biggest mistake of my life. Just by leaving the house, I gave the control over someone else's hand and I also lost any chance of communication. I put my fully paid house in my ex's hand.

It is said right by Robert Schuller:

> *"Never cut a tree down in the wintertime. Never make a negative decision ina low time. Never make your most important decisions when you are in your worst moods. Wait. Be patient. The storm will pass. The spring will come."*

Also, remember that whatever decision we will make will affect everyone around us. My leaving the house affected me, my ex, and my kids.

> *"What we choose affects us and others*
> *So, make your choices right*
> *Do no harm, to ourselves and others."*
>
> – Raj

Anticipation and Vigilance

You cannot avoid the change, but you can be better prepared to deal with it. I believe in two things. One is the anticipation and second vigilance. You need to anticipate in life that things will change. Timing of the change, nobody knows, but we know that things will change. Don't just think of the change in a negative sense but it can happen in a positive way too. Be vigilant. Be ready. Watch where the change can come from. Based on your previous life, learn from it. Learn from every change how will you tackle the future changes.

In the next chapter, you will learn that the change is happening due to a possible predetermined factor that we call destiny. What comes in our lives, when it comes, what goes from our lives and when it goes, is all matter of destiny.

LAW 7

Attachments And Detachments

Are Timed And Destined

CHAPTER 8

Law 7

Attachments and Detachments Are Timed and Destined

What do I mean by this? We have family and friends, who are connected to us in our lives. Do we have any control ovwe which friend is gonna come in our life and when that person goes away? Obviously we know our parents are connected to us genetically but if they are going to be in our lives or not, no one knows for sure either. There had been many cases where only the mother is alive at the time of the birth of the baby. Similarly, some people are rich and some are poor. Later it may change to vice versa. I believe whatever happens in our lives is all destined. According to that destiny, events of our lives are timed. They happen exactly at the time they are destined. I also believe that whatever happens and whenever happens, it happens for good. Now that attachment or detachment at that time feels right to you or not, may be a topic of discussion. Buddha said that attachment or desire is the cause of suffering. According to him detachment from the things, we are attached to, leads to suffering. His solution to suffering is, not to be attached or not to have desires.

Life Is Like A Train

Have you observed a train, from its origin to its destination? The compartments are connected or removed from the engine at different stations. Similarly, this is what happens in real life too. Things or people get connected to us like a compartment and removed from time to time. Just like there is a schedule in which compartment will be added or removed destiny has a schedule that is attached to each one of us or removed at a certain time.

> *"Life is like a train*
> *Things or people are*
> *connected to us*
> *like a compartment and*
> *removed from time to time."*
>
> – Raj

Effects Of Attachment And Detachment

What happens when something is attached or detached in our lives. It is like a chemical reaction. The reaction can bring out happiness or sadness. When we are attached to something we love, it creates a feeling of happiness, satisfaction, and pleasure. When we are attached to something we hate it gives rise to a feeling of hate, sadness. On the other hand when we are detached from something we love it creates a feeling of hate and sadness. And when we detach from something, we hate it gives a feeling of pleasure, happiness, and satisfaction. For example when I got divorced actually it was a feeling of happiness but with that, I had to detach from other things also like my kids, which in turn lead to feelings of sadness, pain, and hatred.

Nothing Can Happen Before It's Time

One day I was going out to run some errands. Maybe I was about to leave suddenly I realized that I forgot something. When I came back inside I saw that I had left the stove on. Have you had something like this happen to you? I feel there must be a purpose of God in making me come back. It was preplanned. Nothing can happen before its time. Whatever happens, happens for a good reason.

Destiny The Predetermined Path

Life is so amazingly strange that it seems like everything is predetermined. In my own story of divorce, I literally tried all the avenues. I tried to make my ex understand. I tried to fix the problems or issues in my marriage. I tried to make a deal. I even tried to give everything away and end it. But NO. It had a time when it was supposed to end. After 4 years of the painful divorce process, it did. April 2017 was the time everything came to an end. I sacrificed a lot. I literally gave away a lot of things in order to just end it. I even felt that the judge was biased and there was a fraud going on. He must have taken money from the other side. Whatever the case was, it just ended and I was happy it ended. This is how this law came. It gave me a feeling that in life you can do whatever you want but if something is not destined to happen at that time, it will not happen.

Be Ready To Detach

How to reduce the impact of detachments? Gautam Buddha said, don't have desires, as these are the cause of suffering Everyone cannot leave the comforts of life and run to the jungle. If we have a body, we need to satisfy it through physical comforts. In my opinion, it is ok to attach yourself to the things you like (of course

"Attach to things as, If at any instant you have to detach from them, you can easily do that."

– Raj

the things you think are socially acceptable) but attach as, if at any instant you have to detach from them you can easily do that.

The Beginning Is The End And The End Is The Beginning

Is it really easy to detach from things? Or to reduce sufferings from the detachments. NO. But Gita has talked about things in it beautifully. We have to understand the fact given in Gita that "nothing belongs to

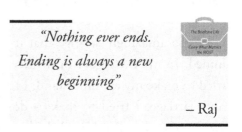

"Nothing ever ends. Ending is always a new beginning"

– Raj

you". We came with nothing and will go with nothing and in between those nothing was everything So even if something you lose or get detached from, it is ok. Also, nothing really ends in this life. Every end is the beginning of something new.

Driving The Life In The Fast Lane

What are we generally doing? We are constantly chasing a dream that we may never achieve. There is never ending want that we create and all our lives we keep running behind it. We are constantly hustling and bustling to get the most we can. In my three lane concept, were driving in the fast lane provides you all the physical comfort but we tend to lose the happiness aspect. We even tend to teach our kids the same thing. We tell them to drive in the fast lane. Be smart. Get higher education. Go for a better job. There is always a competition we create among each other. Our mind can achieve whatever we want most of the time, if the power of belief is strong. We need to really teach our kids the value of life. In the end we leave it all here. We need to learn to create a balance between faster lane driving and slower lane driving so we can on average be in the middle lane as Gautam Buddha suggested. A balanced life is the best life which gives us peace.

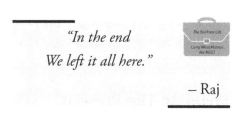

"In the end
We left it all here."

— Raj

How To Deal With Loss

Life is strange. Either we are living in the past or in the future. If we lose something in life which was very precious to us, we break. If someone gets divorced, or if someone leaves someone, or if we took a big

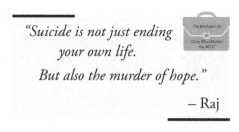

"Suicide is not just ending
your own life.
But also the murder of hope."

— Raj

loss in business, etc etc. it is very hard for us to cope with that loss. People get depressed. People tend to commit suicide. They feel that life is not worth it. They take decisions in an impulse. Remember when you end your life, you are not just ending your life but you are killing hope. Our situation when it is actually happening seems like the biggest one, but at a later time it seems so small.

We should never ever take life so seriously to the point that we take our life. Anger is an instant gratification that is followed by years of pain. If we connect with bad memories of the past It will be very hard to connect with good memories of the future.

Ctrl, Alt, And Del

What happens when our computer freezes? Are we able to do anything? We feel as if we are going to die. Do we? NO. We press CTRL+ALT+DEL and restart our computer. Same way if something bad happens in our lives, that's what we need to do.

Living In The Present

I think this is the key to happiness. Living in the past or present creates fear, worries, and living in today lets us enjoy the present moment. We need to cherish everything and everybody around us. Every single thing created by God is beautiful and there is to enjoy.

So by now, we have learned all the laws. Remember these laws are nothing that we need to just remember. We need to apply these laws in the stressful and painful situations of our lives. Next chapter we will try to explain, how to do that.

How To
Get Rid Of Sufferings
Carry what matters the most:
The briefcase of happiness

CHAPTER 9

Getting Rid Of Sufferings

Carry What Matters The Most:
The Briefcase Of Happiness

So, by now you have probably understood the concept of seven laws. If you really think about them, there is nothing new I have said. One way or the other someone must have told you before. But just knowing them is not enough. Gautam Buddha has said a very beautiful thing. He said, that knowing a lot is not as important as the application of it. That's what I will say too now. If you can learn to apply these seven laws in your life's situations, then I can guarantee that your life will be suffering free. But you must promise me that you will apply it in 100% of the situation. I know it is not possible. And it is ok if you are not able to apply it 100% of the time, just do not complain later that they do not work.

I overcame all my divorce related sufferings by applying all these laws. This would be a very strange statement. In life suffering never ends. Life is dynamic. Your cloud of suffering thoughts keeps coming to you again and again. I am not saying by using these laws I can completely eliminate my sufferings but I am going to be honest with you, that each time I truly apply these laws to my cloud of suffering thoughts, the impact of those suffering is very minimal.

The focus of this book is on improving quality of life by creating a life free of suffering. self-image through positive thinking, having a more positive attitude can make you open to a world of physical changes. In addition to changing your way of thinking, you can also change your behavior and abilities by learning new skills.

What does matters in life? Steve Jobs's final words included the fact that love and relationship matter the most. We spend most of our life in the physical dimension accumulating pleasure especially the early part of our life. Later part of life we spend in the spiritual dimension. Having power, relationships, money, or whatever money can buy are important aspects of life as they give pleasure but my belief is that all those things are timed and destined. If you were destined to have certain pleasures, you will have it, and if you were not then, you will not.

Making money, having power, being in a relationship all are part of the physical dimension and are an important part of life. There are three major purposes in our lives. As previously mentioned physical dimension purpose is achievement of pleasure, purpose of emotional dimension is being happy and the purpose of the spiritual dimension is getting peace.

With divorce often comes a feeling of shame, low confidence, and low self-worth - as if people who get divorced have done something wrong, or failed somehow. It's only natural to feel perhaps scared at finding yourself single again. You may feel alone, isolated, and surprised by who has turned their back on you.

This is normal. However, it needn't be this way. Self-confidence and self-worth have everything to do with having a strong inner core. Often, outer success can hide a weak core, but without a strong core and courage, true happiness is not sustainable long term. The inner core has to do with loving yourself for who you truly are.

Three Key Points About This Life

I have not read Gita entirely but I have heard the teachings of it from many sources. In my belief, it provides very practical knowledge about life. What I have learned through my sufferings and what I have learned from this scripture are the following three key concepts about life.

One is that *"Nothing belongs to us. We came with absolutely nothing and we will take absolutely nothing with us"*. Our life is a gift of God. We are part of that divine energy that can neither be created nor destroyed. This is a very important aspect to understand as all our lives we are spending time and energy collecting physical means.

Second is that *"Change is the only constant of life"*. In this universe, everything is changing. And due to the change comes the third lesson of an unpredictable life.

Third is that life is unpredictable. *"Life can never be planned but only be adapted."* As previously mentioned when I was going to San Francisco from Philadelphia airport in June 2017, and at the entrance of an airport parking, I noticed there was an accident. There was a motorcyclist laying on the ground with blood around his head and neck. He was hit by a car a few minutes prior. I think he was already dead by the time I passed by as people were around him waiting for the authorities. I thought what must have been going through the mind of this young man in a few minutes prior to his death. He probably had no idea this will happen to him. This is how life is. It is unpredictable.

Commonly, suffering happens in the present but is happening due to things of the past or future. It usually happens due to either lack of something we love, or the presence of something we hate. Or it happens due to the change of circumstances from pleasant to unpleasant.

Seven laws in this book are designed to filter your thoughts and clear the cloud of suffering. If you really apply these laws it will provide you with tools to search and destroy your sufferings. In my other book called

Seven ways in Seven days to change your life, the seven techniques will also teach you how to keep away suffering and become successful.

Redefining Our Purpose

The dimensions we live in are the cause and solutions to our problems. Physical dimension creates our purpose of physical needs like satisfaction, the emotional dimension creates our purpose of emotional needs like love and happiness, the spiritual dimension is the supermost which create our purpose of spiritual needs like peace. The ultimate goal is to be free.

We learned the three things about life such as nothing belongs to you, change is inevitable and life cannot be planned but only be adapted. These true facts should help us redefine our purposes in life. Why are we running after physical means when they are really not stable and attached to us forever. When our focus becomes on higher purposes like spiritual needs then we are peaceful, happy, and satisfied.

How To Apply These Laws

Our problems create thoughts. These are mixed thoughts and they cause us to worry about the future. In the end, we have a cloud of suffering thoughts. The thought makes us. These laws filter these thoughts and give them a new worry-free aspect.

So, for example, I was going through a divorce and since it started I had many thoughts which had fear, lack of self-confidence, doubting the possibilities, depression due to loss, lack of control on changing situations, and unpredictable future. When my ex asked for a divorce I had no idea it was coming.

Law 5 made me realize that you have 0% control over what comes to you but 100 % control on how you react to it. I realized that what happened was not in my control at that moment, so I have to accept the situation as is.

Law 6 helped me understand that my relationship with my ex and kids had changed as it is the norm. Everything and anything changes. I realized that things had changed since its start and I had to keep up. Sometimes if time has passed of recovery, then things do not come back where they were and once again we have to accept that fact. I tried to go back which didn't happen, and later I tried very hard to finish the divorce sacrificing everything in life but it didn't happen. One day things came to an end.

Law 7, destiny was something that decides who and what will be in your life and for how long. I understood that you cannot really keep someone of something longer than it is destined. At the start of things, I thought of killing myself many times. I thought the whole thing was so painful that I will die. When things ended I saw myself happy and healthy. I thanked God that everything was happening for good. HE has a plan for you.

Law 1, He makes sure whatever is happening, happening for a good reason. Many times I thought I am not good enough. I did so many things for my kids and suffered as I inspite of doing everything I couldn't get what I wanted.

Law 2, made me realize that I need to put myself on the priority. I could see the change. I was happier. I started doing things for me. I became almost bankrupt. Every month thousands of dollars were going to attorneys. We were fighting for things that were not long-lasting. We were fighting for the money that we were losing every single day in litigation. I was thinking this will not end. I will not be able to rebuild myself.

Law 3, but I believed in myself and restructured my practice. Anything is possible with the belief. In the end the most important aspect I understood that we are all observers. What we see or able to see is our reality. No one is wrong or right. My ex was not wrong or right. I was not wrong or right. It was just our perceptions which were our realities for which we both were fighting. The best thing would have been if we would have seen things through other's eyes. If we would have paid attention to other's perspectives, I can guarantee things would not have to come even to divorce.

Law 4, was the best and most important law that helped me realize that our perception is our reality.

So if you have a cloud of thoughts put the filter of every single law and you will see that you are able to understand and handle the situation better.

Live A Simple Life

We need to make life simple. We create our own complexity. I always say

"Look for simplicity in this complex life.
Not the complexity in this simple life."

– Raj

Life Is An Exam

It is very interesting to know that we have had many centuries pass by and many scholars have tried to figure out the path of life but we all are still struggling and trying to find the best way to live,…suffering free. Some say life is a journey, not a destination. It is full of beautiful experiences. Some say it is a school where time is a teacher and we have to take many exams in this life. Some believe that we are reborn while some believe that we only live once. The fact is that life is unpredictable and there is no one perfect way of living. We should just live in presence, in a day tight compartment and just keep doing, keep moving.

Never Forget God And Death

My father had written on a mantlepiece "*Ishvar aur maut ko kabhi mat bhoolo*" means never forget God and death. You do not have to fear any of those but do not forget as God is everywhere and death can come any time.

The Mind Is Like A Factory

Our perception decides if something will give us pleasure, happiness, or sadness. We perceive from our mind. Our mind is like a factory. It has millions of thoughts every day. It creates or tries to create more and more for us. It's like more product you will produce more trash will accumulate. More trash is the cause of suffering. It is especially important to clean that factory on a regular basis. Cleaning of mind needs meditation, and music. Also, if we produce less, our trash would be less. This is called contentment. If we stay happy with less, then it will cause less sufferings.

Love Is Prime

"When you will look back in time, you will realize that only thing that mattered was love". Another book I am working on is called "3SSS in a Successful Relationships" I have focused on a very important principle we should live our life on is love. Often, we criticize people around us which pushes them away. We should praise and appreciate them. Dale Carnegie said that two things are very important to all human beings, one is sex and other feeling of being appreciated. We should always think from our heart. Also, remember that the most important person in your life is you, so never criticize yourself and praise and appreciate yourself. Do no harm to yourself and others.

Carry What Matters the Most: The Briefcase Of Happiness

We all cannot be Gautam Buddha and leave our physical comforts and live in the jungle. But at the same time attachment with those physical comfort creates suffering on their detachments. So, the answer to this problem is to carry less. On the way of life, the more things you will attach to, may bring happiness but will also bring pain and suffering. Attach to least possible things and attach loose, means like if you must detach from something you can easily do so. This is where emotional intelligence also plays an important role. Remember nothing belongs to you, and nothing will last forever. And whatever you have now will keep changing. So, do not get stuck. Whenever you are thinking of attaching to something also think about exit from it. "Begin with the end in mind".

But the bottom line is, you play a huge part in your happiness by not carrying a suitcase of sufferings but to carry the briefcase of happiness, and you can significantly increase it by taking action and changing your attitude toward yourself. You are responsible for yourself. Your happiness (or your misery) depend in a significant part upon what you tell yourself, how you treat yourself, and how you interpret your world. That is why I say

Believe in yourself and believe that you are capable of handling life's problems because your perception is what determines your reality.

Advance like a hero. Don't be thwarted by anything. How many days will this body last, with its happiness and misery? When you have got the human body, then rise and reach the state of fearlessness! And then as long as the body endures, speak unto others this message of fearlessness. Arise, awake, and stop not until you reach the goal!!!

Contentment is the key. Whatever you have, or whatever you do, be content with that.

Suffering will stay with you all your life.

Stay In The Middle Lane

We are in this world full of suffering. To get rid of suffering, we cannot take the path of Gautam Buddha by leaving the luxury and go to the jungle and just do meditation. Even Buddha after years of following his principles realized that the best path is the middle path, the path of a balanced life.

It is All About Perspective

The central law is "Perception is reality". It is how we look at it. You have the power to create your reality. If it is physically not there, imagine it. Simple imagination and visualization alone can create a beautiful reality.

> **I believe that the goal of everything in this universe is creating a balance between the two forces, the negative and positive, and attempting to reach the state of neutrality. In the same way, the purpose of life is to create a balance between two strong forces the mind and the heart and reaching a state of neutrality "a peaceful soul". There always will be a constant battle between two forces negative and positive. The closest we remain to the soul, which is the middle lane is better.**

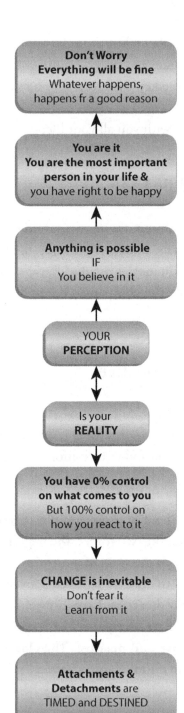

"Life is like a movie.

There are going to be bad scenes and good scenes.

But in the end what matters is just the entertainment and experiences"

NOTHING BELONGS TO YOU

We came with absolutely nothing and we will take absolutely nothing with us. Our life is a gift of God. We are part of divine energy that cannot be created or destroyed. This energy or our life has a soul thatof consists of our Mind, Heart, and Spirit. We are the byproduct of our thoughts. Life is a journey full of beautiful experiences.

CHANGE IS THE ONLY CONSTANT

In this universe, everything is moving which creates the change.

Change is inevitable.

LIFE CAN NEVER BE PLANNED.
IT CAN ONLY BE ADAPTED

Life is unpredictable. Living in the moment is the key. Life is like a movie. There would be good scenes, and bad scenes. In the end, what matters is the entertainment of the experiences.

The Briefcase *Life*

Law 1
Don't Worry: **Everything will be fine**
Whatever happens, happens for a good reason

Law 2
You are the most important person in your life
and you have right to be happy

Law 3
Anything is possible, **if you believe in it**

Law 4
YOUR PERCEPTION IS **YOUR REALITY**

Law 5
You have 0% control on what comes to you
but 100% control on how you react to it

Law 6
Change is inevitable, **don't fear it, learn form it**

Law 7
Attachments & Detachments **are timed & destined**

About The Author

Dr. Rajan Gupta was born and brought up in New Delhi, India. His childhood was in the city of Delhi. He came across many people in his life who have helped shape his present. Every single person who came in his life whether he or she gave good or bad experiences to him, he believes was an important person otherwise his life would not have been the same. So, he is thankful to everyone. He believes that attachments and detachments with people or anything in life are timed and destined. One of the most memorable things for him from childhood was a quote written by his father on a mantlepiece **"Ishwar aur maut ko kabhi mat bhulo" means "never forget God and Death**.

After schooling he went to Ahmedabad for his medical school. This was one of the most beautiful phases of his life where he created so many beautiful relations of his life. Later he traveled to USA and received residency training at St Francis Medical Center (UPMC) in Pittsburgh and his Intervention Pain fellowship at Vanderbilt University in Nashville (Tennessee).

Dr. Gupta has been practicing pain management for over 10 years and has his practices in South Jersey and Philadelphia. He has received multiple awards including the **"Best Hands"** award for intervention pain, **Top Doctor** award in **2015, 2016, 2017,2018, 2019**, **South Jersey Magazine Top Physicians** award in **2017, 2018, 2019**, The Philadelphia Magazine Top Physician award **2018, 2019**, 2020 the **Prestigious Pillar of Community Service** award in **2013** and many more.

He has been a writer all his life. He loves to create things. He is working on few books "7 ways in 7 days to change your life", "Growing to be pain free", "Married with Pain" and "3SSS in a successful relationship", "How to be a modern Buddha". He is also acting, and producing movies like "Cozy Connections", "The Beginning of the End" based on the principles of his books.

He believes that contentment is the key. Whatever you do, whatever you have, just be content with it. That will bring peace. Pain and sufferings are inevitable. He says to follow these laws as filters so that you can "Stop Suffering and Start Living".

Made in the USA
Monee, IL
31 August 2020